# CHICANA (W)RITES on Word and Film

# CHICANA (W)RITES on Word and Film

Edited by

María Herrera-Sobek
and
Helena María Viramontes

Series in Chicana/Latina Studies

Third Woman Press
Berkeley

Typeset by GET SET! Prepress, Oakland, Calif.
Printed and bound by McNaughton & Gunn, Saline, Mich.

This book would not have been possible without a generous grant from the California Arts Council and the support of the Ethnic Studies Department of the University of California, Berkeley.



Cover art: *Portrait of the Artist as the Virgen de Guadalupe*, by Yolanda M. Lopez. Oil, pastel on paper.



Printed on acid-free paper.

First printing 1995
95 96 97 98 99 10 9 8 7 6 5 4 3 2 1

Library of Congress Cataloging-in-Publication Data

Chicana (w)rites : on word and film / edited by María Herrera-Sobek and Helena María Viramontes.
p. cm. — (Series in Chicana/Latina studies)
Includes bibliographical references.
ISBN 0-943219-10-8 (pbk. : acid free)
1. American literature—Mexican American authors. 2. American literature—Mexican American authors—History and criticism. 3. American literature—Women authors—History and criticism. 4. Mexican American women—Literary collections. 5. Mexican Americans in motion pictures. 6. Women and literature—United States. 7. American literature—Women authors. I. Herrera-Sobek, María. II. Viramontes, Helena María. III. Series.
PS508.M4C56 1995 95-40555
810.8'086872—dc20 CIP

For
Eloy Rodríguez
Manuel Gómez
Guadalupe López
Erik Jason Sobek
and
in loving memory of
Hilaria Calvillo Rodríguez,
a mujer for all times

# Contents

**Prose**



**Criticism**

# Acknowledgements

Helena María Viramontes and I owe a great deal of gratitude to all the individuals and institutions at the University of California, Irvine who made the conference "Chicana Writes: On Word and Film" a reality. Without their financial support this volume would not have been possible. We therefore gratefully acknowledge the contributions made by the following persons: Terence Parsons, Dean of Humanities; Eloy Rodríguez, Director of the International Chicano Studies Program; Robert Hickok, Dean, School of Fine Arts; Manuel Gómez, Assistant Vice Chancellor; SAA/EOP, Carla Espinoza Assistant Vice Chancellor Affirmative Action, Equal Opportunity; Department of Spanish and Portuguese; Rachel D. Pardee, Humanities; Sharla Schroeder, Women's Resource Center; and the Latin American/Chicano Studies Program. We owe a special thanks to Sharon Gómez, Debbie Thyssen, Kathy Kennedy, and Crystal Ricaporte for assisting us in accounting and bookkeeping activities. We also thank Joseph G. Sobek for videotaping part of the conference proceedings.

We thank the U.C. Irvine bookstore for the book signing reception they held for our writers.

We would also like to thank Barbara Carrazco for the fine art work she did for the Conference poster.

We acknowledge our debt to the above individuals for believing in the worthiness of this project and for supporting the writing and dissemination of Chicana creative works and scholarship. We appreciate both their moral support and the monetary contributions that made the conference a success.

We thank Susan Bergholz for permission to publish Sandra Cisneros's "Little Miracles, Kept Promises" (Copyright 1990 by Sandra Cisneros, published in *Woman Hollering Creek* [Random House 1991], first published in *Grand Street*, Fall 1990. Reprinted by permission of Susan Bergholz Literary Service New York, N.Y.).

We are pleased to acknowledge our photographer Alvaro Ruffinelli who took Bernice Zamora's picture. We sincerely thank him.

Helena María Viramontes would also like to thank her children, Pilar and Eloy Francisco, for their patience and assistance in helping her get her work done.

María Herrera-Sobek
University of California, Irvine

# Preface

"Chicana (W)rites: On Word and Film" was the third conference hosted at the University of California, Irvine which specifically focused on the creative works of Chicanas. The first conference convened on 4 May 1982 and was the first national conference on Chicana writers ever hosted by a major university. Several pioneers in Chicano/a literature braved the heavy rains that poured on the day of the conference, including our beloved late Chicano novelist and U.C. Riverside Chancellor Tomás Rivera, who was a firm supporter of Chicano/a literature. I was very grateful for Chancellor Rivera's support because, although I was unable to offer him an honorarium or even reimburse him for travel expenses, he graciously served as our morning session's keynote speaker and chairman of the morning panel. Several Chicana critics participated at this event including Rosaura Sánchez, Carmen Salazar, Margarita Nieto-Gómez, Sylvia Lizárraga, Marta Sánchez, and Tey Diana Rebolledo, who was the keynote speaker for the afternoon program. Other Chicano/a critics specializing in Chicana authors and issues were also present. These included Francisco Lomelí, Eliud Martínez, and Carlos Cortés. I shall be forever grateful to these Chicano/a scholars because they participated without any financial compensation. I did commit myself to publishing the proceedings. I kept my promise and the articles read at the Conference were published in the anthology *Beyond Stereotypes: The Critical Analysis of Chicana Literature* (1985). I feel gratified this collection proved useful to the scholarly community. It has received a very positive reception and is quoted in numerous publications, in addition to being used as a textbook in many literature classes.

The second conference focusing on Chicana writers convened on 23 April 1987. This time Helena María Viramontes was the motive force propelling the initiative for the Conference. Her initial idea of having two Chicana critics and two writers interact in a university setting sounded exciting and provocative. Helena's idea, however, soon developed into a full-fledged conference. The conference was titled "Charting New Frontiers in American Literature: Chicana Creativity and Criticism." Lorna Dee Cervantes, Evangelina Vigil, Lucha Corpi, Denise Chávez and Marisela Norte graced us with their presence and their readings. Critics such as Tey Diana Rebolledo, Julián Olivares, Yvonne Yarbro-Bejarano, and Norma Alarcón provided us with a forum in which Chicana literary theory could be discussed. Again, the proceedings from this Conference were published as *Chicana Creativity and Criticism: Charting New Frontiers in American Literature* (1988). The book has received numerous excellent reviews and is extensively quoted.

It was with the above two successes in mind that Helena and I were emboldened to host a third conference at U.C. Irvine in 1990. We titled the conference "Chicana Writes: On Word and Film." This time Helena decided that we should include Chicana filmmakers in order to showcase the work that these talented women have been doing in a highly competitive environment. We divided the presentations into three sections: Criticism, Literary Creativity, and Filmmaking. We were pleased at the tremendous turnout that we had and the enthusiastic support from various individuals and institutions who are extremely supportive of Chicana creative efforts. At this Conference writers of such caliber as Sandra Cisneros, Ana Castillo, Mary Helen Ponce, and Demetria Martínez read from some of their works. Critics such as Elizabeth J. Ordóñez, Angie Chabram, and Genaro Padilla presented their most recent scholarship. We also had a theatrical reading by Diane Rodríguez. We are very appreciative of all these critics, writers, filmmakers, and actresses who gave of their time and talent so graciously and made the conference a resounding success. We acknowledge our debt to them. It is from the presentations at this conference that the present volume is mainly derived.

In addition to the 1990 readings we requested articles and literary works from critics and poets, such as Bernice Zamora and Elba Sánchez, who did not attend the conference. We also have an exclusive interview of Bernice Zamora by Elsa Li. Other critics include Erlinda Gonzales-Berry, Norma Alarcón, Hector Torres and Juan Bruce-Novoa. We feel very lucky to have the contributions of these critics and poets, for we believe their works complement and augment those of the other contributors.

University of California, Irvine
María Herrera-Sobek

# Introduction

*María Herrera-Sobek*

The strength, vigor, and beauty of Chicana creative writings and now filmmaking (in its infancy) can be seen in the works included in this anthology. We believe Chicana productivity will continue to delight us and intellectually stimulate us. It will also continue to challenge existing canons by redefining and amplifying the conceptualization of what "literature" is or ought to be. Chicana writings likewise will continue to invigorate and charge with new blood the field of Chicano/a studies. The comments that follow are designed to highlight the contributions Chicana writers and critics are making in Chicana literary studies.

## Poetry

Bernice Zamora's poem "A Book on Goodness" is a metaphysical discussion on the concepts of Good and Evil. The poetic voice redefines the religious male's conceptualizations of the two concepts and proposes her own definitions of the terms. The poems included here follow in the footsteps of her previous work published in her collection of poems *Restless Serpents* (1976). Zamora's strategy is to juxtapose a male weltanschauung against a female one. In "A Book on Goodness" there is a marked difference between the two subject positions. The poetic voice, who we assume is female from the poem's content, asserts her loyalty to her female self and the community of women. The poetic persona expresses her views on "A Book on Goodness" i.e. the Bible and through a feminist optic posits her own conclusion regarding its teachings. William, the patriarchal voice of authority, is deconstructed into Willy (as in "willy, nilly"). In a sarcastic mode she inverts the names Willy and William rendering William as the nickname and Willy as the name. ("Willy, William for short, . . ."). The first line of the poem unauthorizes William and his voice of authority, who the female subject in the beginning (as in "in the beginning was the word and the word was God") admires for his supposedly lucid ability to distinguish Right from Wrong.

> Willy, William for short, could take
> A volume of backpages and gain
> a sermon indicative of good
> Real search on God.

The closing line provides an ironic finality to the first part of the poem. The "I" is introduced in the last line as a counterpoint to William, and again in a sardonic image between males bathing their feet and contemporary holy water fonts. In spite of this, the poetic persona reiterates her belief in a Good and Evil world with God incarnating the Good.

An abrupt change issues in the second half of the poem and redirects the focus of the text away from a male world and into a female one. Not only is the reader now forced to focus his/her gaze on the female poetic voice, but this female speaking subject is brought to a lower level, spatially speaking, and to a mundane level, spiritually speaking, in lines ten and eleven:

> A woman like myself, plumped
> In a chair, adjusting a
> Bra strap, leaning forward

The lofty search for good is brought to a human level, to a feminine level, for the speaking female subject appropriates the Word and transforms it into a happy discourse. Through the Word in the woman's mouth the world can soar to Himalayan heights. The appropriation of the Word by the female subject reveals new insights for now the speaking subject is more sure of what Good and Evil are. Good is "happy discourse" and Evil is redefined "As possible evil I imagine/Such a woman as dragged among/ The God givers." For the poetic persona Evil resides in the institutionalization of religion.

While "A Book on Goodness" redefines the ethical concepts of Good and Evil, and does this from a feminist perspective thus displacing patriarchal order, "The Wine of Romance" is a caustic indictment of married life with an alcoholic man and the position of women and children within this dysfunctional married relationship. The poetic voice flatly recounts the few options women have in life, mainly one—to get married. "I married with one option." The poetic persona was supposedly forewarned, however she did not heed the warning: "In so many moral ways I laid/Down the guard and Guardian/of a winning life." The narrative voice evinces nostalgia for another life that could have been successfully realized and that she allowed to slip away. The second stanza narrates in the third person the bitter results, i.e. the nightmare of living with an abusive, alcoholic husband who imprisons wife and children in his iron-clad tragic grasp. The narrative persona, however, places the blame directly on the wife herself. The poem seems to be a guilt-ridden confession of a woman who threw caution to the wind (albeit having few options) and married a drunk. The hell forthcoming from this marital situation does not effect only the wife herself, but the helpless children are also thrown into a nightmarish inferno of violence and oppression.

Zamora's last poem "Theater" is a relatively long philosophical dissertation on the changing fate of the sexual act. Her central metaphor of sex as theater brilliantly captures the many scenes sex has played out in the past four decades (1950-1991). The sexual stage begins in the fifties, a decade we all remember as an innocent sexual age. It was an era, nevertheless, notorious for back-seat-of-the-car necking and petting and the ever present sexual scene played behind the barn, the emblematic 1950s' warning of "Nice girls don't" frequently forgotten.

The sexually liberating sixties and early seventies were a time for experimentation, and the poetic voice who is really not too keen on sex witnesses (experiences?) the performance of sex:

> Sex upstage, behind doors—
> Barns and barrelled—up street
> Towned and tarred, backed in alleys,
> Bound or burned, legal and illegal,
> Licit and illicit, stretched or
> Fetal, moral—oh, ever moral—

However, as the AIDS epidemic emerged in the eighties, sex all of a sudden acquired terrifying proportions

> . . . the plot abandoned
> Now. Colorfully packaged condoms

Tickets to a failed play
Passed freely as a failed ploy,
Clutter cemeteries
Crematoriums and stages,
Prosceniumed and unsizzling,

The AIDS epidemic has indeed shut down many a foreplay, the consequences of engaging in "free love" now unmentionable and terrifying. Zamora's poem achieves perfect closure with the lines

And, out behind the barn,
Summer rehearsals are closed.

The "behind the barn" sexual metaphor of a more innocent age has brought closure to our sex plays.

As the poems demonstrate, Zamora's creative works are characterized by a deep metaphorical and philosophical strain. Her metaphors are generally abstract and complex and the reader has to use his/her intelligence to grapple with the issues delineated within the poems. Zamora's poetry is not easy to read; it requires active involvement on the part of the reader. However, after careful reading of the poems, the reader is rewarded with the keen insights on life this splendidly talented poet has to offer us.

Demetria Martínez, a young Chicana from New Mexico, offers us poetry impregnated with images of love, war, and nature. Her literary output evinces a close communicative spiritual state with the mountains and landscape of her native New Mexico. Here nature and humans are one living in harmony and peace. It is only the destructive tendencies of people that disturb the balance and bring pain and suffering into the world. Her poem "Landscape, Alcalde, N.M." is typical of Martínez's nature oriented poems. It describes the sun peeking between two hills as a "squash/blossom/necklace."

Love is also ever present in Martinez's work. Her poem "The Idol" is an ironic comment on the vagaries of a love relationship not fully realized; perhaps gone sour. The poetic voice acknowledges the distance between her lover "Far off/as God" and herself: she only receives postcards. The poetic voice becomes reconciled at not having this unattainable love object and in an ironic tone closes:

I am a
lucky woman.
You can't
hurt me.
All I lack
in the world
is you.

Martínez's other six poems "Point Blank," "Postscript," "War," "The Conquest," "Power," and "Ceasefire" are all imbued with sharp images critical of a world where children go to sleep hungry; where the gun and the rifle are the only voices heard; where the conquered struggle daily to keep a firm hold on reality and not succumb to alienating myths of half truths and outright lies.

The poet is skillful in conflating the everyday, the quotidian with violent images of war and destruction. In "Point Blank" the natural imagery of a New Mexican(?) sunrise is associated with a verb connoting violence.

Through lace curtain
sun explodes
color of papaya

The verb "explodes" intimates of violence to come. The following strophe reiterates the hint of a violent human world juxtaposed against a peace loving natural cosmos.

dirt yard
saguaro cactus
like fingers
sing of peace

The natural world begs for humans to end their bellicose conflicts. Peace is nature's way.

The beginning stanzas intimate the development of a violent universe. And indeed the strophes that follow delineate a woman's efforts to obtain a vest (bulletproof?) from a sheriff friend for a priest in El Salvador. The everyday activity of the anonymous woman contrasts sharply with her request. Scenes from a war-torn El Salvador: i.e. the murdering of Jesuit priests, nuns, and civilians enters the readers consciousness. Martínez does a masterful job of integrating slices from everyday life in America with the violent activities taking place in El Salvador.

"Postscript," another poem, continues the above theme of war in El Salvador. Here the poetic persona recounts the idealistic dreams of a couple who wanted to change the world. With wine glasses high they toasted, loved and planned a new world order. The poem closes with the death of the male lover.

> In Morazan you died
> defending a chicken wire
> clinic, a doctor who wrests
> bullet from bone

The female voice ends her romantic/revolutionary interlude with

> All I saved, Pedro,
> were these corks.

That is to say, all the poetic persona has left is the memory of those wine-filled nights of love and idealism.

The poem "The Conquest" comes closer to home and the incessant war of words Chicanos/as are forced to use in the streets and homes of the United States. New Mexico's state motto is "The Land of Enchantment," but for Chicanos and Native Americans it is a land of constant confrontation, battling dehumanizing myths and a history tinged with the horror of lynchings, massacres, etc. The poet angrily answers an unknown interlocutor (a tourist?)

> You say you envy
> my roots.
>
> You don't know
> how little I sleep,
>
> . . . . . . . . . .
>
> How I bruise
> on a pumice metate,
>
> grinding like dry corn
> the myths you cherish,

The two last poems included in Martinez's selection, "Power" and "Ceasefire," are in the autobiographical mode. The poetic persona, a militant voice in the sixties, is finding peace and harmony in the present. In "Power" the poet states

At 30 you bury
those years
like umbilical cord,
return to mornings
listening,
coffee, blank book,
language of
trees.

And in "Ceasefire"

day darkens
like dishwater,
quiet, wind
on the lip
of a bottle,
old man hoses
down sidewalk,
you're home.

Elba Rosario Sánchez's collection of poems can be divided into three categories: feminist issues, social protest, and erotic love poems. In the first category we can include "In a Dream my Sisters," "Mirror Image: Womanpoetry," "Espejismos: Mujer Poesía," "Moon Corn," "Maíz Luna," "Codex," "Lizard," "Lagartija," and "Woman's Word." In the second category are poems reflecting concern with social issues: i.e. war, poverty and worker's exploitation. Included in this category are the poems "There Is a War Going On," "Cruzando Fronteras," "Watsonville: Más de dos años después" (in reference to the cannery strikes taking place in that northern California agricultural town in recent years). The third category provides us with a glimpse of Sánchez's sensual erotic poetry: included here are "Rumbamos" and "Moon Harvest."

Sánchez's poetry evidences a strong artistic talent for the construction of delicate but incisive metaphors. In her poem "In a Dream my Sisters" we have the metaphor of two women poets—

the poetic voice speaking to an interlocutor—ostensibly Lorna Dee Cervantes, a well-recognized poet, since the poem is dedicated to her. The poetic persona finds inspiration and feels a strong bonding with her interlocutor, with whom she identifies spiritually. Interlocutor and poet merge in this sea of spirituality and creativity. There is great admiration and love for this Other woman, who is described as having the wisdom of the "ancient one," a nature goddess—the fount of beauty and inspiration.

In "Mirror Image: Womanpoetry" the brilliant and famous Mexican painter Frida Kahlo is the source of inspiration and homage. Frida is perceived as a powerful role model for women. Sánchez's poetic voice also finds inspiration in ancient Mesoamerican goddesses such as the Moon Goddess, the Corn Goddess, and Coatlicue. All of these are female deities with whom the poetic voice intuits a special relationship and creative bond.

On the other hand, in her poem "Lizard" the poetic voice finds in Self her own source of power, beauty, and inspiration In "Woman's Word" the poetic persona is even more aggressive in expressing her newfound woman power.

Sánchez's protest poems deal forthrightly with issues of war, i.e. the United States' involvement in wars such as the Persian Gulf War (1991) and the Chicano's frequent meeting with death in these confrontations. The irony expressed is that Chicanos fight in wars when the real battles are against drugs, poverty, racism, ignorance and other ills besetting this minority group right here at home in the United States. Her other two poems, "Cruzando fronteras" and "Watsonville," broach such issues as family separation due to the necessity of working in a far-away land, and poverty due to poor wages and unemployment. There is a bittersweet tone to Sánchez's protest poetry, for although it may be a militant type of social protest poetry, the artistic manner in which she elaborates her message give the poems both depth and beauty.

Sánchez's erotic poetry celebrates the rhythms of love, of life, of sensuality. In "Rumbamos" lovemaking is metaphorically described as a dance, as an exciting rhythm similar to the rhythm of fiercely beating drums. And in "Moon Harvest" a sensual, delicate description of a love scene in the darkness of the moon is rendered in sensuous, mystical imagery.

**Prose**

In "Little Miracles/Kept Promises" Sandra Cisneros introduces us to the world of the *retablo* or exvoto. The *retablos* are paintings depicting a special favor or miracle granted by a particular saint to a devotee who had prayed and devotedly asked for this particular miracle. The recipient of the miracle makes a manda or "promise" to have a retablo painted with a picture of the Virgin, Jesus, or a saint, and a scene describing the miracle if the request is granted. A short narrative describing the nature of the miracle accompanies the painting, usually inscribed below or along the side of the drawing. The paintings are usually executed by folk artists and are done in a primitive, sometimes almost childlike, style.

Cisneros has brilliantly integrated this religious folk art and religious belief-system (the milagro, or miracle, and the manda, or promise) and transformed it into an original creative work of fiction. However Cisneros has not only successfully integrated the various folk genres and belief-systems, but she has done so with strong doses of feminist ideology and social protest—and she has done all of this with a sharp sense of humor.

Cisneros' narratives incorporate with great poignancy and humor the travails, needs, and hardships of working class Chicanos/as. Through the succinct narratives, most are only a few lines long, the reader experiences the hard life of the proletariat. We learn of the poor health of Chicanos and lack of proper medical services, the exploitation of the poor, the undocumented who work and are not paid their wages (they fear deportation if they go to the police). We witness the struggles of staying in school in a school system that is not relevant to the needs of the Chicanos and has an alienating culture. A fine example of this is the request from Eliberto González from Dallas, Texas who asks Saint Jude, Patron Saint of Lost Causes: "Help me pass my English 320, British Restoration Literature class and everything to turn out ok." Through the narratives we hear the voice of the dispossessed, the powerless, the working poor whose only recourse is to appeal to supernatural forces for miracles.

In Cisneros' *milagritos* we also hear a strong feminist voice. Feminist ideology is expressed in various *milagros*, and in particular the last one. The devotee Rosario "Chayo" de León has a long monologue with the Virgin de Guadalupe/Tonantzin/Coatlaxpeuh where she articulates her feminist concerns: (1) refusal to follow in the passive, submissive tracks of her female forebears, (2) placing a high value on her independence—she prefers to live alone—and loves her solitude and freedom to think for herself, (3) but most of all she does not want a man to marry and lord it over her. She is self-sufficient. For this show of independence and self-reliance she suffers the taunts and jeers of relatives and friends. She experiences strong pressure to conform to a patriarchal culture that wants to force her back into the fold, the mold.

Cisneros demonstrates through her creative energy the political force and impact a folk genre such as the *retablo milagro* narrative can have in the hands of a talented writer.

Mary Helen Ponce's short story "It" explores the travails of a pre-teen Chicanita who longs to have her menstrual cycle started. In a humorous tone, Ponce describes the day to day and month to month anxious moments of a young girl who longs to be like her other teenage friends who are already experiencing their menstrual cycle. Ponce's story "It" falls within her previous work of chronicling the warm, comical, bittersweet growing up experiences of Chicanos/as living in the San Fernando Valley in California during the 1950s and 1960s.

Helena María Viramontes' short story "The Jumping Bean" is an excellent example of her splendid ability to delineate characters. With a fine stroke of the pen her characters acquire life and draw the reader into their fictional world. In this story the figure of the father is particularly striking. In her delineation of a hard-working Latino father, we come to know and understand the difficult and painful life of a man struggling for both spiritual and physical survival. The reader begins to understand that the violence inflicted on the soul of a man in a cruel, racist society is not left at the doorstep of his home but is indeed brought inside the hearth and visited upon his innocent children. The children too are presented as survivors; they are delineated as a bright and sensitive brood who try their utmost to make the best of a difficult situation. María de la Luz, child-surrogate mother, takes charge of the household chores upon her mother's chronic illnesses. But it is the invisible child—the child from whose point of view we read the story—that tugs at our heartstrings. She, the invisible, nameless one, introduces us to her world of surprise and wonder. Her links to the natural world, i.e. the snake and the moth, present her as an innocent primordial being whose pain at a puzzling world becomes our pain. At the conclusion of the story, nevertheless, the "invisible child" blossoms and acquires a new sense of being and self-confidence when she takes the initiative and swallows the contested jumping bean. Through her quick action she saves her father from the difficult quagmire he had walked into. Her new-found self-esteem leaves the reader with a pleasurable feeling—with a sense of optimism—that life will turn out okay for the young, vulnerable child.

Ana Castillo's contribution to this volume is an excerpt from her 1990 novel *Sapogonia*. The selection included in this anthology is Chapter XXXVIII where we find Pastora Velásquez, the principal protagonist of the novel, in jail serving a prison term for transporting undocumented workers in Michigan. Pastora, a committed activist, had been under surveillance when she was asked by a local pastor to transport Dory Sierra Madeira (the ex-wife of one of Pastora's lovers) and her child residing without legal documents in Michigan and in need of transportation to a church sanctuary in Chicago. Pastora agrees to the task but unfortunately is caught and incarcerated.

During her prison term Pastora befriends Mary Lou Acevedo, a Latina with whom she has an intimate lesbian relationship. The narrative explores the friendship between the two women as they wait their release from jail. Mary Lou is a frail woman easily manipulated and intimidated by others. Her relationship with Pastora imbues her with a sense of confidence. At the same time Pastora becomes cognizant of some aspects of her personality she had not been aware before. Pastora's problems with the bully inmate Elaine McElroy who is jealous of her because of her relationship with Mary Lou makes her realize she needs to develop a stronger courageous self if she is to avoid trouble in the future. The prison term proves to be productive in the sense of Pastora's acquiring a new self-knowledge and inner growth and strength. Since her "crime" had been in the service of humanity the reader empathizes with Pastora and learns from her spiritual growth and experience, however harrowing or unpleasant this may have been.

Castillo's strength in narrative development lies in her perceptive understanding of the relationship between two women. In *Sapogonia* a major portion of the novel is this constant journey into an exploration of the bonds developed between two women. In this sense *Sapogonia* continues the narrative thread her previous novel *The Mixquiahuala Letters*, 1986, had woven in her continuing depiction of women and their intimate relationships as they struggle to gain subject positions within a phallocentric world.

**Criticism**

By appropriating the confessional mode the above Chicana authors are deconstructing male-dominated narratives and re-inscribing themselves as subjects and acquiring their own voice. Chicanas are therefore breaking the silence Chicano hegemony had imposed on them in the name of ethnic unity.

Erlinda Gonzales-Berry, in her article "*The* [Subversive] *Mixquiahuala Letters*: An Antidote for Self-Hate," illuminates our understanding of Ana Castillo's outstanding novel. Gonzales-Berry perceives *The Mixquiahuala Letters* (1986) as subversive toward patriarchal hegemony, but liberating for Chicanas. She identifies several strategies Ana Castillo uses in the novel to dismantle or deconstruct male dominance. As an example, Gonzales-Berry points to the epistolary form of the novel, the dialogue with Julio Cortázar—i.e. the dedication to Cortázar—and the various possible readings of *The Mixquiahuala Letters*. Cortázar's game plan for the reading of his novel *Rayuela* is to offer two approaches: to read *Rayuela* in a linear fashion, or as Cortázar has instructed. However the readers are divided into two: a Lector Macho (active) and a Lector Hembra (passive), with the Lector Macho (or "Cómplice") being privileged and the Lector Hembra devalued. Castillo on the other hand, offers three possible readings: (1) conformist, (2) cynic, and (3) quixotic. A fourth possible reading of course is to read the work chronologically. Castillo offers yet another choice to the reader—any way he/she chooses to read it—thus undermining her own authority as author, and in the process exposing Cortázar's patriarchal leanings and breaking the slavery pattern of "Father" or "Master" to daughter, as was alluded to in the epigram to Anais Nin: "I quit loving my father a long time ago. What remained was a slavery to a pattern."

It becomes apparent, as in the case of Moraga and Chávez, that Chicanas are writing their own script and challenging master narrative discourses, while in the process re-inscribing themselves as subjects of these new narratives.

Hector A. Torres also examines Ana Castillo's *The Mixquiahuala Letters* in his excellent article "Story, Telling, Voice: Narrative Authority in Ana Castillo's *The Mixquiahuala Letters*." He perceptively points out how Castillo cleverly uses the epistolary genre to critique patriarchal ideologies extant in Latino and Anglo Cultures. Castillo appropriates a phallocentric genre—i.e. the novel—and stamps her own voice on it. Through her storytelling devices she is able to invade the linguistic domain long dominated by male articulations. *The Mixquiahuala Letters* presents the voice of one Chicana retelling the development and maturing of friendship with another woman. Through their adventures in Mexico and the Unites States the protagonist, Teresa, and her interlocutor, Alicia, the addressee of the letters, come to know themselves and each other, and in the process discover strategies for dealing with the male universe that surrounds them. Torres asserts that through writing, Castillo gives herself, and by extension other Chicanas, a subject position. In gaining narrative authority the writer challenges a phallocentric discourse that misrepresents women. Thus, by her gaining access to writing, Castillo authorizes Self and other Chicanas to become subjects. In the process of giving voice to a marginalized group she also calls into question and challenges the established American literary canon.

In my article "The Street Scene: Metaphoric Strategies in Two Contemporary Chicana Poets" I examine two poets, Evangelina Vigil and Beverly Silva, who through their writings demonstrate a certain ambivalence toward public and private space, and thus the metaphors of *casa* (private space) and *cantina* (public space) appear and reappear in their works. In the early 1980s when Vigil's *Thirty an' Seen a Lot* (1982) and Silva's *The Second Street Poems* (1983) were published, Chicanas were beginning to assert their independence, as reflected in their works. Vigil's and Silva's literary *oeuvres* were also early indications of a desire to free themselves from the Chicano master narrative script. Thus they inserted themselves not as devoted *mamacitas*, *abuelitas*, or *jefitas*, but as women in charge of their lives. Women who walked the streets, not as prostitutes, but as subjects exploring their own neighborhood streets which had been forbidden to them in the past. But not only do the poetic persona in the writings of these two poets open the locked doors and sealed windows, but in addition to walking out into the world they invade the once-forbidden strictly male domains such as the cantinas. Previously, dance halls and cantinas belonged solely to males, or to those despised and even more marginalized women —the vilified whores. Silva's protagonist, in an uncharacteristic manner (for Chicanas as perceived by the Chicano gaze), leaves husband and the comfort of a middle-class home to explore the world, her Chicana roots, and to "find herself." Likewise, Vigil's poetic voice, again in an uncharacteristic fashion, instead of supporting Chicano machismo reacts against it in no uncertain terms, and in the process invades male linguistic domains of forbidden expression as exemplified by the use of such expletives as "Chingón," "motherfucker," "huevos," etc. Thus these two authors rewrite the script and insert themselves as subjects.

Elizabeth Ordóñez, in her study "Webs and Interrogations: Postmodernism, Gender, and Ethnicity in the Poetry of Cervantes and Cisneros," demonstrates how the poetry of two Chicana authors falls within the purview of postmodernist politics. She posits that the "modernist urn" has been "cracked" and the new liberating movement—i.e. postmodernism—challenges old conceptualizations of what is aesthetically correct and pleasing. Postmodernism provides the liberating context in which tradition can be broken and new modes of expressing reality can be explored.

Ordóñez analyzes the works of Cervantes and Cisneros, who she views as falling within the postmodernist project of "challenging master narratives" and "questioning dominant cultural codes." Both Chicana writers reposition the Subject within their writings and engage in a reinscription of said Subject in a radically different way than the male patriarchal gaze has done in the past. Cervantes employs memory in her quest for deconstructing male narrative plots. Cisneros employs various strategies, including a rewriting of master narratives of love. Both authors, however, are not completely free of modernist aesthetics, and their work, according to Ordóñez, is a synthesis of both the modernist and postmodernist projects.

Although there are few Chicana novelists, interest in the few authors who do write novels is growing, as evidenced by the articles focusing on Ana Castillo and Sheila Ortiz Taylor. Ortiz Taylor has been neglected by Chicano/a critics in the past and in "*Faultline*: Sheila Ortiz Taylor's Third Woman Utopia," Juan

Bruce-Novoa speculates that perhaps this is due to lack of overt identification with her Chicana identity and perhaps, in part, because she belongs to another marginalized group—lesbians. Bruce-Novoa examines her novel *Faultline* from the perspective that through its construction—both formally and content-wise—the work offers a radical view of subjectivity, identity, and the nature of reality itself. The very title conjures up a jagged image between two surfaces with a space in between, thus erasing neat lines of opposition and offering a more fluid view of reality. According to Bruce-Novoa, "from the very beginning the text simultaneously sets up a system of logical, bipolar terms (witness/jury, accused/accuser, text/reader) and infuses the system with apparently anarchical, even chaotic content and form." This is intentionally done since the protagonist Arden, a lesbian, is in litigation with a heterosexual husband, Malthus, who "insists on the possibility of varying and even contradictory interpretations of any event, of the joy of interpenetrating fields, of intersecting lines and dialoguing spaces." Bruce-Novoa avers that through *Faultline* Ortiz Taylor, a lesbian, is positing a Third womanist position where "identity is not either/or but the process itself which bonds elements in constant flux."

While Ordóñez, Bruce-Novoa, Herrera-Sobek, and Gonzales-Berry examine Chicana authors and their literary writings, in "Cognitive Desires: An Allegory of/for Chicana Critics" Norma Alarcón focuses on the precarious position of the Chicana critic. Alarcón perceives the Chicana critic wedged between two literary critical theory movements: Anglo-American and European feminisms. Alarcón charges that both systems of literary interpretations place the Chicana in an uncomfortable position, since they both not only neglect these minority women's sociohistorical positions, but indeed silence her with charges of "déclassé" and of practicing essentialist notions or, worse yet, of being ethnocentric. The Chicana critic soon realizes that there is no space in the Academy for her and is bounced from Spanish Departments to English Departments, to Ethnic Studies Departments, to Women's Studies Departments, not really fitting in any of them. Alarcón perceptively reasons that this inability of the academic system to find a space for the Chicana critic forces her to become a "migrant worker," traveling from one university to another, never finding a proper home.

Even so, Alarcón posits that Chicana writers and their texts are presently more likely to "succeed" in academia since their texts have been found to have use-value within the parameters of diversification—i.e. the politics of cultural diversity. For now, however, the Chicana critic can still be classified as "homeless."

In her brilliant article " 'And you know what I have to say isn't always pleasant': Translating the Unspoken Word in Cisneros," Katherine Ríos revisits the Malinche myth in Sandra Cisneros' short story "Never Marry a Mexican." She dissects issues of race, gender, and class and accurately pinpoints Cisneros' critique, from a unique feminist Chicana optic, the contradictions found in both white brown/white sisterhood as well as Chicano nationalist concerns with identity and solidarity.

Alvina E. Quintana, likewise, in her article, "Beyond the Anti-Aesthetic: Reading Gloria Anzaldúa's *Borderlands* and Maxine Hong Kingston's *The Woman Warrior*," explores how minority women writers wage battle against racist and unauthentic representations of them both in mainstream literature and minority male writings.

Both Ríos and Quintana underscore how minority women writers give "voice" to those subjects who have been silenced.

**Film**

The issue of marginalization and misrepresentation is taken up by Rosa Linda Fregoso in her ground-breaking article "Chicana Film Practices: Confronting the Many-Headed Demon of Oppression." As in the articles discussed previously, Chicana filmmakers have not fared any better, regarding acceptance of their works, than other Mexican American women in the literary and visual arts. Unfortunately, the battle for *cineastas* is fought in two fronts: in mainstream culture and with minority filmmakers themselves. The present anthology seeks to highlight the contributions these women are making in this field.

Filmmaking and novel writing are two areas of endeavor that have been alien territory, for the most part, to Chicanas. Some Chicana novelists are making great strides in achieving recognition in this area, as demonstrated by Ana Castillo and Sheila Ortiz Taylor. Similarly, in filmmaking a few Chicanas are making inroads in that difficult-to-enter artistic field. Frances Salomé

España and Lourdes Portillo are two such pioneers in the film industry. We are very fortunate to publish their comments in this anthology.

In "On Film Making—A Personal Odyssey" España offers us a personal commentary on her career as a filmmaker. She attributes her success in this art form to her own tenacity and the spirit of creativity erupting in the 1970s under the impetus of the Chicano Movement. The Chicano Movement opened España's eyes to the surrounding discrimination existing in the East Los Angeles barrios. It also reaffirmed the Chicanos/as' right to pursue their own interests and instilled a confidence in themselves to do it. The slogan "¡Sí se puede!" ("You can do it!") shattered the walls of defeat and racism and empowered Chicanos/as to pursue their dreams and aspirations. España felt the call and with her innate talent and perseverance has been able to enter in the filmmaking industry.

Lourdes Portillo's article "On Chicanas and Filmmaking—A Commentary" provides us with an overall view of the status of Chicanos/as in filmmaking. She particularly focuses on the difficulties Chicanas encounter in the field. Portillo insists there is great prejudice against entrusting women (and even more so Chicanas) with the enormous amounts of money necessary for a filmmaking enterprise. Until this particular type of sexism and racism is abolished it will be very difficult for Chicanos/as to enter and succeed in the field. This in spite of the all-American myth that anyone can succeed through hard work and personal initiative. The filmmaking industry is still one of the strongest bastions of racism and sexism.

**Conclusion**

As can be deduced from the above collection of creative works and critical writings, Chicanas are continuing to produce at full speed outstanding pieces of poetry, prose, and more recently films. This literary renaissance begun in the 1970s is currently being reinvigorated by a group of Chicana lesbian writers as evidenced by the recent publication *Chicana Lesbians: The Girls our Mothers Warned Us About* (1991). Given the continued and growing interest in Chicana creativity and criticism the two areas will continue to flourish and prosper in the years ahead.

# Poetry

# A Book on Goodness

*Bernice Zamora*

Willy, William for short, could take
A volume of backpages and gain
A sermon indicative of good
Real search on God. I took to God
Early on, lapped the puddles Willy
Left in the water fonts (Weren't
They once footbaths for Christ's
Disciples?); I took, too, to trusting
God as good and evil as not good.
A woman like myself, plumped
In a chair, adjusting a
Bra strap, leaning forward
For happy discourse, pockets
Eight people large enough to hold
As hostages flying over the Himalayas,
I took as good. As possible evil I imagine
Such a woman as dragged among
The God givers.

## The Wine of Romance

*Bernice Zamora*

I married with one option.
"What is the matter with you?
        You'll get hurt;
        You can't do that on two drinks. . ."
I rode the tail of freedom
On a champagne trail of that
Particular war between gamblers.
In so many moral ways I laid
Down the guard and Guardian
Of a winning life.

The wife of a drunk ruins
The children she bears him.
The children of drunks cry
In the night prison of his long life.
The wife of a drunk, let us note,
Is a dry drunk who nails
And bars children in a cage
To hold hostage to the dry
And dead lives encaged forever.

# Theatre

*Bernice Zamora*

Once I found the remains,
I wandered ever slowly toward
The serious side of method acting.
What one calls bride-swapping aims
At center stage chills the shins.
Over-heated legacies, these bones
Governed long before puberty,
Long before the Catholic age
Of reason, back when out
Behind the barn was out
Behind the barn. Could it be
Curiosity for suffering sex
All too quickly died the proper
Death in me and then went
To heaven? Or did the
Resurrection act as my protector
These long years of suffering
Sex upstage, behind doors—
Barns and barrelled—up streets
Towned and tarred, backed in alleys,
Bound or burned, legal and illegal,
Licit and illicit, stretched or
Fetal, moral—oh, ever moral—
And immoral according to drunken
Laws conceived for public view
Like finely chiseled tombstones or
Well-wrought passion plays,
Obscured or subtle street dealings,
Sailing or unsailing, sanctioned
And unsanctioned but never,
Never condemned, strictly speaking

In the strictly sporting sense
Of male play. And play
They played, the plot abandoned
Now. Colorfully packaged condoms,
Tickets to a failed play
Passed freely as a failed ploy,
Clutter cemeteries,
Crematoriums and stages,
Prosceniumed and unsizzling,
And, out behind the barn,
Summer rehearsals are closed.

# The Idol

*Demetria Martínez*

Far off
as God,
you mail
cards I
prop up
in a niche
over the
fireplace,
San Ysidro's
old spot,
wood nose
and toes
scoured off
by a hundred
years of May
processions
to bless
ditches
and fields.

Your love
at least
is pure,
unattainable,
perfectly
realized
on 3 × 5's
that crop up
like flowering
chamisa in

adobe ruins
of my life.

I am a
lucky woman.
You can't
hurt me.
All I lack
in the world
is you.

# Landscape,
# Alcalde, N.M.

*Demetria Martínez*

Hanging
low
as
a
squash
blossom
necklace

sun

drops
between
hills,
bosom
of
the
world

# Point Blank

*Demetria Martínez*

1.

Through lace curtain
sun explodes
color of papaya

dirt yard
saguaro cactus
like fingers
sign of peace

2.

On the tub edge
wrapped in a towel
a woman shaves her legs
glazes them with
cornhuskers lotion

phone in her free hand
she asks the sheriff
a personal friend
for a vest
for a priest in El Salvador
hangs up
lights cedar incense
pinches mint
from a pot
wonders what her sons
want for dinner

3.

She is not extraordinary
she forgets to salt the beans
falls asleep with books
never finished on her lap

but she makes rain
and doesn't know it

that day clouds broke open
like a communion host

rain wrapped summer's leftovers
in sheets of foil

## Postscript

*Demetria Martínez*

Winter, summer
intersect,
on the corner
of Edith and Osuna
autumn grips a rake,
cardboard sign offers
work for food.

Twenty-five an hour,
my red pickup,
at the recyclers
bottles chink
like spare change,
1.5 liters
of revelations
we didn't know
we know until
we spoke.

Always on a couch,
cross-legged like yogis.
In Salvador, you said,
we have 14 words
for upheaval,
I want you, I answered,
echoing in canyons
of wine glasses.

Managua, Berlin,
north Edith,
we were going

to save worlds,
1.5 liters
of revolutions
launched on a couch,
faces flush
with spring.

In Morazan you died
defending a chicken wire
clinic, a doctor who wrests
bullet from bone.

All I saved, Pedro,
were these corks.

# War

*Demetria Martínez*

Olive branch,
oil rig,

fig leaf,
gas mask.

President and dictator
on T.V. defend

their individual evils
while the *arroyo*

between those who eat beef
and those who eat insects swells,

its waters surging
faster than blood

to the heart.
The world is beating, beating:

the parade's lead drummer,
flags shuddering like wheat,

a child clapping
on a dirt floor

dreaming of something
to eat.

## The Conquest

*Demetria Martínez*

Spain Mexico United States
On the plaza flags snap

in wind like
the closing of coffins,

bones of Indians
in museums,

necks of Mexicans
lynched by gringos.

Tourists snap pictures
of the land of enchantment

but the cries of those
whose stories aren't told

fill the Old Town kiosk
with static.

My life is a dial
I turn again and again

to make out what I can.

You say you envy
my roots.

You don't know
how little I sleep,

memorizing grammars
of my people,

how I bruise
on a pumice *metate*,

grinding like dry corn
the myths you cherish,

tours of Christmas *luminarias*,
truth clenched, a fist in the dark.

# Power

*Demetria Martínez*

God
in the bread,
peyote, Spanish bible,
at 20 you killed him,
learned English,
talked your way
into beds of men
you did not love,
everywhere testified
against amerika,
cracked and spit
the empire's myths
like piñón nut.

At 30 you bury
those years
like umbilical cord,
return to mornings
listening,
coffee, blank book,
language of trees

# Ceasefire

*Demetria Martínez*

1960
Grandpa's
meat market,
now beer bottles
ripen like
ears of corn
in the Andes.
When uprisings of
daily life seed
your mind,
grains of glass,
cross this lot,
women pin
white towels
on wire,
scrape fat,
dog pans,
wipe hands,
aprons embroidered,
days of the week,
cry *suppertime*,
word older
than warfare,
smelling of
garlic,
*cilantro*,
day darkens
like dishwater,
quiet, wind
on the lip
of a bottle,
old man hoses
down sidewalk,
you're home.

# In A Dream My Sisters

*Elba Rosario Sánchez*

*To Lorna Dee*

In my dream,
two women:

we stand
eye to eye
your charcoal
hair awash in
flicks of colors
a reed
nurtured in
lagoons in
marshes
we speak in
new tongues
entwined
around each other
our hands reach out
pull down the walls
and begin
together
gently mixing
lagoons and shores
I kiss you then
our kiss
gurgles laughter
you shake your head
pull back
I smile and
tell you:

—I see the ancient one in you
la anciana
the one whose breath
bore ours
who passes down
water and awakening
agua y despertar
kernels in flower
maíz a flor
I see her in you
I feel your hands
hers ours
I see her in you
ancient one

# Mirror Image: Womanpoetry

*Elba Rosario Sánchez*

*To Frida*

this one doesn't
stand before you
dressed in lace
nor does she come
mincing words
no
this one doesn't arrive
dressed in little flowers
smelling of a rose
no sir

this one comes before you
womb fist
rock bone
veil foam
root offspring
arms hands
thorns pierce
her tongue

at times she offers
honeyed threads
orange blossoms
at times
she flings poison

this one
this one comes

to give testimony
express her pain
opening the door
to her reality
shouting truths
firmly embracing
her passion

# Espejismo: Mujer Poesía

*Elba Rosario Sánchez*

*A Frida*

ésta no viene engalanada
vestida de encajes
ni tampoco viene
con pelos en la lengua
no
ésta no llega
adornada de florecitas
a rosa olorosa
no señor

ésta viene
vientre puño
piedra hueso
velo espuma
raíz fruto
brazos manos
espinas le curten
la lengua

a veces ofrece
hilos de miel
flor de naranjo
a veces
arroja veneno

ésta
ésta viene
a dar testimonio

expresar su dolor
abriendo la puerta
a su realidad
gritando verdades
abrazando con fuerza
su pasión

# Moon Corn

*Elba Rosario Sánchez*

In the mirror
of night
under a slip
of a moon
I pick ears of corn

I touch you     cornstalk
heart     are you
ripened flower
burst
in seed     are you

I begin   I part your leaves
in my hands   your
moist sweet brown
hair
in dew     bathed

*diosita maíz*
tiny goddess of corn
this humble one
this voice
comes to take your fruit

I begin
you yield   your corn limbs
offer me   milk tender
kernels
life mother     your smile

## Maíz Luna

*Elba Rosario Sánchez*

En el espejo
de la noche
pisco estrellas

palpo    tu corazón
milpa eres
madura espiga eres

comienzo a deshojarte
acariciando tu pelo
de turrón café húmedo

diosita maíz
esta voz humilde
pide tomar tu fruta

abres tus hojas ofreciéndome
granitos de leche
mamá vida

tu sonrisa

# Codex

*Elba Rosario Sánchez*

written on the walls
in the belly
of the pyramids
of the time
of the moon
at once past
and present time

life steeped in
ancient rituals
puffs of clouds
from women's mouths
flights taken
on puffs of clouds
a dance
with my ancestors
*yo ánima*/ I soulmate

a time steeped
in metaphors
metaphors
of resistance
metaphors to          hold onto
the herbs
the tobacco
the sea shells
the corn

metaphors for

the prayers
the feathers          offerings
to all precious

living ones
the deer
metaphor for
life in flight

it was
a time of
*Coatlicue*
like a circle round
like life round
*Coatlicue*
mirrored serpent
wrapped around
the hoop of life
wrapped around
the hoop of death
*madre serpiente*

it was a time
of the women
*las creadoras*
who celebrated
the cycles of their
moons
*ellas*
they pray
they heal
they work
they know
the children
children
stars
that fall
becoming rain

life
for their cornfields
life blood
sacred
*como las yerbitas*
their children

# Lizard

*Elba Rosario Sánchez*

here I am
contented lizard
I spend my days
belly to the sun
stretching out
without fearing
the dagger
of my imperfections
I am who I am

I awoke
from a long dream
ate the spiderwebs
that entangled
my eyelashes
blindfolding me

I do not eat
flies any more
nor am I cold blooded
I am
my own midwife
showing off scales
of earthen copper
from head to tail
give birth to myself

# Lagartija

*Elba Rosario Sánchez*

aquí me ves
lagartija contenta
me paso los días
panza al sol
cuerpo extendido
sin miedo
al filo
de mis imperfecciones
soy quien soy

desperté
de un largo sueño
me comí las telarañas
que antes me enredaban
las pestañas
vendándome los ojos

ahora ya no como
moscas
ni soy de sangre fría
yo misma
mi propia partera
luciendo escamas
de cobre terrenal
de cabeza a cola
me doy a luz

## Woman's Word

*Elba Rosario Sánchez*

life  woman  herstory
I sustain
in my memory
the one you want
to mutilate
to domesticate
with your alphabet

you have wanted me mute
since childhood
once
silence
was my abyss
your frothing words
placated
your eyes sternly
warned
  —don't think
   you're prettier that way

once
I would hide
my forbidden voice
in the pleats of my silences
cities trapped in my throat
until my tongue gave birth
to the word
challenging
what was
once accepted

## There Is a War Going On

*Elba Rosario Sánchez*

maimed hearts
torn hearths
hearts torn
in horror of
cratered homes
and bodies
in the sand
heartsandeyes
dazed
aglow from the
endless rain of
fire bombs

screams and sirens
silver slashes tatoos
oozing red
over ripped flesh
*El hijo de Doña Irene*
El Smiley *muerto*
he couldn't get a job
his spirit frozen
his brain cells
deadened by
meth and crack
he was just a homeboy
from the other side
of town

over and over
promises and pleas
over and over

she's reeling back
pulled by the hair
her face
grinds against
the wall
her jaw is ripping
in his grip
woman's spirit
numbed
and despairing
in a windowless room
filled with children
*mi hermana*
*mujer*

who dies on the war line?
who pays on the home line?
there is a war going on
right there
right here

## Cruzando Fronteras

*Elba Rosario Sánchez*

*a mi madre, quien en México, esperaba*
*las cartas de mi padre en Chicago*

perseguida por tu ausencia
el pito del cartero
me hace correr
mis manos se adelantan
vuelan
extendiéndose como pista
para que sobre ellas aterrice
el sobre esperado
las conocidas letras

quizás habrá una mancha
un hilo
un cabello
una foto
un algo que me acerque
un poco más a tí

al otro lado
todavía sudas a chorros
te despiertan y acuestan
retorcijones de entrañas hambrientas
algunas mañanas y muchas noches
te sientes morir estando tan lejos
de tu suelo
de tu gente

yo busco tu aliento en esas cartas
quizás al desdoblar las hojas

sentiré el calor de tus manos
quizás así llegue a mí
el olor de tu sudor
el sabor de tus palabras risas besos
vía aérea
vía aérea
vía aérea

# Watsonville

*Elba Rosario Sánchez*

*más de dos años después*

tu delgado dedo
y el gordo
pico de café pájaro
guían la colilla del cigarro
tus labios la aprietan
y chupas con fervor
chupas
como si fuera
tu último suspiro
como si se te apagara
la vida
como para
contener todo tu mundo
en esa chupada
cierras los ojos

—horas enteras
he caminado horas enteras
tu entonces frágil figura
se dobla bajo el peso de la ropa
—ocho años de jale
más de un año en huelga
jíjole, eso si que fue difícil
ahí sí que aprendí
aprendimos todos
me acaban de decir
que sólo me darán
cuatro horas al día
seis

si es que pueden
¿te imaginas? ¿qué voy a hacer?
tus escasos cuarenta años
se multiplican en las rutas
que cruzan tu frente
y giran alrededor de tus ojos
estábamos sentadas en Winchell's
recuerdo las bancas
plástico amarillento frío
por la ventana
veíamos el tráfico y la gente
pasar

# Rumbamos

*Elba Rosario Sánchez*

sacred is this dance
as sacred is the drum
communion of
hand and skin
   touch   touch   kiss   kiss
one pulse
one heart
two sticks beat the air
heat and rhythm
         that we thrill in
naked to our skins
   taca   taca   dun   dun
      taca   taca   dun   dun
hearts   in   a   gal   lop
syn
   co
      pa
         ting
to this *guaguanco*
to this *tumbao*
to our *rumba* of love

# Rumbamos

*Elba Rosario Sánchez*

sagrada es esta danza
como sagrado el tambor
comunión de
mano a cuero
toca toca besa besa
un pulso
un corazón
dos claves en el aire
calor y ritmo
que gozamos
a cuerito encuerados
taca taca dun dun
taca taca dun dun
corazones ga lo pan tes
sin
co
pan
do
a este guaguancó
a este tumbao
a nuestra rumba de amor

# Moon's Harvest

*Elba Rosario Sánchez*

I search for you
in the darkness

guided
by the moon's threads
my hands find
your cornstalk limbs

between my fingers
moistbrown silk
cascades over
moon kernels

in the darkness
I find you

# Prose

# Sapogonia (excerpt)

*Ana Castillo*

You wake on your own in the morning, gather your things set at the foot of the bed the night before, and make your way to the bathroom at the far end of the long room. You urinate, brush your teeth, wash your face and hands, run a brush through your hair. You wear no makeup; even the dashing black mascara, rouge, and lipstick that you were once accustomed to in the world of men has been discarded, deemed unnecessary and a worthless expense. You slip on the panties and bra, and one of your three button-down blouses or one of your three T-shirts, each stenciled with one slogan or another, and one of your two pairs of jeans or your cotton pants. You always wear athletic shoes. Because it is chilly these mornings, you throw on a windbreaker to run across the courtyard to the cafeteria.

You are on kitchen duty for the breakfast shift. This is your assignment. It is your job, although you don't get paid. Most of the women working with you are silent because sleep, like cobwebs, inhabits their brains and they're dwelling on dreams, which are private and luxurious.

Only Mary Lou Acevedo talks. She chews gum, she talks. She smokes a menthol cigarette and talks. She talks and doesn't care if anyone listens. You listen to Mary Lou because she is the one familiar object that reminds you of where you come from. Mary Lou told you on your first day on kitchen duty that she lived many years before on Peoria St., one block from where you did as a child. She is five years your senior and moved away before you started school. She left to 18th St. with her parents, her twin brother, and six other brothers and sisters.

On 18th St.—it was 16th and Racine actually—just past the viaduct, the Acevedo family lived in an old shingled house upstairs from the junk store her father owned and made his living from. Mary Lou's mother found him on the toilet seat one morning, his eyes lost up in his head, his mouth wide open, dead. Something inside him had burst open and poisoned him.

Mary Lou's older sister dropped out of high school pregnant and got married to her first boyfriend, who was black and always had a lot of girlfriends. They have six kids now and live on 17th and Racine. Her husband helps run the junk store.

Mary Lou's twin brother shot himself in the head three years earlier, leaving a Boricua wife and baby daughter behind. No note. His widow went to a spiritualist in Puerto Rico who told her he killed himself because he had another woman who'd put a hex on him when he refused to leave his wife for her.

Mary Lou's younger brothers and sisters had all grown up too fast, learning too much about the wrong things and not enough about what was good for them.

Mary Lou was put in jail because she kidnapped her own kids. Her ex-husband had warned her, do it again and I'll call the authorities on you. She took the children to Florida. Nearly a year later she was found and put away. But her husband had gone one better. He had let the police know that Mary Lou in part made her living from selling dope. She was also given time for possession of a quantity of marijuana and cocaine sufficient to keep the partiers of any swank NY night club satiated for an entire weekend.

Mary Lou looks younger than her age. She is dark, small with thin legs, no calves, and has a black mole right on the corner of her chin and the distressful eyes of a caged rabbit. It is the look in those eyes and the incessant chatter that tell you why Mary Lou found it necessary to attach herself to a *stud-broad*.

After breakfast there is a meeting with the counselor. The rest of the day you work as the college advisor's assistant; for this you are paid forty dollars a month. On designated evenings, you attend an aerobics class. In the dayroom late in the evening when you can't sleep, you stay up talking with one or two of the women. At night, sometimes, you go into the laundry room, closing the door behind you, and you play your guitar.

On Sundays, you have band practice, which specializes in rhythm and blues, but in the laundry room, where no one's preference of music overrules your own, you play sixteenth-century Spanish music with the principle of variation. You play the compositions of Fernando Sor, his *Variations on a Theme by Mozart, Opus 9*. The theme was from *The Magic Flute*, whose music also provided Beethoven with a theme for one of his sets of variations. The music makes you happy.

Human beings are creatures of habit and it has been barely six months when you have already accustomed yourself to the routine, the lack of privacy, the snoring of the woman who sleeps on the cot next to yours. You have trained yourself to be only so friendly, and never to not be friendly, whether the person presented before you in your personal estimation deserves your attention or not.

When Mary Lou was with her husband, she got involved with a woman. Her husband found out, threw her out, and sought an immediate divorce. He was given custody of the children. The judge, a woman, told Mary Lou that she wasn't giving the children to her husband's care because of her lesbian tendencies, but because promiscuity for a married individual was a bad example of morality to give to children, regardless if it was with the same sex.

Mary Lou's outside lover was kind and attentive. She was like a mother sometimes, when Mary Lou needed mothering, and she was a loyal sister when Mary Lou needed a confidante, and she was very warm and very good to be with. Mary Lou received a letter from her once a week.

Mary Lou, who is older than you, you first regard as a younger sister because of her character, which always makes her easily persuaded, unsure about her own opinions. She tells you one morning that Elaine McElroy, one of the most notorious stud-broads around, wants to marry her.

Mary Lou and you are in the dayroom one evening, smoking and talking. "I've got eighteen months to go," Mary Lou says, exhaling a puff. "You think I'll make it?" She laughs that little nervous laugh of hers.

"You'll make it," you respond solemnly. You yourself have seven months left, each day marked off in your head the moment you open your eyes in the morning.

"Think my kids'll ever forgive me?" Mary Lou doesn't laugh this time, but plays with a hangnail.

"Your kids have nothing to forgive you for, Mary Lou," you say quietly. "What have you ever done wrong? You left a man who beat you?"

Mary Lou shakes her head, "I left their father to be with a woman."

"She loves you, doesn't she?" you ask.

"I think so, but it's been so long. And now Elaine. . ."

You look away from Mary Lou. In a corner is a group of black women, dancing to the radio, in another, a group of white women playing cards, at the far end, a few brown women talking in Spanish. "There's that one who said something to you yesterday," you whisper discreetly, noticing a haughty look being sent your way from the group of Spanish-speaking women.

"You mean la puertorriqueña?" Mary Lou asks. You nod. "She's always saying something to someone!" Mary Lou says. "I just ignore her! Ignore her. It's the best thing, Pastora."

You nod again. Elaine McElroy walks in. She calls to Mary Lou and Mary Lou gets up to go to her.

"Wait," you say, and the spontaneous gesture of your hand on her forearm surprises you. Elaine is intimidating because of her size, but you pity how your friend's docility toward the woman is so obvious. Mary Lou hesitates. She doesn't want to go to Elaine, but she will. She only needs a reason to stay.

*Tell her to stay.* Elaine is big and tough, with at least six residents as lovers. They give her cigarettes and money. She has sex with them and when they have a problem she gives them protection. They run to quake beneath the great wings of their very own guard. It is because marriage seems so unlikely for Elaine that you have been persistent to have Mary Lou reconsider marrying her.

"Wait," you repeat, quietly, hardly moving your lips. Mary Lou sits down. Elaine McElroy is watching from across the room. She lights a cigarette. "Let's go," you say to Mary Lou and you both leave the room together.

Someone whispers in your ear in the cafeteria the next day, "Watch out! Elaine's mad at you, honey, for messin' with one of her women!" Nothing happens that day. Days pass. At band practice on Sunday, someone else repeats the warning, "Elaine says she's gonna kick your ass good for trying to steal Mary Lou from her. . ." Nothing happens.

One morning you can't find one of your T-shirts. You think you may have misplaced it, but several of your commissaries are missing, too: a new bottle of shampoo and a fresh pack of cigarettes, as well as the porcelain box you keep the hair bands and barrettes in that hold your hair up when you scrub pots, when you play your guitar. One of the residents in your cottage hints that she knows who has been in your things, but she won't say who.

After breakfast another woman tells you that she saw one of Elaine's women wearing your T-shirt. There was no mistake that it was yours because on the back was stenciled "*Música de las Américas*," and no one else in the entire state has one like it.

Elaine works out in the gym. She is known to give a hard punch. It isn't her size or her strength that makes you ignore her instigation. You are being considered for a work release program in Chicago. It's almost as good as being home so long as you maintain a clean record.

Mary Lou knows where to find you when you aren't in the dayroom in the evening. In the laundry room, she smokes a cigarette while you play that fancy music she thinks you are a genius for knowing. She liked Elvis Presley as a kid. She also like María Victoria because her father took her and the family to the Teatro Zenith when they were children and María Victoria was there performing live. "Do you know 'Paloma negra?' " she asks you, and you sing it for her.

"¿Te vas a casar con ella?" you ask without looking at her, who smokes a cigarette and stares at her gym shoes. She sticks the butt under the shoe and puts it out, her small hand lingering along the shoelace. Her eyes are on the foot; your eyes are on the hand, the fingers playfully walking over the tip of your own shoe. She pulls at it and laughs a little. She shrugs her shoulder. "No sé."

"And your friend, the one who's waiting for you outside?" you ask. You are aware that your voice is unsteady suddenly, awaiting her response. She feels your need to know. If Mary Lou were someone else, she would lie. But she doesn't know how to lie. "She seems so far away right now."

Mary Lou has said this looking at you, right into your face, that kind of innocent directness that invades all your barriers. *Look at her, meet the dark, open face, and as you do, it is now only inches away from your own.*

Mary Lou's mouth is very small and thin against yours. Her dishwasher's hands are hard against your ribs and hips. You taste her with your mouth, your hands, her smell, the texture of her hair and skin.

"And who's waiting for you out there?" Mary Lou whispers, a gruff voice in your ear, along your neck.

"No one," you answer, your throat full, so that the words are hardly uttered, "But I won't forget you." And Mary Lou has entered you, so that you haven't had to say that.

*You will take Mary Lou with you. Mary Lou, who is the abandoned buildings you explored with a child's courage; rooftops jumped; fast double-dutch tournaments; black girls who pulled your red-ribboned braids; pink and white roses offered to the Virgin the month of May; Christmas pilgrimages which taught you the hymns that gave you the gift of song; urban renewal and the upheaval of your Mexican world; white city workers who relocated each family after its building was marked with an X in a circle, the next one to be torn down; your father who left, and the mother's next husband who never spoke your name or looked you in the face until you were thirteen and he tried to have you in bed; your mother, who stopped being Catholic after your confirmation and went to Protestant church meetings in a storefront every night; Abuelita who took care of you from the age of three months and taught you about the healing of the body with herbs and of the soul with your own; Mary Lou, who banished the devil of your childhood.*

Elaine's animosity continues in the form of hurling personal insults when she happens to run into you. Others overhear her and you are constantly assured by witnesses that you must maintain your calmness, that you can't let Elaine's acrimony get the better of you. And you don't.

It happens in aerobics class one Wednesday night. You're near the instructor, facing her, when others, who see her coming in, report later that Elaine rushed toward you like a bull who saw red. She threw her whole weight on you, who were caught completely off guard, knocking you to the floor immediately. By the time officers were able to get hold of Elaine, she had bent back your right foot and left arm to the point of spraining them both.

Elaine is ticketed and sent to the floor for two weeks. Because of your previously unblemished record and because of the vast testimony on your behalf that Elaine had been wanting a fight with you, who repeatedly avoided it, you are not put in segregation, but you are ticketed, temporarily restricted from being in the band, going to aerobics and to the dayroom. You have also lost the hope to be put out on work release. It is the committee's assessment that you could have avoided the whole incident had you not insisted on advising Mary Lou Acevedo when you knew what the possible consequences were.

# Little Miracles, Kept Promises

*Sandra Cisneros*

Exvoto, Donated as Promised

On the 20th of December of 1988 we suffered a terrible disaster on the road to Corpus Christi. The bus we were riding skidded and overturned near Robstown and a lady and her little girl were killed. Thanks to La Virgen de Guadalupe we are alive, all of us miraculously unharmed, and with no visible scars, except we are afraid to ride buses. We dedicate this retablo to La Virgencita with our affection and gratitude and our everlasting faith.

Familia Arteaga
Alice, Texas
G.R. (Gracias Recibido/Thanks Given)

Blessed Santo Niño de Atocha,

Thank you for helping us when Chapa's truck got stolen. We didn't know how we was going to make it. He needs it to get to work, and this job, well, he's been on probation since we got him to quit drinking. Raquel and his kids are hardly ever afraid of him anymore, and we are proud parents. We don't know how we can repay you for everything you have done for our family. We will light a candle to you every Sunday and never forget you.

Sidronio Tijerina
Brenda A. Camacho de Tijerina
San Angelo, Texas

Dear San Martín de Porres,

Please send us clothes, furniture, shoes, dishes. We need anything that don't eat. Since the fire we have to start all over again and Lalo's disability check ain't much and don't go far. Zulema would like to finish school but I says she can just forget about it now. She's our oldest and her place is at home helping us out I told her. Please make her see some sense. She's all we got.

Thanking you,
Adelfa Vásquez
Escobas, Texas

Dear San Antonio de Padua,

Can you please help me find a man who isn't a pain in the nalgas. There aren't any in Texas, I swear. Especially not in San Antonio.

Can you do something about all the educated Chicanos who have to go to California to find a job. I guess what my sister Irma says is true: "If you didn't get a husband when you were in college, you don't get one."

I would appreciate it very much if you sent me a man who speaks Spanish, who at least can pronounce his name the way it's supposed to be pronounced. Someone please who never calls himself "Hispanic" unless he's applying for a grant from Washington, D.C.

Can you send me a man man. I mean someone who's not ashamed to be seen cooking or cleaning or looking after himself. In other words, a man who acts like an adult. Not one who's never lived alone, never bought his own underwear, never ironed his own shirts, never even heated his own tortillas. In other words, don't send me someone like my brothers who my mother ruined with too much chichi, or I'll throw him back.

I'll turn your statue upside down until you send him to me. I've put up with too much too long, and now I'm just too intelligent, too powerful, too beautiful, too sure of who I am finally to deserve anything less.

Ms. Barbara Ybáñez
San Antonio, Texas

Dear Niño Fedencio,

I would like for you to help me get a job with good pay, benefits, and retirement plan. I promise you if you help me I will make a pilgrimage to your tomb in Espinazo and bring you flowers. Many thanks.

César Escandón
Pharr, Texas

DEAR DON PEDRITO JARAMILLO HEALER OF LOS OLMOS

MY NAME IS ENRIQUETA ANTONIA SANDOVAL I LIVE IN SAN MARCOS TX I AM SICK THEY OPERATED ME FROM A KIDNEY AND A TUMOR OF CANCER BUT THANKS TO GOD I AM ALIVE BUT I HAVE TO GET TREATMENTS FOR A YEAR THE KIMO I AM 2½ YEARS OLD BUT MY GRANDMA BROUGHT ME THAT YOU AND OUR LORD WHO IS IN THE HEAVENS WILL CURE ME WITH THIS LETTER THAT I AM DEPOSITING HERE ITS MY GRANDMA WHO IS WRITING THIS I HOPE EVERYBODY WHO SEES THIS LETTER WILL TAKE A MINUTE TO ASK FOR MY HEALTH

ENRIQUETA ANTONIA SANDOVAL
2 AND A HALF YEARS OLD

I LEOCADIA DIMAS VDA. DE CORDERO OF SAN MARCOS TX HAVE COME TO PAY THIS REQUEST TO DON PEDRITO THAT MY GRANDDAUGHTER WILL COME OUT FINE FROM HER OPERATION THANKS TO GOD AND THOSE WHO HELPED SUCH GOOD DOCTORS THAT DID THEIR JOB WELL THE REST IS IN GODS HANDS THAT HE DO HIS WILL MANY THANKS WITH ALL MY HEART.

YOUR VERY RESPECTFUL SERVANT
LEOCADIA

Oh Mighty Poderosos, Blessed Powerful Ones,

You who are crowned in heaven and who are so close to our Divine Savior, I implore your intercession before the Almighty on my behalf. I ask for peace of spirit and prosperity, and that the demons in my path that are the cause of all my woes be removed so that they no longer torment me. Look favorably on this petition and bless me, that I may continue to glorify your deeds with all my heart—santísmo Niño Fidencio, gran General Pancho Villa, bendito Don Pedrito Jaramillo, virtuoso John F. Kennedy, and blessed Pope John Paul. Amen.

Gertrudis Parra
Uvalde, Texas

Father Almighty,

Teach me to love my husband again. Forgive me.

s.
Corpus Christi

Seven African Powers that surround our Savior—Obatala, Yemaya, Ochún, Orunla, Ogun, Elegua, and Shango—why don't you behave and be good to me? Oh Seven African Powers, come on, don't be bad. Let my Illinois lottery ticket win, and if it does, don't let my cousin Cirilo in Chicago cheat me out of my winnings, since I'm the one who pays for the ticket and all he does is buy it for me each week—if he does even that. He's my cousin, but like the Bible says, better to say nothing than to say nothing nice.

Protect me from the evil eye of the envious and don't let my enemies do me harm, because I've never done a thing wrong to anyone first. Save this good Christian who the wicked have taken advantage of.

Seven Powers, reward my devotion with good luck. Look after me, why don't you? And don't forget me because I never forget you.

Moises Ildefonso Mata
San Antonio, Texas

Virgencita de Guadalupe,

I promise to walk to your shrine on my knees the very first day I get back. I swear, if you will only get me the Tortilleria la Casa de la Masa to pay me the $253.72 they owe me for two weeks work. I put in 67½ hours that first week and 79 hours the second, and I don't have anything to show for it yet. I calculated with the taxes deducted, I have $253.72 coming to me. That's all I'm asking for. The $253.72 I have coming to me.

I have asked the proprietors Blanquita and Rudy Mondragón and they keep telling me next week, next week, next week. And it's almost the middle of the third week already and I don't know how I'm going to do it to pay this week's rent, since I'm already behind, and the other guys have loaned me as much as they're able, and I don't know what I'm going to do, I don't know what I'm going to do.

My wife and the kids and my in-laws all depend on what I send home. We are humble people, Virgencita. You know I'm not full of vices. That's how I am. It's been hard for me to live here so far away without seeing my wife, you know. And sometimes one gets tempted, but no, and no, and no. I'm not like that. Please, Virgencita, all I'm asking for is my $253.72. There is no one else I can turn to here in this country, and well, if you can't help me, well, I just don't know.

Arnulfo Contreras
San Antonio, Texas

Saint Sebastian who was persecuted with arrows and then survived, thank you for answering my prayers! All them arrows that had persecuted me—my brother-in-law Ernie and my sister Alba and their kids—el Junior, la Gloria, and el Skyler—all gone. And now my home sweet home is mine again, and my Dianita bien lovey-dovey, and my kids got something to say to me besides who hit who.

Here is the little gold milagrito I promised you, a little house, see? And it ain't that cheap gold-plate shit either. So now that I paid you back, we're even, right? Cause I don't like for no one to say Victor Lozano don't pay his debts. I pays cash on the line, bro. And Victor Lozano's word like his deeds is solid gold.

Victor A. Lozano
Houston, TX

Dear San Lázaro,

My mother's comadre Demetria said if I prayed to you that like maybe you could help me because you were raised from the dead and did a lot of miracles and maybe if I lit a candle every night for seven days and prayed, you might maybe could help me with my face breaking out with so many pimples. Thank you.

Rubén Ledesma
Hebbronville, Texas

Santísma Señora de San Juan de los Lagos,

We came to see you twice when they brought you to San Antonio, my mother and my sister Yolanda and two of my aunts, Tía Enedina and my Tía Perla, and we drove all the way from Beeville just to visit you and make our requests.

I don't know what my Tía Enedina asked for, she's always so secretive, but probably it had to do with her son Beto who doesn't do anything but hang around the house and get into trouble. And my Tía Perla no doubt complained about her ladies' problems—her ovaries that itch, her tangled fallopians, her uterus that makes her seasick with all its flipping and flopping. And Mami who said she only came along for the ride, lit three candles so you would bless us all and sweep jealousy and bitterness from our hearts because that't what she says every day and every night. And my sister Yoli asked that you help her lose weight because I don't want to wind up like Tía Perla, embroidering altar cloths and dressing saints.

But that was a year ago, Virgencita, and since then my cousin Beto was fined for killing the neighbor's rooster with a flying Big Red bottle, and my Tía Perla is convinced her uterus has fallen because when she walks something inside her rattles like a maraca, and my mother and my aunts are arguing and yelling at each other same as always. And my stupid sister Yoli is still sending away for even stupider products like the Grasa Fantástica, guaranteed to burn away fat—It really works, Tere, just rub some on while you're watching TV—only she's fatter than ever and just as sad.

What I realize is that we all made the trip to San Antonio to ask something of you, Virgencita, we all needed you to listen to us. And of all of us, my mama and sister Yoli, and my aunts Enedina and Perla, of all of us, you granted me my petition and sent, just like I asked, a guy who would love only me because I was tired of looking at girls younger than me walking along the street or riding in cars or standing in front of the school with a guy's arm hooked around their neck.

So what is it I'm asking for? Please, Virgencita. Lift this heavy cross from my shoulders and leave me like I was before, wind on my neck, my arms swinging free, and no one telling me how I ought to be.

Teresa Galindo
Beeville, Texas

Miraculous Black Christ of Esquipulas,

Please make our grandson to be nice to us and stay away from drugs. Save him to find a job and move away from us. Thank you.

Grandma y Grandfather
Harlingen

M3rle5l45s Bl1ck Chr3st 4f 2sq53p5l1s,

3 1sk y45,L4rd, w3th 1ll my h21rt pl21s2 w1tch 4v2r M1nny B2n1v3d2s wh4 3s 4v2rs2ls. 3 l4v2 h3m 1nd 3 d4n't kn4w wh1t t4 d4 1b45t 1ll th3s l4v2 s1dn2ss 1nd sh1m2 th1t f3lls m2.

B2nj1m3n T.
D21 R34 TX

Milagroso Cristo Negro de Esquipulas,

Te ofrezco este retrato de mis niños. Wáchelos, Dios Santo, y si le quitas el trago a mi hijo te prometo prender velitas. Ayúdanos con nuestras cuentas, Señor, y que el cheque del income tax nos llegue pronto para pagar los biles. Danos una buena vida y que les ayudes a mis hijos a cambiar sus modos. Tú que eres tan bondadoso eschucha estas peticiones que te pido con todo mi corazón y con toda la fe de mi alma. Ten piedad, Padre mio. Mi nombre es Adela O.

Elizondo.
Cotulla TX

Milagroso Cristo Negro,

Thank you por el Milagro de haber graduado de high school. Aquí le regalo mi retrato de graduation.

Fito Moroles
Rockport, Texas

Cristo Negro,

Venimos desde muy lejos. Infinitas gracias, Señor. Gracias por habernos escuchado.

Familia Armendáriz G.
Matamoros, Tamps. México

Jesus Christ,

Please keep Deborah Abrego and Ralph S. Urrea together forever.

Love,
Deborah Abrego
Sabinal, Texas

Blessed Virgen de Remedios,

Señora Dolores Alcalá de Corchado finds herself gravely ill from a complication that resulted after a delicate operation she underwent Thursday last, and from which she was recovering satisfactorily until suffering a hemmorhage Tuesday morning. Please intercede on her behalf. We leave her in the hands of God, that His will be done, now that we have witnessed her suffering and don't know whether she should die or continue this life. Her husband of forty-eight years offers this request with all his heart.

Señor Gustavo Corchado B.
Laredo, Tejas

Madrecita de Dios,

Thank you. Our child is born healthy!

Rene y Janie Garza
Hondo, TX

Saint Jude, patron saint of lost causes,

Help me pass my English 320, British Restoration Literature class and everything to turn out ok.

Eliberto González
Dallas

✣ ✣ ✣ ✣ ✣ ✣

Virgencita...

I've cut off my hair just like I promised I would and pinned my braid here by your statue. Above a Toys "R" Us name tag that says IZAURA. Along several hospital bracelets. Next to a business card for Sergio's Casa de la Belleza Beauty College. Domingo Reyna's driver's license. Notes printed on the flaps of envelopes. Silk roses, plastic roses, paper roses, roses crocheted out of fluorescent orange yarn. Photo button of a baby in a *charro* hat. Caramel-skinned woman in a white graduation cap and gown. Mean dude in bandanna and tattoos. Oval black-and-white portrait of the sad uncle who never married. A mama in a sleeveless dress watering porch plants. Sweet boy with new mustache and new soldier uniform. Teenager with a little bit of herself sitting on her lap. Blurred husband and wife leaning one into the other as if joined at the hip. Black-and-white photo of the cousins *la* Josie *y la* Mary Helen, circa 1942. Polaroid of Sylvia Rios. First Holy Communion, age nine years.

So many *milagritos* safety-pinned here, so many little miracles dangling from red thread—a gold Sacred Heart, a tiny copper arm, a kneeling man in silver, a bottle, a brass truck, a foot, a house, a hand, a baby, a cat, a breast, a tooth, a belly button, and evil eye. So many petitions, so many promises made and kept. And there is nothing I can give you except this braid of hair the color of coffee in a glass.

*Chayo, what have you done! All that beautiful hair.*

*Chayito, how could you ruin in one second what your mother took years to create?*

*You might as well've plucked out your eyes like Saint Lucy. All that hair!*

My mother cried, did I tell you? All that beautiful hair. . .

I've cut off my hair. Which I've never cut since the day I was born. The donkey tail in a birthday game. Something shed like a snakeskin.

My head as light as if I'd raised it from the water. My heart buoyant again, as if before I'd worn el Sagrado Corazón in my open chest. I could've lit this entire church with my grief.

I'm a bell without a clapper. A woman with one foot in this world and one foot in that. A woman straddling both. This thing between my legs, this unmentionable.

I'm a snake swallowing its tail. I'm my history and my future. All my ancestors' ancestors inside my own belly. All my futures and all my pasts.

I've had to steel and hoard and hone myself. I've had to push the furniture against the door and not let you in.

*What you doing sitting in there in the dark?*

I'm thinking.

*Thinking of what?*

Just. . . thinking.

*You're nuts. Chayo, ven a saludar. All the relatives are here. You come out of there and be sociable.*

Do boys think, and girls daydream? Do only girls have to come out and greet the relatives and smile and be nice and *quedar bien*?

*Its not good to spend so much time alone.*

*What she do in there all by herself? It don't look right.*

*Chayito, when you getting married? Look at your cousin Leticita. She's younger than you.*

*How many kids you want when you grow up?*

*When I become a mommy. . . .*

*You'll change. You'll see. Wait till you meet Mr. Right.*

*Chayo, tell everybody what it is you're studying again.*

*Look at our Chayito. She likes making her little pictures. She's gonna be a painter.*

*A painter! Tell her I got five rooms that need painting.*
*When you become a mother. . . .*

* * *

Thank you for making all those months I held my breath not a child in my belly, but a thyroid problem in my throat.

I can't be a mother. Not now. Maybe never. Not for me to choose, like I didn't choose being female. Like I didn't choose being artist—it isn't something you choose. It's something you are, only I can't explain it.

I don't want to be a mother.

I wouldn't mind being a father. At least a father could still be artist, could love some*thing* instead of some*one*, and no one would call that selfish.

I leave my braid here and thank you for believing what I do is important. Though no one else in my family, no other woman, neither friend nor relative, no one I know, not even the heroine in the *telenovelas*, no woman wants to live alone.

I do.

Virgencita de Guadalupe. For a long time I wouldn't let you in my house. I couldn't see you without seeing my ma each time my father came home drunk and yelling, blaming everything that ever went wrong in his life on her.

I couldn't look at your folded hands without seeing my *abuela* mumbling, "My son, my son, my son. . . ." Couldn't look at you without blaming you for all the pain my mother and her mother and all our mother's mothers have put up with in the name of God. Couldn't let you in my house.

I wanted you bare-breasted, snakes in your hands. I wanted you leaping and somersaulting the backs of bulls. I wanted you swallowing raw hearts and rattling volcanic ash. I wasn't going to be my mother or my grandma. All that self-sacrifice, all that silent suffering. Hell no. Not here. Not me.

Don't think it was easy going without you. Don't think I didn't get my share of it from everyone. Heretic. Atheist. *Malinchista. Hocicona.* But I wouldn't shut my yap. My mouth always getting me in trouble. *Is* that *what they teach you at the university? Miss High-and-Mighty. Mis Thinks-She's-Too-Good-for-Us.* Acting like a *bolilla*, a white girl. *Malinche.* Don't think it didn't hurt being called a traitor. Trying to explain to my ma, to my *abuela*, why I didn't want to be like them.

I don't know how it all fell in place. How I finally understood who you are. No longer Mary the mild, but our mother Tonantzín. Your church at Tepeyac built on the site of her temple. Sacred ground no matter whose goddess claims it.

That you could have the power to rally people when a country was born, and again during civil war, and during a farmworker strike in California made me think maybe there is power in my mother's patience, strength in my grandmother's endurance. Because those who suffer have a special power, don't they? The power of understanding someone else's pain. And understanding is the beginning of healing.

When I learned your real name is Coatlaxopeuh, She Who Has Dominion over Serpents, when I recognized you as Tonantzín, and learned your names are Teteoinnan, Toci, Xochiquetzal, Tlazolteotl, Coatlicue, Chalchiuhtlicue, Coyolxauhqui, Huixtocihuatl, Chicomecoatl, Cihuacoatl, when I could see you as Nuestra Señora de la Soledad, Nuestra Señora de los Remedios, Nuestra Señora del Perpetuo Socorro, Nuestra Señora de San Juan de los Lagos, Our Lady of Lourdes, Our Lady of Mount Carmel, Our Lady of the Rosary, Our Lady of Sorrows, I wasn't ashamed, then, to be my mother's daughter, my grandmother's granddaughter, my ancestor's child.

When I could see you in all your facets, all at once the Buddha, the Tao, the true Messiah, Yahweh, Allah, the Heart of the Sky, the Heart of the Earth, the Lord of the Near and Far, the Spirit, the Light, the Universe, I could love you, and, finally, learn to love me.

Mighty Guadalupana Coatlazopeuh Tonantzín,

What "little miracle" could I pin here? Braid of hair in its place and know that I thank you.

Rosario (Chayo) De León<br>Austin, Tejas

# It

*Mary Helen Ponce*

I remember well my twelfth birthday, a cold Sunday in January. The icy wind that blew through the pepper trees and bedroom window kept me awake most of the night. I felt sick. My head ached; my stomach hurt.

The day before, when we were dismissed from el catecismo, Virgie, Concha, and I rushed back to Don Jesús's store, anxious to sample los dulces, the Mexican candy only he sold. Virgie quickly found what she wanted: jelly beans, gumdrops, and cacahuates, peanuts in the shell, sold in tiny bags. Concha bought two pieces of calabaza, sweet pumpkin jelled into squares. I walked around the store, my shoes scraping against the wooden floor, but couldn't decide what it was I wanted. The pan I usually loved so much appeared dry, unappetizing. I wanted something different from the usual candy that stuck to the roof of my mouth and clung to my teeth, but all I saw were shelves of arroz, leche de bote, and dusty cans of Campbell's soup. I fingered ripe tomatoes and crispy green chiles nestled in crates near the entrance, and was about to pinch grapes from a tray, when I spotted the patas de cochi, pink pigs' feet swimming in a jar. The patas, including the hooves, were kept in a wide jar next to the cash register; their wrinkled skin shimmered in the brine. Pigs' feet, kids on Hoyt Street said, were a favorite of the winos who hung around the alley behind the store. Still they *were* different.

I turned the jar around as the feet slapped against the glass, and pondered. Did I really want a pata? Should I spend my nickels on wino food? Hungry for something and eager to get home to my chores, I asked Virgie for my share of our bottle money, selected the biggest pata, paid, then ran out of the store. We walked back along the dusty path next to Doña Chonita's house. As I gnawed on the gristly skin I smiled at Virgie, whose mouth was smeared with chocolate.

I pretended the pig's foot was delicious, determined not to gag on the vinegar. Once at home I changed clothes, then went about my Saturday chores: washing out my underwear and cleaning the dining room chairs, both of which I hated. When finished with the loathsome jobs, I pulled back the cotton spread on my bed and lay down in the bedroom I shared with Trina.

I felt sick. My stomach was making funny noises. I could taste the vinegar, la pata. I began to moan and groan as I rubbed my stomach. Trina, busy plucking her eyebrows, became alarmed at my cries and ran to fetch Elizabet. The two of them stood in the hallway, dark heads pressed close, whispering in low, muted voices.

"Her stomach hurts. . ."

"Hummm, well, she *is* twelve."

Elizabet went into her bathroom, then returned with a purple box, which she silently slid under my bed. Then she filled the hot-water bottle from the kitchen faucet and gave it to me to press against my tender middle. She tiptoed out of the room, then softly closed the door. I laid in bed, pale and wan, waiting for It.

It seemed I had been waiting for It for so long! At least since the summer before, when Nancy got It and acted even more superior. Upon hearing Nancy's news I moped around the house, feeling terribly juvenile and left out. Later that year, when Virgie, a smug look on her round face, announced she was now a señorita, I became even more depressed. It just wasn't fair! Morning, noon, and night, I checked my calzones, frantic to see signs of It. I was sorely disappointed not to find even a trace.

I still wore camisetas, undershirts which I couldn't wait to replace with lacy bras. I also hated the cotton slips with the tiny tucks in the front that looked so childish, infantile really. My itching breasts were beginning to push against my dresses. My clothes were all wrong, I grumbled to my mother, refusing to wear the prissy dresses with white collar and cuffs from the previous year. When Trina wasn't looking, I would squeeze into her clothes, feeling terribly grown-up; until one day when I burst the zipper of her favorite skirt. Determined to update my wardrobe, I took my mother's sewing basket and hid in the bathroom to hike up the hem of my favorite skirt. All in preparation for It.

I had a mustache, which I hated. I had hairy legs that I was not allowed to shave. Sometimes I could almost smell my sobacos, a smell I attributed to the scraggly armpit hairs I had recently sprouted. The long black hairs on my arms appeared longer each day; at times I wound them around a pencil. And hated it. I resorted to wearing long-sleeved dresses even on hot days. And I hated that, too.

My curly black hair was unmanageable. It surrounded my face like a dark juniper bush. On wet and rainy days it got even frizzier, so that it resembled Brillo Pads. But I detested the Shirley Temple curls that were earlier my trademark and refused to wear the common trenzas that I associated with elementary school kids. On school days an amused Elizabet secured my unruly hair with shiny barrettes bought in town, saying I looked fine. But once out the door, I yanked them off, stuck them in my pocket, then slipped a handful of bobby-pins into place.

One March day while Mundo, Concha, and I were playing kickball, we needed a fourth player.

"Can Virgie come out?"

"No."

"¿Por qué?"

"Ummm, she is sort of sick . . ."

Virgie, I was told, could not play for at least three days. I immediately knew why. So did Mundo and Concha. Virgie had It. Later in our game I fell and scraped my knee; I stopped the blood with the hem of my dress, then ran home. When my mother saw the stains on my dress she told me to go wait for her in the bathroom. Her face held a look of respect. Clearly she thought I had It.

When she realized I had only cut my knee, however, she scolded me por andar en la calle and ruining a good dress. Doña Luisa, never too far from a crisis, cautioned me not to run around too much. "No es good for you," she said, her eyes troubled, "no es good." She then walked me to her house, stoked the wooden stove, and fed me warm milk and bread. Satiated with cinammon toast, I sat back to wait for It.

That evening, when it was my turn to wash the supper dishes, I began to moan.

"My stomach hurts. Me duele el estómago."

"Estómago. And do you feel dizzy too?"

"Sí."

I was excused from clearing the table, washing dishes, and sweeping the kitchen floor. Told to lie down in my bedroom with the hot water bottle, I did just that.

Then Concha got It. And Josie too, followed by Terry who was only eleven! And then it was June, July. Childhood games of hide-and-seek bored me, as did bike rides down Hoyt Street. I now preferred to spend the afternoon beneath a cool pirul, my favorite pepper tree, to embroider flowers and birds on bleached sacking. I sat with my legs primly crossed, the skirt of my dress pulled low. Just in case It creeped up on me.

I began to stuff Kleenex inside my underwear, just in case It caught me unawares, until one day, while running across el llano, I dropped a batch.

My mustache grew darker. I sneaked Pancake Number 2 from Nora, wet a sponge, then smeared it across the offensive black veil, but it still showed. I then sought out la Nancy, who knew everything.

"I hate my bigote."

"Well bleach it! Como yo."

I ran to the store, bought the necessary supplies, then I locked myself in the bathroom. In a small bowl I mixed peroxide and white henna, making sure to use a wooden spoon. I slathered the smelly potion on my upper lip, then (while Josey pounded on the bathroom door) washed off the dried powder and stared into the mirror. I was dismayed to see no immediate results. Within days, however, my mustache turned first a brownish-red, then a bright yellow.

Each month my legs got hairier and hairier. I dared not wear summer shorts, but began to borrow Norbert's Levi's, making sure not to roll them past my calf. When I could stand it no longer, I waited for Berney to leave, then shaved my legs with his trusty Gillette razor, making sure I had first secured the bathroom door. I then spent hours applying alcohol and adhesive tape to the many cuts that decorated my legs. All the while I longed for It.

More than anything, though, I hated my hair. Nancy now sported un permanente that was the envy of the girls on Hoyt Street. Not to be outdone, Concha had her hair cut in cute bangs. Desperate to be rid of the curl and having read that braiding kinky hair made it straight, I began to braid my hair at night. Each morning I fought to be first in the bathroom. With mounting excitement I would unbraid my thick trenza, but my hair sprang out around my face like a dark bush again.

When school started in September of my twelfth year, I was sent to the school nurse for a routine checkup. I was weighed and measured; my eyes, ears, and throat checked, and my reflexes measured with a tap on the knee. The nurse then read my chart and asked if I had experienced any changes since school let out. It was disappointing to have nothing new to report. Check!

And then a new girl came to our school. Her name was Barbara. I hated her because she had an American name, two dimples, and had already started It! I now hated anyone with dimples too. I began to sleep with a pinto bean attached with surgical tape to each cheek, confident that in time I, too, would have dimples. When I swallowed a bean in my sleep, and nearly gagged, I decided that dimples were not all that important. Certainly not as important as It.

During Christmas I stuffed myself with my mother's sugar tamales. I ate so much masa I got a stomach ache. Once more I was put to bed with the trusty water bottle. And then it was January once more. I would soon be all of thirteen. A teenager! A tall teenager who still had not gotten It! I began to cross off each day on a calendar hidden from Trina's prying eyes. I waited until evening to make an X across the date; just in case It arrived during the day.

As my birthday approached, I began to panic. I begged Elizabet to take me to the doctor in San Fernando. "Something is wrong," I wailed, "something's wrong with me!" But Elizabet only smiled and went about her business. In my bedroom I kicked the purple box against the wall. It had not helped me at all!

I dared not miss Mass; I was diligent in taking Holy Communion. But I avoided sitting next to viejitas said to be "barren," thinking I might catch their disease. I made sure not to eat meat on Fridays, certain that God in all His glory would reward this sacrifice. I prayed to all the female saints to intercede with the Virgin Mary on my behalf. "Saint Teresa of Avila, please send It. Santa Cecilia, help me get over It. All ye holy saints in Heaven, tell God I can't live without It."

I feared living out my life as an old maid, relegated to dusting church pews and caring for plaster saints. A vestir santos. I could never marry without It, that much was certain. Nor could I have children! Only when a girl has gotten It could she have babies, as everyone on Hoyt Street already knew. And so I waited for God to send me a sign of It.

My thirteenth birthday came and went. I now stood at five feet five inches in my bare feet. I was taller than my sisters and mother; I towered over Doña Luisa and most of my friends. My green winter coat came to above my knees; the waist of my red jumper rode above my midriff. My shoe size jumped from six to seven to eight. This made my older sisters, all of whom wore size five and six shoes, smirk with satisfaction.

And then one day, as if by magic, my arms lost their hairy look. My yellow mustache grew out; the dark veil no longer was visible. My legs grew long and lean, with less and less hair. I threw out las camisetas and was bought a cotton bra. When my mother wasn't looking, I hiked up my skirt hems, then opened up the slits on each side. I lavished Palmolive soap on my face, then followed with Ponds Cream, for that seven-day complexion wonder. My thick hair fell across my shoulders in a wavy pageboy.

I studied the movie magazines in search of my face type: oval? Square? Heart-shaped? I experimented with tweezers and wound up with two bloody, crooked lines, which I filled in with an eyebrow pencil snitched from Nora. I bought a cheap lipbrush and replaced Tangee Natural with Tangee Fire Red. I bought a red plastic belt (size 22 waist) for $1.99, and inherited, from a reluctant Trina, my first pair of high heels, on which I tottered to church each Sunday.

And then finally I got It! I was on my way to the store, about to climb the fence that led to the alley, when I detected signs of It on my beige culottes. I straddled the fence, not knowing whether to jump over or slide down, in a lady-like manner. My tomboy days were clearly over. I disengaged my legs, smoothed down my pants, and walked home feeling dizzy, elated. At last! At last I was a bonafide teenager! I itched to blurt out my news to Nancy, Virgie, and Concha, but told only Elizabet, who once more brought out the purple box.

That balmy night as I lay in bed, the hot-water bottle secure against my belly, I flipped through the booklet in the purple box. I think it was entitled "What Every Teenage Girl Should Know." I memorized everything about fallopians, ovaries, and twenty-eight day cycles. I snuggled under the covers, sipping té de canela, cinnamon tea, said to be good for It. I touched myself down there, just to make sure I still had It, then turned over and went to sleep.

# The Jumping Bean

*Helena María Viramontes*

He cocked his fisherman's face, seared and rumpled and buoyant in the sea of glass, combed the Tres Roses pomade onto his hair jamming three fingers to make a slick, shimmering wave. From where she stood, the gold-plated crucifix which anchored his neck sparkled in the mirror until he buried it beneath his shirt buttons. The young girl thought her papa pretty in his oversized salt-and-pepper suit jacket, the triangular lapels so wide they peaked to his padded shoulders.

He had no reason to see her. She was just one of the many children he labored for, carrying wet cement and grit on the bridge of his back. The others, the gringo plasterers, called him the jumping bean not for his pencil-thin mustache and Spanish surname, but because of his ability to scale a ladder towing more than his weight in cement with the speed of a man half his age, as circles of salty sweat rung like the age of a tree on his work shirt. Even as the wooden poke of the hod stabbed against his belly like the spiked heat of midday, he had never thought to quit this work. Even when the thorny whiskey could no longer drown the sound of his own bones aching, he would never abandon his own children. He reminded her mother constantly of his contributions and all of them were made to feel indebted to his relentless back and the two hands he rinsed with vinegar daily to relieve the burn of the abrasive, gray grit powder. He was a finch of a man, a sparrow of nerves, his fingers swollen live wires too dangerous to touch.

He spotted her reflection and his smile made her feel as though it were permissible to approach him. He turned to her real self, fished his hand into the deep pit pocket of his ironed trousers, jiggled loose change, reeled out a white coin. His head came forward to hers, his nose wide and flat from a boxer's punch, his eyes black as burnt stone, his teeth tinted tobacco against an unfamiliar face. He handed her the coin, his thumb nail bruised, and she stared at the disc, licked off the cement dust to discern that it was a buffalo nickel. She brushed his cheek with her lips, then disappeared into the kitchen voices of her family while he disappeared, the flask of Wild Turkey clinking against his house key.

She was the only one with the patience to do it, lull her mother back to sleep with long brush strokes. So when her oldest sister, María de la Luz, woke her with "Mama's not sleeping again," the youngest girl dragged her heavy feet to where mama sat, an Avon brush by her side. The young girl's heart bucked wildly when she saw the prayer cards filed in a parade of saints on the kitchen table, as if by her mama for the pot banging miracles that never came.

"Don't be afraid," María de la Luz whispered. But the young girl stayed away anyway. Mama had the look of cold sin in her eyes. María gently rubbed the heated olive oil with concentrated effort on Mama's temples to ease and loosen the tumor of disappointment, and when she saw the girl, motioned for her to come. After a while, María bent to thaw Mama's feet in warm, clear water while her own knees itched from the cold floor.

"It's okay," María said. She cupped water over Mama's left foot gently, the trickling pebbles of water drops the only sound in the room. "Go on now. Brush her hair."

The young girl approached them. The fall of Mama's long hair reassured her, and she began unraveling the hemplike braid. The white dandruff flakes drifted silently to the bones of Mama's shoulders as she brushed. Brushed. She leaned on one foot then the other to keep herself awake, brushed, but dreamed anyway; dreamed of snowcapped mountains, brown saintly faces that tumbled away like dead leaves on a rising wind.

A grayish phosphorescent stream flowing from the window was enough for the young girl to decipher a slithering form. She brushed faster. She waited for María to say something about the long, white snake which s'ed its way under the table, its forked tongue savoring the cool autumn air, but María talked to her Mama instead.

"You do what you have to do to live," said María when Mama broke like the morning light, broke into sobs because she kept her daughters up half the night. "That's what you taught us." Mama cried passionately, never realizing there was so much grief inside her.

"You're tired, Mama, is all," María replied, too tired herself to speculate on the demons Mama was battling. She caught water in a pot, turned the faucet off, put on the flames to boil.

The snake slipped under the murky gray morning like wet soap until the young girl felt the slithering tube slide over her bare feet, and the chilling sensation prompted her to drum her toes on the worn floor. She wanted to speak, but was silenced by the snake which spiraled itself around her ankles and tightened its grasp. She held her breath, felt her body swell with terror. She tried in vain to interrupt the exchange between the two women, but they had no reason to see her.

"You're not going crazy," María warned her Mama, while she stirred the last of the Quaker Oats into the boiling water. The snake had disappeared. It was the first day of school, and the children would be hungry.

The Foreman, the junior of the company, liked Papa. He felt this Spanish man had heart. But the plasterers, welders, bulldozer drivers resented his centaur ability to endure the work, creating a standard they would inevitably be compared to. In turn, they created their own standards and exiled him to exist only in their peripheral vision.

He worked in their oblivion. They denied the sweat that bled like torrents over his eyes when he climbed the scaffolds with one hundred and sixty pounds of cement on his back, balancing himself on the thin planks, two stories, three stories high. They never imagined his rebelling bones collapsing like noisy spoons at the end of the day, where he lay on their living room floor, his arms and legs spread wide, the children tiptoeing around him; or the midnight whiskey that made him resentful and violent to those who tiptoed too loudly. They never imagined that his was a body too, made of flesh and bone and bleeding blood and had hit the canvas hard years ago. It was only from the monumental fear of going hungry that he rallied his strength, raised and buckled his knees, cast himself into the sweating heat, to draw or pull what was necessary to yield another meal. He feared many things, but work was not one of them.

Papa sat on his haunches, outside the lopsided circle of workers, and chewed on a sandwich he insisted be made with Wonder Bread, sipped lukewarm coffee from his plastic thermos cup. He watched the men laugh, offer cigarettes, crumble wax paper into a ball, and discard it without a care. One of the plasterers chewed on a toothpick. Theodore, the one man he knew by name, poked his ear, scrutinized the wax he pulled out as if he had just created a perfect corn roll.

"Hey Jumpin'! Don't you like us or what?" Papa knew that some people hated more easily than others for reasons which were as thin as balloons and just as empty. He knew because he was one of these. He was beginning to hate this man.

"Do we smell or what?" One man chuckled at Theodore's comments. "Come on. I gotta question to ask you." Papa straightened up, carried his lunch box and coffee cup, joined the circle. Theodore smiled. He lifted one steel toe boot on the step of the bulldozer, looked down at Papa.

"I gotta question for you." Theodore pointed a finger at Papa. "What's the difference between a spic and a drunk?"

The man with the toothpick removed it from between his teeth to speak, "You're a real asshole, Theo."

"Can't take a joke, Ray?"

"You're gonna get your ass kicked some day." Like a line traced in the dirt, Papa understood the words to mean a challenge of some sort between the two men though spoken too quickly for him to understand them all. The man bit on his toothpick again, kicked gravel with his mustard colored construction boots. The gravel twisted beneath his boots as he walked away.

Someone sneezed loudly, another pinched pebbles in the center of the circle.

"The difference is a drunk will sober up, but a spic will always be a spic, ain't that right Jumpin?" A few plasterers laughed. Papa watched the men with their mouths open in big round O's. Theodore slapped Papa on his back causing him to spill his coffee. Others sat silently, smoking cigarettes, downcast eyes inspecting their cement-caked boots.

Papa missed the solitude of the sea and he felt no shame being insignificant against its immensity. There, without the pounding of the jackhammers, pieces of sun glittered on the water. There, adrift, he would cast the net, feel the challenge of resistance in his hands whenever he pulled in the reins of his livelihood. He did not understand what Theodore was saying. He would memorize the question, repeat it to María de la Luz, have her explain it to him. And yet, the urge to quash Theodore was overwhelming.

Papa turned to view the men clustered on the corner of Sixth and Central in downtown L.A., men like himself, scanning the oncoming traffic in hopes of some signal that would promise a day's work, a chance to prove their worth, to carry tools, work with iron, shovel cement, any chance, any work. The urge was overwhelming, but he forced a smile anyway. The foreman stepped out of his trailer to see what the commotion was about.

Papa screwed the cup of his thermos in place, put his thermos in his lunch box, and forced himself up on his haunches.

"A real company man" a plasterer said, no longer laughing, watching Papa, who began work before the others. Not waiting for the cement truck, Papa scooped three shovels full of gravel into a metal trough, scooped three shovels full of sand, one shovel of cement, the powder bathing him and he held his breath, shut his eyes until the dust settled. He ran the water hose to the trough, turned it on, took a handful and splashed it on his neck, his face, to remove the residue before it began burning his skin. Once filled with enough water, Papa began kneading the cement with a long poked hoe and his resistant muscles pulled forth the hoe, scraping the bottom of the trough, folding and sloshing the mix then pushing, again scraping, pulled, pushed, fold, pull, push, fold the cement into thickening grit.

"Don't he know he's cutting in on our lunch hour?" asked the truck driver.

"Who the hell does Jumpin' think he is?"

"His spic," Theodore replied, gesturing to the foreman who stood on the trailer steps and exaggeratedly pointed to his watch. The plasterers watched the foreman put his arms akimbo in mock impatience. Theodore spit to one side as the foreman approached them angrily when no one moved from the circle.

María de la Luz knew nine was an unlikely number. It was the number of pills prescribed to her Mama and it was the number of cigarettes her Mama smoked a day. It was the number of mouths which had to be fed, the number of towels, calzones, socks, shirts, shorts, blouses that were washed on Thursday, hung out to dry on Friday, ironed on Saturday, worn on Sunday. And it was the number of nights that María didn't sleep because she waited up for her brothers or the children caught colds and ran fevers and coughed and had nightmares.

On the ninth week of Mama's illness, the truant officer arrived. His appearance edged the neighborhood dogs into junk yard madness, yapping and growling and throwing themselves against the chain-link fences. From behind the curtains, peeking between the laths of venetian blinds, the neighbors stared at the officer who stumbled his way into a maze of clean laundry hung on slack wire lines, asked themselves about this official-looking gringo with a clipboard whose shirt buttons strained to dam back a flooding belly. The officer loosened his red tie, looked behind him suspiciously, knocked again on the screen door, and the young girl with a runny nose hid behind María de la Luz. The officer addressed her as "Mrs." and asked why her daughter, "Mar ee a Loose" (he said the name so that it sounded real crooked to the young girl's ears), had been truant nine weeks from school.

"My mother isn't feeling good," she told the officer. She held a broom and he wrote something on his clipboard. The young girl didn't like all this writing he was doing and put her fingers in her mouth.

"Stop biting your nails," María reprimanded.

He said, "Is this the kinda life you wanna have, huh? Washing clothes, shoveling dog turd? You need to be learning."

María returned the incredulous stare. Didn't he understand what she said? Her Mama wasn't feeling good. The young girl wiped her nose with the sleeve of her sweater.

"You'll end up like some old lady in the shoe."

"Fuck off," she told the officer (which also sounded crooked to the young girl's ears) and María slammed the door, edging in another wave of crazy dog frenzy. A few moments passed, and the girl looked up at María who stared at the closed door. Finally, María palmed her loose hair back, placed the broom behind the door and went to another room. The dogs settled down to their mid-noon naps.

The girl found María in the only room in the house with a lock. The girl touched the knob and with a certain warmth in the palm of her hand, was able to unlock the door. She poked her head in to see María with an open book, sitting on the seat of the toilet. María looked up, marked a page with her finger, closed the book.

"Let me be, so's I can figure this out," she told the young girl. María was sure she had locked the door, but knew too the young girl had a knack for doing things like this. Since her sister didn't move, María tried to ignore her, opened the book, began underlining a sentence with her finger. "Let me alone, goddamnit!"

The young girl went into the kitchen, her fingers in her mouth, passed her Mama who sat silently at the table, flipping a stack of playing cards in a game of solitaire, cigarette smoke in a corkscrew above her head. The smoke made the young girl sneeze, and she went outside and sat on the porch, watched the hanging sheets flap flap senselessly like sails on a ship wreck.

It was her Papa's words addressing María. The words came into the bedroom in the form of a white moth, wing span of her hands, and landed on the wall, its wings spreading and rising in slow meditation. The young girl watched. She lay between two sisters; one sister threw her arm over her chest, the other a hefty leg, and she felt smothered like a fly caught in a cobweb of limbs.

María drudged through the fragile thin ice of morning, stumbled over beds and blankets, settled her bones on a roll-away cot next to their bed. Her arm fell to the side, limp, like a dead animal. Outside, the lamp post shone a foggy yellow glow. The white moth fluttered to the window and banged itself against the glass endlessly with dull and scratchy thuds.

The young girl had heard the words from the other side of the door. Mama wasn't well enough to come home from the hospital for Christmas.

The girl tried to levitate her body to open the window but was firmly vised between her sisters. She whispered María's name, saw the name mist linger in front of her, then slowly evaporate. She began to see small streamers like molten silver, streak gently downward on the window glass. The moth stood silent, its wings rising and spreading, waiting for her.

Icicles fell like Christmas tinsel from the ceiling. No one would believe that the window and the ceiling bled tears. Her sisters slept soundly and every once in awhile one of them would grind her teeth or pass gas. But the girl was the daughter of her mother, and she rose to the occasion until her body banged against the glass, felt the chill against her cheek. She strained to break the window, but felt her arm pulled away, felt weak against the gravitational force, filled her lungs to release.

María opened the window to a blast of cold wind. The moth fluttered out. She slammed the window down.

The young girl cried. If only she had the capacity to walk barefoot on broken jagged words like María, then she wouldn't have to release the words, and she could smash them into a thousand pieces of glass, just like she wanted to smash the window. But María pulled her close to her, sealed her mouth, hushed her for nothing was worth this much unbroken silence.

One of the trucks sped by loaded with the last of the scaffolds, leaving dust behind, grinding gravel beneath its tires. The welders worked above him, sparks raining to the sides of them, reinforcing the window sealants. Papa looked up at the building while standing on the top step of the foreman's trailer, admired the erect and shiny structure in all its newness, felt a certain pride, then felt ashamed of that pride. He wiped his boots before entering the trailer. It was unusually hot for a spring day. The foreman swung his chair back, and without standing up handed him a check, talked in a tight stitched sentence over the buzzing of the air conditioner.

"I do weekend jobs, nothing big, a little extra cash on the side, maybe you can work for me then."

Papa nodded, stared at the check. He studied his name in block printed type, felt the texture of official paper, stared at the amount engraved above his name. He studied the amount as the foreman talked, translated the amount to a down payment on the pick-up he had set his eyes on a few months before. The used truck was in good working condition. The fact that it had a new shiny spare chained to the back made him content. He folded the check neatly so as not to smudge the name or amount, placed it in his billfold, asked in crooked English if he should leave now or hang around until his shift was over; wondered what to do next. He offered his hand to the foreman who shook it with a hardy grip.

Outside the sun blazed, making the smoky air stick to his lungs. Spring was here too soon. If he couldn't find work by summer, they would have to move to where the migrant work was guaranteed: tomatoes in Indiana, asparagus in Illinois, strawberries in Michigan. But until then, he planned to hammer and chisel the cemented walkway near the laundry lines, make room to plant nopal, verdulagas, chayotes. Of course, things would get better. He was a good worker, one of the best, not afraid to use his back. His lemon tree did not yield this year, but the pomegranates cracked with beet red juice. Things would get better.

He lifted his lunch box, but when he opened it, he discovered a crinkled bag stuffed to the side of the thermos. On the palm of his hand he shook out the contents, held a handful of jumping beans, watched the half moon beans itch and shake in the heat of the sun.

He remembered repeating the question to María about the spic and the drunk, asked that she explain it to him. She said that he worked with a bunch of assholes, and he slapped her for saying a bad word, and she pushed him aside to get out of the house, holding her hand on her mouth. The children cried, judged him with accusatory eyes and he began yelling at them, calling them beggars and leeches and told them to hide or he would kill them all and they scattered, the young girl hiding under the bed where he found her hours later, fast asleep.

It made him wonder about his wife who believed demons possessed her, about his sons who stayed out half the night, the children who scattered in fear, and his beautiful daughter María whom he had slapped with all his might, made him wonder if he was the one being possessed by the questions he did not understand.

He decided against throwing the beans out, returned the contents to the bag. The beans would be a reconciliatory offer to his children and the thought make him content. He walked home to save the bus fare, the beans quiet in his lunch box.

By mid-afternoon he entered their small walkway which led to their back yard. He called the children and the neighbor's children over. They rushed and circled around him, craning their necks to see what Papa held in the brown paper sack. He poured the contents on the porch where a strong beam of sun spotlighted the tranquil beans. The children watched, unimpressed by the beans which stood as still as stones. Suddenly, like popcorn bursting, the beans began to twist, tremble, finally jump, and the children laughed in utter astonishment. "Is it magic?" one of the children asked, and the young girl turned to Papa for an answer.

María de la Luz opened the screen door to look down at the

heads watching the beans jumping. "How do the beans jump?" another asked María, for Papa never gave answers. Curious, María picked up one and bit it open against Papa's protests. Inside the cracked opening, a small white caterpillar unfolded its larva body.

"Leave it alone," Papa ordered, but María immediately bit open another and another.

"They're trapped. They wanna to get out." It seemed unfair to her to find enjoyment in the entrapment of other living things. The children grimaced, contorted their faces from nausea as they watched María crack the hard bean between her teeth with delicate force.

"Leave it alone," Papa said in a voice the children were afraid of.

"They're gonna die." First the children looked at María cracking the beans, then turned to look at Papa whose voice was turning louder. The young girl panicked, put her fingers to her mouth.

Papa's temper rose like his nostrils. As of today, he was unemployed, had a sick wife, now couldn't even win over his children's forgiveness without being accused of something. He raised his hand at her insubordination, but before he could strike her, before the children began their screaming and crying again, she caught his raised hand in mid-motion, and it stunned him, this betrayal of her nature. María had managed to let free all but one caterpillar. She grasped Papa's hand, the one with the blue thumbnail, laid his hand open. Her eyes melted with red anger. She pressed the single bean in the palm of his hand, steadied her trembling voice.

"Go ahead," she said, a tear streaming down her cheek, "If it means that much to you, keep it."

Go ahead and what? he thought. What was he supposed to do? He had to make of her an example for the rest of the children. If he let the caterpillar go, she would certainly feel she had won, which would only be the beginning of her rebellion. If he killed the caterpillar, let it bang itself inside the brown bean, something else would die as well. He just couldn't figure out what. The children stared at his every move and he stared at the single bean.

The young girl shoved her way closer to her Papa. She looked up at María de la Luz, her nose running, looked at Papa, small and twitching and frightened, looked up at the blank door frame where her Mama would be standing right now and putting a stop to all of this madness. Without thinking, the young girl removed the fingers from her mouth, swept the bean from the palm of her Papa's hand. For once, everyone's attention shifted to the young girl. She put the bean in her mouth and swallowed it.

The day her mother returned from the hospital, was the day the young girl tasted the sweetest, reddest juiciest watermelon she had ever had. Mama looked pale, her cheeks fallen and waxen, her nose red as if she suffered a cold. She looked nervously about at her brood of children, but smiled just the same. The children, the smaller ones like the young girl, stiffened up, shoulders back, mouths quiet except for a whispering question, here and there. For them it was such an unnatural position that even María de la Luz and Papa felt their bones contort. Mama decided it was best that she sleep first, then get up and make some arroz con pollo, fresh tortillas. The children clapped and laughed and were relieved for they were tired of María's Hamburger Heaven, Beto even calling it Hamburger Hell. They felt the rigid air ease when Mama left the room, felt the lazy heat make their eyes drowsy.

They had packed the clothes and belongings in boxes and piled them like a pyramid in the walkway, ready to load them up in the pick-up come tomorrow. Today, María plugged an extension cord and dragged her prized GE radio outside and turned it to her favorite oldies station, sat cross-legged on the little patch of grass, her dress over her knees. Papa changed from his salt-and-pepper suit to a paper thin speckled shirt which he didn't button, and which flapped open from a slight summer breeze.

Spreading some newspapers on the porch, he placed the green watermelon, green as the brine of the Belvedere Park lake, on top and then he plunged the knife in, the watermelon cracking like thunderbolts into two halves, the juice bleeding droplets on the newspaper. He carefully removed the seedless center of the melon and put it on a plate for Mama who always got the heart. After that, Papa sliced and gave, sliced and gave, and the young girl took two boat pieces, handed one to María and sat, cross-legged next to her.

The young girl bit into the red flesh of the watermelon slice and the flavor burst like confetti on her tongue. The juice dripping from the sides of her mouth tickled, and she wiped her face clean with María's dress. María stopped spitting out the black seeds using her ducking brother as a target, stopped spitting to scold her. She scolded the young girl with such a funny face, calling her a silly goose, you silly little goose, the young girl laughed so hard, felt so happy, she couldn't help but feel like something as red, sweet and full of confetti was in the making.

# Criticism

# The [Subversive] Mixquiahuala Letters: An Antidote for Self-Hate

*Erlinda Gonzales-Berry*

Ana Castillo's *The Mixquiahuala Letters* is a Chicana novel which is read widely in Chicano and feminist literature classes in American universities. Nonetheless, it has generated little critical attention, perhaps because it is a novel that, at first glance, appears to be riddled with contradictions. A close reading reveals that it is, more accurately, a novel that delights in transgression and in subversion. Three aspects of the novel that interest me are: 1) its dialogue with Julio Cortázar's *Rayuela*; 2) the subversion of genre as a strategy used to inscribe the female subject; 3) rage as a catalyst for the expression of love among women. A thread that links the three topics is Castillo's commitment to the undermining of hierarchies and the games and discourses that sustain them. This commitment is introduced immediately with the following epigram: "I quit loving my father a long time ago. What remained was a slavery to a pattern" (Anais Nin, *Under the Glass Bell*). The pivotal signs in this quote, *father* and *slavery*, herald the exploration of male-female relations as constituted within the perimeters of the "law of the father," that is, within a patriarchal paradigm. It is, consequently, baffling to encounter on the following page this inscription: "In memory of the master of the game, Julio Cortázar." The reader is perplexed, not so much because Castillo dedicates the novel to a male, but because she chooses the epithet *master*, a concept so central to patriarchal discourse. Add to this the fact that Castillo, in her structuring of *The Mixquiahuala Letters*, emulates the structure of this master's masterpiece. Is Castillo aware of the contradiction that leaps out at the reader in the initial pages, or is she, perhaps, setting (up) Cortázar as her model only to turn the game tables on him? The latter possibility warrants some consideration.

In structuring *Rayuela*, Cortázar offers the reader the choice of two approaches to the text. One is a traditional chronological reading of the first 56 chapters. The second involves the interpolation of chapters 57 through 155 amongst the first 56 chapters according to a plan devised by the author. This second reading results in a non-chronological skipping-about the text, requiring what Cortázar calls a *lector cómplice*. Cortázar emphasizes in a note to the reader that the important element here is *choice*, the implication being that he relinquishes his voice of author(ity), allowing the reader to determine the most appropriate way to read the novel. The problem here is the following: what self-respecting reader would choose the ordered, but *partial*, reading of the text? In effect, the non-traditional option stands as a blatant challenge to the reader. As such, the seemingly democratic author, who despite his otherwise transgressive *écriture* in which he posits *la otra orilla*, or the pre-oedipal mode which precedes that of the phallocentric symbolic, as the desired mode for inscribing the text,[1] is not able to extricate himself from the weight of the "law of the father." Cortázar, in fact, manipulates the reader in such a way that allows him to prove that he is not only *spielmeister* of the game of manipulation, but also master (read: voice of authority) of his text. Add to this the fact that the philosopher Morelli, whose ideas greatly influence the characters of *Rayuela*, refers disparagingly to a passive reader who refuses to play the role of *lector cómplice* as a *lector hembra*. If we apply this Morellian reasoning to Cortázar's text, we understand that the reader who fails to elect the more challenging reading is also a *lector hembra*. Cortázar's adherence to a patriarchal discourse that marks femaleness, or *lo femenino*, as inferior cannot go unnoticed.

Let us now examine Castillo's game. Like Cortázar, Castillo offers the reader some alternative reading strategies: one for the conformist, one for the cynic, and one for the quixotic. The readings differ in that each begins and ends in a different manner, and in each some letters are omitted. Castillo places her reader in the very uncomfortable position of having to make a choice based on an act of self-scrutiny and self-definition. Should the reader be loathe to engage in such an endeavor, (s)he can, of course, do a traditional chronological reading, which, incidentally, is the only complete reading. The temptation, of course, is to do the complete reading, as well as all of the optional readings, in order to appreciate Castillo's perception of cynic, quixotic, and conformist.

Should the reader do just that, (s)he in fact creates an additional option. But regardless of which reading—or readings—is finally chosen, the point is that while Cortázar goads the reader away from the *lectura hembra* toward what he, as authority of the text, considers a superior reading (*a lectura macho*?). Castillo succeeds, in good post-modernist form, in inspiring a subversive reading of her text, thereby undermining her own author(ity). In this light her inscription, "in memory of the master of the game," bears the mark of irony, for Castillo's emulation of Magister Ludi Cortázar constitutes her own ludic endeavor, whereby she leads the reader to decode Cortázar's complicity with a code of patriarchal authority and her own subversive stance vis-à-vis that code. Thus Castillo takes her first step in breaking that pattern of slavery alluded to in the epigram.

## Genre and Dimensions of Self

The author's choice of the epistolary as the sub-genre through which she explores facets of the self and the process of inscribing subjectivity is a curious one.[2] In the first place, it is an outdated genre, in the second, it is strictly codified and hardly seems compatible with the postmodern tendencies which obtain in Castillo's text.[3] These tendencies occur precisely because Castillo's iconoclasm does not allow her to recognize, nor to acquiesce, before the authority of master codes, be they genres codes or modes of perceiving alterity.

In this letter-writing project, the letter simultaneously functions as a bridge *and* as a boundary between subject and object. It verbally links the receiver, (Other), to the sender, (Self), but it also posits the other as the impenetrable mirror that reflects the specular image of the speaking-writing subject. The opposition between subject and object is reinforced by physical descriptions that form a binary paradigm that seems to correspond to a Spain-Mexico, Cortés-Malinche, or master-slave relationship. Castillo seems to be treading dangerous hierarchical waters here, but wait, there is a twist which points once again toward subversion: the attributes of the subject are not those that are normally attributed to the dominant entity in the pair, but rather to the subordinate one and vice versa:

| subject (Teresa) | object (Alicia) |
|---|---|
| morena | fair skinned |
| round, fleshy contours | thin, muscular contours |
| Indian Ancestry | Anglo-Spanish Ancestry[4] |

Through this inversion of binary opposites, Castillo begins to deflate the paradigm of its traditional trappings. The transgressive nature of this act, however, is not immediately clear, for the sovereignty of the subject is simultaneously underscored as Teresa recalls the past experiences of *both* subject and object. Despite her knowledge-experience of these events, Alicia listens passively, thereby surrendering her authority of experience and situating the speaker in the privileged position of omniscient narrator. The use of the second person pronoun accentuates the sense of hypnotic control of the object by the subject:

> No one had come to meet you at the bus depot. You did the rare thing of catching a cab to the tenement, out of fear of getting mugged with such tempting cargo, odd objects wrapped in newsprint that protruded from brightly colored straw bags. . . . It had been a long journey home, so long that you were in no rush to get inside, more so because you knew you were about to enter not your apartment but transcend from one reality into the other. (42)

Dwelling on details of opposition between self and other, the subject describes the other, in letter fourteen, in terms that barely conceal the dialectic desire to unite herself to the object, thus overcoming separation. This desire surfaces again in letter eleven, in which Teresa describes to Alicia having watched her engage in sex with a male lover. The italics used in this passage underscore the power of the voyeuristic gaze, which translates as pure desire:

> He kneaded
> the small hollow of your lower back
> and you let out
> an almost inaudible moan
> the elastic waistband of your panties
> pushed down over the swollen profusion
> of your buttocks
> with the help of his confident hands

worked past thighs horizontally
        clumsily
over calves and each naked foot
on the sofa
        across the room
i closed my eyes
        went on
        with my nap (39)

But given the dominant position from which the subject addresses the object, the reader wonders whether union is envisioned exclusively under the domain of the subject, thereby corroborating a hierarchical configuration of identity that is absolute and oppressive (Saldívar 1984, 155). If this is the case, Castillo appears to be working herself into a snare of contradictions.

Not to despair postmodern readers, oh ye seekers of the demise of hierarchies, for gradually there begins a breakdown of this pattern: failure to date letters, a confusing mixture of pronouns, a missing greeting here, an absent farewell there, no signature. The very conventions of the genre which traditionally have marked the boundaries between self and other begin to disappear, and ambiguity shows her tantalizing face. The reader questions: Is this or isn't this a letter? Is Teresa really writing to another woman, or is she writing to herself—using the letter as a pretext for the "talking cure" or the reconciliation of a schizoid identity?[5] These doubts lead us to question also whether the illogical nature of the correspondence—that is, the subject's narrating of past events for the object, as if the object were not capable to recalling *her* past for *herself*—really constitutes a power-play as we had initially supposed, or if it is, rather, an act of subterfuge (the gradual change of pronouns from "you" to "we" supports this latter speculation).

And what of letters that read like impressionistic rambling and that are printed on the page as poems:

        We call it by name:. . . 1974, '76, a moment
of Southwestern influence, our Aztlán period
                TIME IS FLUID
The days are eternal dry hot a drought began water
measured precious oil        we call it January, June
autumn leaves constant green
        Wonderland

> lay back trip out on street mime clowns jugglers peddlers
> of invisible magic dust sometimes in a barren apartment
> we roll back the rug and dance (38)

Can there be any doubt that Castillo is attempting to leave the realm of logocentric rationality? That she is striving to reach Anzaldúa's "Coatlicue State"?[6] That poetry should be the vehicle which carries Teresa in the direction of this pre-oedipal state should not surprise us, for as French critic Hélène Cixous reminds us: "Poetry involves gaining strength through the unconscious and because the unconscious, that other limitless country, is the place where the repressed manage to survive" (1983, 283-284). And it is precisely in the territory of the pre-symbolic, of *la otra orilla*, which Cortázar's Oliveira so desperately sought to reach, that self and other come together, not in the phallogocentric tradition of absolute, fixed opposition, but rather in difference—plural, fluid, fragmentary. Cixous describes the process and later links it to the very essence of a feminine libidinal economy:

> To admit that writing is precisely working (in) the between inspecting the process of the same and of the other without which nothing can live, undoing the work of death. . . . A process of different subjects knowing one another and beginning one another anew only from the living boundaries of the other: of multiple and inexhaustible courses with millions of encounters and transformations of the same into the other and into the in-between, from which woman takes her forms. (1983, 287)

Castillo, in the subtle fashion in which she writes against the epistolary grain, obviously engages in working the "transformations of the same into the other." But she also explores the "living boundaries of the Other" in an explicit manner:

> Our first letters were addressed and signed with the greatest affirmation of allegiance and in good faith
> passion bound
> by uterine comprehension. In sisterhood. In solidarity. A strong embrace. Always. We were not to be separated. A fine-edged blade couldn't have been wedged between our shared consciousness, like two huge slabs of stone placed adjacent with inexplicable precision by the Incas.(18)

And on another occasion we witness "different subjects beginning one another anew":

> For the first half of the decade we were an objective one, a single entity, nondiscriminate of the other's being. It wasn't limited to hikes through scented woods, listening to passionate folk music, the tranquility of reading aloud from passages that drew meaning into our linear lives; not solely bound by the synchronization of tai chi when in the midst of chaos we began cranelike movements in slow motion one and its mirror. (122)

My detour through Cixous in order to arrive at a reading of Castillo has helped me to answer the question raised earlier: Is Teresa writing to herself? The answer is yes and no. This ambiguity inheres in the text precisely because Castillo subverts the epistolary cannon to encode the subject's identity in the paradox of difference within which self is self *and* it is other.

Critics have pointed that this mode of identity, while not exclusive to, nor inherent in, women's writing, certainly forms a pattern. Judith Keagen Gardiner, drawing on the theory of Nancy Chodorow, attributes this pattern to the flexible nature of ego and body boundaries in the female (Gardiner 1982, 186). These permeable boundaries are the result of a symbiotic merger with the mother, which the daughter imitates and replicates when she becomes a mother. Close relationships thus form the foundation of feminine gender identity. Masculine individuation, on the other hand, is the result of an abrupt and alienating separation from the mother and an abstract identification with the absent father. Consequently, masculine gender identity is more governed by "denial of relation and dependence" (Rosaldo and Lamphere 8). Thus masculine ego boundaries tend to be more fixed and rigid, and it is not uncommon for the crossing of boundaries by males to be realized as acts of aggression (Gardiner 1982, 186). Castillo's treatment of male-female relations sustains this notion.[7] In her writing, such relations are not developed through a poetics of difference. They are, instead, governed by alienation, a pattern inherent in a patriarchal master-slave paradigm. Castillo's female characters emerge from their encounters with males as victims of abandonment, abuse, and violence. These experiences contribute to a mounting sense of rage:

> Your eyes are pinned to the rumpled figure on the kitchen floor. Abdel lies perfectly still. His eyes haven't been closed and they stare at you like those glass ones in stuffed deer heads. . . . I didn't even know you had a gun' you said to no one in particular. I didn't know you had a gun! I DIDN'T. . . KNOW. . .! MOTHER OF GOD, HELP! TERESA. . .? ABDEL; YOU SON OF A BITCH!
> Motherfucker, why didn't you just leave? (132)

The shouting implied through upper case print in these last lines obviously belongs to Alicia. The very last statement of the text, however, is set off graphically, in lower case print, from Alicia's angry outburst. We realize from the tone that her appropriation of the crass, masculine phrase that she launches as the ultimate accusation against Abdel is not gratuitous. It, in fact, contains a grain of truth, for, as Susan Rubin Suleiman observes in her illuminating article on pornography in Bataille's *Story of the Eye*, in that Eternal Oedipal drama: "the confrontation between the all powerful father and a traumatized son, [is] a confrontation staged across and over the body of the mother" (132). It is as if with this last statement Castillo attempts to do what Cixous threatened in "The Laugh of the Medusa": "Now, I—woman am going to blow up the Law. . .in language" (1983, 291). In this case Castillo's dynamite is the father-son's own language.

Teresa's expression of rage, however, is not hysterical but, rather, the calm, calculated statement of one who has reflected and finally understood. It is so precisely because Teresa has exorcised her rage, and she has done so through the act of writing. In this manner, she has been able to engage in what Norma Alarcón, drawing on Kristeva, calls "An analysis 'after the fact' of the treacherous route on the way to becoming a 'woman' " (1987, 150). But the journey is not complete until she shares it with Alicia. In the act of sharing, Teresa discovers her love for Alicia. Castillo thus arrives at what Yvonne Yarbro-Bejarano calls the ". . . heart of Chicana writing, for without this love they could never make the courageous move to place Chicana subjectivity in the center of literary representation, or depict pivotal relationships among woman past and present, or even obey the first audacious impulse to put pen to paper" (1987, 144). I believe Castillo would agree with this statement, for she herself has stated that if there is any message in her poetry it is "a call for the Hispanic woman to love herself" (Binder 37). Implicit in *The Mixquiahuala Letters* is the notion that in order to love themselves, and each other, women must learn to undermine and subvert discourses of authority and domination which have taught them so much self-hate.

## Notes

1. Distrusting the order imposed by reason, and the potential of symbolic signifiers for representing reality, Morelli, a fictitious writer-philosopher, engages in meditations such as the following: "Como.... Sin palabras llegar a la palabra...sin consciencia razonante aprehender una unidad profunda" (Cortázar 1966, 99).

2. Yarbro-Bejarano calls attention to this process in the brief paragraph that she devotes to *The Mixquiahuala Letters*. Nonetheless, she fails to analyze the intricacies involved in Castillo's manipulation of the genre in her treatment of alterity. Yarbro-Bejarano states: "The narrative voice not only engages in a process of self-exploration through writing, but the form of writing—letters—foregrounds an explicit exchange with a reader to whom the writing is directed. The novel defines subjectivity in relation to another woman, and the bond between the two woman further cemented by the epistolary examination of their relationship is as important as the exploration of self through writing" (1987, 144).

3. From the point of view of feminine aesthetics the epistolary does not seem so incongruent for, as many critics have pointed out, much of women's writing springs forth from lower forms of written discourse: diaries, letters, nursery rhymes. Her use of the epistolary, however, does not imply that Castillo is writing as an 18th century female writer, who because of social immobilization was unable to act in the world (Miller 1986, 278). She writes her letters as a contemporary woman bearing testimony to the discrepancies between women's desires to act and define themselves and the world's reception and suppression of those desires.

4. One could make the case that Alicia is Teresa's double, the split occurring on her first trip to Mexico. Alicia would thus represent Teresa's "Anglo" self, a self that often emerges for Chicanos when we come in contact with Mexicans and realize that they view us as "pochos." The fact that Castillo herself at one time studied art—Alicia is an artist—supports such "biographical" reading of the text. Such a reading would expand the dialogue with Cortázar if compared to his treatment of the doppelgänger motif as it relates to Oliveira and Traveller (1966, 185). However, Oliveira and Traveller remain separate characters, though Oliveira refers explicitly to Traveller as his doppelgänger. The boundaries between Alicia and Teresa are more precarious. This reading suggests that the doubles merge over the dead body of Abdel—the inert corpus of

patriarchal discourse—when Alicia calls out Teresa's (her own?) name. The text would thus stand as a metaphor for the reconciliation of the divided female self. Elements of the present analysis would still apply.

5. See note 4.

6. In her text on crossing borders, Anzaldúa writes: "I see *oposición e insurrección*. I see the crack growing on the rock. I see the heat of anger or rebellion or hope split open the rock, releasing *la Coatlicue*. And someone in me takes matters in our own hands, and eventually, takes dominion over serpents—over my own body, sexual activity, my soul, my mind, my weaknesses and my strengths. Mine. Ours" (1987, 51). I very consciously use the words "strives to reach" because I believe that Castillo does not totally succeed in making the leap to the space of écriture. The urgent sense that permeates the novel, of having to "order" the "chaos" of the past through memory and narration, work against this end.

7. One might question whether Chodorow's model is appropriate for evaluating questions of gender development as they relate to women of color, since the model can be construed to explain the conflictive mother/daughter relationship which often obtains among white women. While the white mother may be seen as overbearing and threatening to the daughter's autonomy, Chicana mothers are more often than not viewed positively in their role as nurturers and protectors. When the mother indeed abuses the daughter's space it is not uncommon for the grandmother to step in to mediate. I believe that the proverbial presence of the grandmother in Chicana literature bears testimony to her role as mediator between Chicana mothers and daughters.

# Story, Telling, Voice: Narrative Authority in Ana Castillo's *The Mixquiahuala Letters*

*Hector A. Torres*

> Perhaps this is the time to stress *technique* again? To renounce for the time being the sovereignty of thought in order to forge *tools* which will permit the exploitation of these resources, these unexplored mines. Perhaps for the time being the serene contemplation of empire must be abandoned in favor of taming those forces which, once unleashed, might explode the very concept of empire. A detour into *strategy, tactics, and practice* is called for, at least as long as it takes to gain vision, self-knowledge, self-possession, even in one's decenteredness.
>
> —Luce Irigaray, *Speculum of the Other Woman*

Although critical appraisal of Ana Castillo's *The Mixquiahuala Letters* is to date slim and lacking, what critical response we do have consistently takes note of Castillo's provocative use of the epistolary genre to articulate a Chicana feminist thematics.[1] The social role from which Castillo makes the letters available to a public reader bespeaks a writer who is confident in her art, able to transform the epistolary genre into a powerful mode of storytelling. With this literary genre—the art of letter writing—Castillo addresses and critiques the complex ideological forces that govern both Anglo and Latin cultures. In making *The Mixquiahuala Letters* available to a reading public, Castillo knows full well that she sends her reader into a narrative labyrinth. The play of the possible narrative orders and thematic arrangements all hint at this narrative labyrinth constituting *The Mixquiahuala Letters*. If A.C. sends the reader off with a, "Good luck which ever journey you choose!" (9), it is with good reason. The labyrinth is necessary if the *Letters* are to use the language of patriarchy at the same time that they turn it against itself, making it address the concerns of Chicanas and other women of color. For Castillo, the narrative labyrinth is a way of tracing through the thin line that separates politics from art, of giving expression to one in the other. The narrative games Castillo proposes upon the opening of the *Letters* serve as an introductory address to the reader—an invitation to enter into dialogue with a writer committed with equal intensity to her politics and her art. This essay is a response to that invitation to dialogue, reading Castillo's text for its storytelling voice and the expression of narrative authority that it carries.

## Of Narrative Authority in *The Mixquiahuala Letters*

In this study I raise the issue of narrative authority in Castillo's *Letters*, addressing the twin questions of how Castillo makes her narrative authority known and on what she bases it. For Chicano literary discourse, narrative authority is no trivial issue, and much hinges on it. How Chicano/a writers appropriate for themselves the authority to tell their stories has much to say about how Chicano/a literary discourse defines itself *relative* to the received canon of American literature in all genres. What Chicano/a writers base their authority on has much to say to this canon—to its constitution and presuppositions about itself.

Ramón Saldívar has well-established the historical and ideological bases for both these twin questions in his recent critical study *Chicano Narrative: The Dialectics of Difference* (1990, 3). In the introduction to that work, Saldívar announces the arrival of the time to acknowledge the role that Chicano literary discourse has had vis-à-vis the Anglo-American canon of literature and its attendant critical practices. "It is time to see Chicano narrative," he argues "as something more than a simple mirror of the life and folklore of a heretofore invisible segment of American society" (1990, 6). Saldívar's complex thesis—that Chicano narrative sets itself in opposition to Anglo American society and that the *corrido* is a socially symbolic act representing this opposition—implies that Chicano narrative does not expect to enter the canon of Anglo American literature simply to be assimilated as one more voice clamoring for attention. Chicano "narrativizing" has stood its historical ground even when Anglo American society has been disposed to deny it any social status or aesthetic value. Thus, it will come as no surprise that, in claiming and expanding its historical space in the American literary landscape, Chicano literary discourse will not easily or comfortably assume the postmodern values informing Anglo American literature and criticism. The irony in this dilemma—that Chicano narrative is a literary discourse whose time has come precisely at the historical moment that postmodernism presides over the scene in Anglo-American letters—has not escaped the attention of other critics.

Rosaura Sánchez has carefully analyzed this historical moment for Chicano literary discourse, concluding that this discourse is a long way from being swept up into the celebration of postmodernist literary tenets:

> Thus, despite parody, fragmentation of time and space, and decentering of subjectivity, Chicano literature continues to be characterized by counter practices that are contestatory and critical of dominant ideologies and practices. Within this literature there is still existential anguish, a notion of collectivity, a search for history, and a longing for subject status. . . as long as the literature continues to be marginal and deterritorialized, Chicano literature, albeit within the cultural dominant of postmodernism, will be only tangentially postmodernist. (1989, 12)

Thus, for both Sánchez and Saldívar, Chicano literary discourse is a subject unwilling to abandon its historical grounds.

Furthermore, if the search for subject status in the form of narrative authority is a pressing issue for Chicano literature, it is even more so for Chicana literature, which, from all appearances, has been marginalized *within* Chicano literature itself. That Chicanas have actively begun the process of establishing their right to be speaking subjects through the social act of writing has been critically surveyed by Norma Alarcón (1989a). Alarcón shows how the historical figure of Malintzin serves as a "paradigmatic figure of Chicana feminism." Surveying the work of Adelaida R. del Castillo, Carmen Tafolla, Cordelia Candelaria, Sylvia González, Alma Villanueva, Lucha Corpi, and Cherríe Moraga, Alarcón demonstrates the various and sundry ways in which these writers have appropriated the figure of Malintzin in order to reinvent themselves as speaking subjects. Although the impact of such an appropriation is not a uniform one for Chicana feminism, there is no denying that, as Alarcón puts it, "... since Chicanas have begun the appropriation of history, sexuality, and language for themselves, they find themselves at the cutting edge of a new historical moment involving a radical though fragile change in consciousness" (1989a, 83). As Chicanas find in Malintzin a paradigmatic figure for Chicana feminism, so it is that in the social act of writing itself they construct their own authority to be speaking subjects.

In this respect, the *Letters* represent a significant contribution to the Chicana's collective social act of writing. Castillo's *Letters* translate into literary form the social experience of a Chicana whose sensibilities are highly attuned not only to oppression in its many forms but also to the global scale on which it operates. Castillo is a shrewd observer of the ways of patriarchy; she understands them enough to offer in the *Letters* a critique of both its Anglo and Latin versions. As Norma Alarcón has put it in a critical study focusing on the sexual thematics of Castillo's work from *Otro Canto* (1977) to *The Mixquiahuala Letters* (1986), the *Letters* index a set of complex heterosexist ideologies stemming from both of these American cultures. In fact, these ideologies, Alarcón contends, drive a wedge between the two protagonists, Teresa and Alicia (1989b, 98).

More to the point, what is at stake for a writer like Castillo—as for other Chicana writers—is: (1) the authority to represent their experience, its basis in social reference and real oppression, and (2) the authority to decide *how* to tell their stories, *what* narrative strategies they want to use in telling their stories.

With this in mind, no one to date has posed the question of narrative strategy in the *Letters* more cogently than Raymund Paredes in his critical review of the work:

> The letters that constitute the novel are written by Teresa to her friend and traveling companion but often rehearse the physical facts of the women's experience together. What is not clear is why anyone would write such elaborate letters simply to retell, without analysis, what the recipient already knows. (1987, 128)

Hence, for Paredes, how Castillo tells her stories in the *Letters* constitutes an aesthetic fault in the text, a narrative strategy that seems to call for some kind of explanation. In contrast, for critics Barbara Brinson Curiel, Erlinda Gonzales-Berry, and Norma

Alarcón, Castillo's narrative strategy contains the potential for a radical critique of Anglo and Latin cultures.

In her study, Curiel is concerned with Castillo's opening discourse to the novel, wherein Castillo proposes three thematic trajectories, one for the conformist, another for the cynic, and still a third for the quixotic. Curiel groups the three trajectories under her own proposal, which she calls the conventional, because it moves from cover to cover. Thereupon she privileges the quixotic trajectory, basing her reading on the Bakhtinian concept of heteroglossia. The appeal to heteroglossia allows Curiel to draw from the quixotic reading those themes carrying a critical charge so as to represent the dialogic structure of the *Letters*. In doing so, she concludes by stating that, "The success of Ana Castillo's *The Mixquiahuala Letters* lies in that it does precisely what Bakhtin recognized that the novel must do: to represent the open-ended and dynamic nature of culture and ideology" (1991, 22).

Erlinda Gonzales-Berry, in a more psychoanalytic approach, sees in the *Letters*, "a novel that delights in transgression and in subversion" (1993). Gonzales-Berry reads in the *Letters* a psychoanalytic space in which Teresa and Alicia share an identity which is never stable, settled, or continuous. As Gonzales-Berry points out, in the act of writing the *Letters* Castillo affirms this mode of identity, standing against the patriarchal modes of identity. The *Letters* subvert the patriarchal desire to dominate identity, to keep it linear, uni-dimensional, bound to a logocentric address. On this view, the *Letters* become a space in which Teresa and Alicia must share an *always never simple* identity, in opposition to patriarchal discourse. As an act of writing, what the *Letters* represent, in effect, is a challenge to the logos of patriarchy. For Gonzales-Berry, the *Letters* articulate the implicit discourse that, ". . . in order to love themselves, and each other, women must learn to undermine and subvert discourse of authority and domination which have taught them self-hate" (1993).

From this sketch, it is interesting to note—and not surprising—that the available criticism of the *Letters* is very much concerned with attending to the question of Castillo's narrative technique. It is not surprising because Castillo is an artist who wants to dialogue with her readers, men and women alike, about the issues that concern Chicanas and other Third World women of color. The epigram, dedication, and reading proposals all attest to the structure of this desire to dialogue, which counts as a complement to Castillo's storytelling voice. But at the same time, the complexity of her mode of narration also indicates that she would dialogue and tell her stories without reproducing patriarchy's discourse of domination. On the site of this relation of complementarity we begin to reinscribe into a critical language what is already in her text —the narrative authority to pen the *Letters* such as they are.[2]

## Clauses, Time, and Chicana Feminism in the *Letters*

Castillo's storytelling voice, that voice that recognizes a need "to narrativize" the events in the lives of the two principal subjects of the *Letters*, Teresa and Alicia, is that voice that first addresses the reader, and is underwritten by the initials A. C. It is also that voice that tells stories because it knows no other thing to do, telling stories being what it does best. Once the reader chooses a journey, Castillo delegates her storytelling voice to Teresa because she is, of the two protagonists, the one who works with words. As canvas and colors are Alicia's medium, so words are Teresa's. (For Alicia's version on canvas and paints of the stories the *Letters* tell, see letter thirty-four). Of course, the delegation does not sanction the reader to identify Castillo with Teresa.

Instead, the delegation requires that Teresa, as teller and participant of her own stories, tread the imaginary line between the selection of events and their interpretation. Not only must she select what to write about, but she must also arrange those events into tellable form.[3] In as much as the task of writing is Teresa's, it is up to her to make sense of their lives, turning the events of their lives into something worth refle(fra)cting. Castillo, in assigning this difficult literary and critical task to Teresa, does not leave her storyteller without the appropriate linguistic *matériel* to take on the challenge of making the patriarchal modes of narration serviceable to Chicana feminism.

As Castillo herself knows, because each of the letters reads as a separate entity, each also represents a radical discontinuity in narrative time with every other letter in the *Letters*. Without the ability to place the letters into minimal temporal sequences,[4] it is impossible to determine the time and scene at which Teresa writes each of the forty letters. That is, while the narrations within each letter contain stories that depict events in their temporal sequence, the letters themselves do not give the necessary linguistic clues that would place them in some definite time and scene of inscription. It is this potential for narration to suspend its own linguistic ground that Castillo exploits so well in order to turn the logos of patriarchy against itself.

Here, one may notice the generosity Castillo displays with her text through the complex dialectic she weaves between the politics and the art of her text. In making the letters available to a reading public, Castillo clearly wants to talk about the conformists, the quixotics, and the cynics among us. The introductory address to the reader registers this contribution to the dialogue. With the same gesture, she ushers the reader into a narrative labyrinth that never turns into an exit, a space from which to diminish the number of potential and uncharted journeys promoted by the forty letters. Castillo sanctions *The Mixquiahuala Letters* as a labyrinth of infinite interpretations—no one reading ranking over another—when she calls to the reader in exclamatory mood wishing her/him good luck on the journey. In effect, the reader is on her/his own to make of the letters what s/he will. Still, by the same token, Castillo never abandons the right over those narrative clauses that would ground each letter to some determinable time and scene of inscription.

For Castillo, the right to these clauses is a stylistic choice about how to represent in literary form the personal and social fragmentations that occupy her two protagonists, and by metonymic reference, the lives of many Chicanas and women of color. Thus, the linguistic condition that enables Castillo to transform the lives of Teresa and Alicia into a literary speech, act, and event is at the same time a strategy of resistance made material in the social act of writing. When Castillo withholds from the reader those clauses that would potentially ground Teresa's narrations, she simultaneously shields her storytelling protagonist from the monologic forces of language, handing her a narrative syntax that plays off the negative capabilities of language. As the epigrammatic voice to this essay suggests, perhaps this notable absence in Castillo's narrative syntax has its estranging effect precisely because it functions as a tool that derives its semantic resources from unexplored mines. This narrative syntax and style is the topic of the rest of this essay. My journey begins with letter three, which initiates the cynic's prescribed order, and I stop not far from there.

If letter three occupies first position in the cynic's prescribed order, this does not mean that Castillo introduces the reader into this thematic trajectory as if it were a story that begins with letter three and ends with letter thirty-eight. Rather, it means that, like the other two thematic trajectories and narrative orders, letter three asks the reader to read from a temporal standpoint that is neither the beginning, nor the end, nor the middle of the narrative. As a consequence, the prescribed readings *de facto* displace the model of the line and install in its place a model of reading that favors cross-reference by story and topical lines. To be sure, such a model of reading does not render time irrelevant. Quite the opposite is true. As letter three makes clear, narrative time is all-important to the *Letters* precisely because its fragmentation requires the reader, as Paul Ricoeur puts it, to "refigure" it.[5] In the process of refiguration, each letter takes on a referential power that transforms Castillo's narrative labyrinth into a picture of the fragmentation that characterizes the lives of Chicanas and other women of color. With this in mind, letter three is exemplary for the oblique picture it presents of Castillo's narrative labyrinth.

In letter three Teresa tells a story of the past and present differences that have made her and Alicia fast friends *and* divided companions. At the scene of inscription, Teresa looks back on the events surrounding the first time they meet, their first summer together, and their eventual parting. As the telling proceeds, it becomes evident that Teresa, in casting the events of that summer into story form, is reflecting back over a considerable temporal distance. Not all at once does the reader get a sense of the temporal distance that separates the time of the story contained in letter three and Teresa's time and scene of inscription. Slowly we learn of the temporal distance separating Teresa from the events she is recalling. Further, in refiguring the distance between story time and inscription time the reader also comes to decode the general illocutionary force of letter three, a force which wavers somewhere between representative and directive[6] (declarative and imperative in the more informal categories of traditional grammar). But again, as with the narrative time, only slowly does the reader come to register the strength and scope of this illocutionary force. With letter three Teresa is in effect trying to repair broken lines of communication with Alicia.

To accomplish this task, Teresa weaves letter three from the events of that summer, which, as we learn from letter six, is a time they have come to call their "first summer's odyssey" (27). In this telling, Teresa reminds Alicia of how, from the beginning of the friendship, they have time and again managed to work out their differences such that they have been brought closer together. The first hint that a grave silence has separated them now for a considerable gap of time comes in the opening salutations that Teresa sends Alicia. "Our first letters" Teresa reminds Alicia, "were addressed and signed with the greatest affirmation of allegiance..." (18). With this opening line, Teresa gives enough information to implicate that their first shared summer, whatever else may have happened thereafter, served as a ground for truly strong friendship. But already, even with such an optimistic opening, the reader gets a sense that all is not well in the present with them. When Teresa adds, "We were not separated. A fine-edged blade *couldn't* have been wedged between our shared consciousness..." [italics on modal verb are mine] (18), she further implicates, with the use of the modal verb denoting inability, that what was impossible in their distant past is now more than a possibility in the immediate present. From the standpoint of the amount of information with which Teresa opens letter three, it is clear that the single consciousness they once shared has slowly waned away.[7]

With the narration that ensues Teresa recalls for Alicia how hard they fought to build that shared consciousness, and in the process silently suggests what a loss it would be if they were to let the relationship slip away for good. The story of their first summer's odyssey begins in Mexico City at a time when the two are probably no more than twenty and both are looking for traces of their cultural and linguistic roots. In a sense, what begins as something like a search for origins ends up as the find of their life. More than finding an authentic site and code upon and with which they can build their individual identities, Teresa and Alicia find in each other a friendship that is more instructive about their present and immediate identities than any simple return to some essential source might have afforded them. That Teresa travels from her native Chicago to Mexico in hopes of finding a new sense of herself is clear from the first clause that begins the narration that tells of how she got there, and of the disappointment she feels with the school: "i had worked at odd jobs for the tuition and boarding expenses..." and thus insinuates that for her the trip had been hard-earned, and further, that is was to be more than "...an existential summer of exotic experiences" (18). As she saw it, this was precisely why the other students were there—students who travelled with the sufficient class privilege of white Anglo America to confuse, or want to confuse, Spanish with Italian. Going to Mexico expecting to be part of the language and culture, Teresa recalls once again that: "My shock bored a 3 inch hole into my native spirit, expecting to study with and under brothers and sisters only to find California blonds and eastern WASPS, instructors who didn't speak Spanish. (Is it *grazi* or *gracia?*)" (18). Later in narrative time, at the scene of her first encounter with Alicia, Teresa is more candid about her reason for going to Mexico, as we shall see.

Gloria Anzaldúa, in addressing the way in which people of color often experience racism, talks about the notion of "blank spots" or "selective reality", defining it as the "narrow spectrum of reality that human beings select or choose to perceive and/or what their culture 'selects' for them to 'see' " (1990, xxi). In this respect, what Teresa has to deal with, first with the other students and instructors and second with the hostesses of the school, is very much like Anzaldúa's concept of "blank spots." In the situations Teresa describes, the blank spots she must deal with have something like the force of indifference: "Didn't they tell anything by my Indian-marked face, fluent use of the language, undeniably Spanish name? Nothing blurred their vision of another gringa come to stay...." (19) asks Teresa of the hostesses, a question that could apply equally to her student colleagues. But this indifference to her person as a person of color from the United States stands in marked contrast with the intense attention that Alicia confers on Teresa the first time they see each other's face.

In telling the story of their first encounter, Teresa foregrounds the critical role that Alicia played in first bringing them together. When Teresa states: "i'm not certain what your first thoughts were of me, studying the dark newcomer from across the dining table...." (18) she acknowledges that in simply being concerned with what Alicia thought of her implied that from the very start neither could be indifferent to the other. Unlike the blank spots she experiences from the others, Teresa is unable to escape Alicia's careful gaze. In effect, Alicia does not let Teresa play her own game of indifference. Alicia, by breaking through Teresa's stand-offish behavior, is responsible for initiating their first summer's odyssey. Teresa, by retelling this story of first encounters, implicitly acknowledges to her friend this critical role in their friendship. On this view, it is no accident that Teresa, at the scene of inscription, uses the subjunctive mood to shade this story of first encounters:

> You scrutinized me with artist's eyes: the curious manner in which i smothered avocado on the corn tortilla *as if* it *were* butter, mixed the beans with the vermicelli soup, spoke only when asked a direct question, looked at no one unless it was necessary, then, it was with an air of defiance *as if* my presence *were* being challenged. [italics on subjunctive markers mine] (19)

With the contrary to fact subjunctive mood Teresa implicates that her stand-offish behavior did not fit the situation. That is, Teresa was not so much being challenged as much as she was simply being ignored. And when she *was* addressed, she reacted to reproduce the same discourse of indifference that the other promulgated on her as a matter of habit. Hence, for her to recount this story of their first encounter is not only to admit old faults but also to affirm new perspectives. Such perspectives, the telling suggests, were gained because Teresa learned an important lesson on that day of first introductions—the lesson of learning how to recognize a friend and an ally. Through this telling what Teresa cedes to Alicia is the affirmation that because of Alicia they became fast friends.

Further, when Teresa writes "You scrutinized me *with artist's eyes*," she implicates that nothing about Teresa escaped Alicia's notice, the adverb of manner giving an already highly evaluative predicate an even more specific sense. In attributing this mode of perception to Alicia, Teresa lets her know via inference how she came to realize at the moment of their first meeting that outrunning her troubled life back in Chicago was going to be difficult. Stated succinctly, Alicia reminds Teresa of why she (Teresa) is in Mexico. When she notices that Alicia's gaze is fixed intently on her wedding band, Teresa is reminded of her marriage back in the States. And when Alicia asks her about it, at that moment Teresa relinquishes any possibility of putting aside concerns of the dying marriage that awaits her back in Chicago. Alicia shatters any illusions that Teresa might have had about what that summer was to be for her. Instead of those illusions, Teresa finds a friend for life as she undergoes a summer in which she has a chance to look at her life and ask what it is that she really wants for herself.

What Teresa really wants we read about in summary form in letter three. In letter nine Teresa tells the whole story of how that summer was among the first in a series of steps that lead her to leave a marriage that had already lost its wind, sails, and rudder. When Teresa's husband arrives in Mexico she has largely come to the conclusion that she "...was no longer prepared to face a mundane life of need and resentment, accept monogamous commitments and honor patriarchal traditions..." At the end of that summer, Teresa is aware that what she wants is "...to be rid of the husband's guiding hand, holidays with family and in-laws ...", no longer wanting to be "...led by a contradicting God, society, road and street signs..." And not least among the things that Teresa wants to throw off is, as she puts it, "...my poverty. Its drabness" (22-23). In sum, it is that first summer's odyssey that leads Teresa to the multi-faceted conclusion that she must be the one to take her life into her hands and change it into what she wants it to be. In reaching these conclusions Teresa recognizes the indispensable role that Alicia played in her life, as she puts it so elegantly, "...that faraway summer of our fledgling womanhood ...." (19) As letter three moves to its close it is this debt that Teresa wants to acknowledge to her friend, and in doing so, recall for her the price they have paid for their friendship. At the scene of inscription, it is this relationship—parable in the making—that is in danger of coming to an abrupt and unnecessary end.

But only indirectly does Teresa make this point, which gains its full force only in the closing paragraph of the letter. With the narration that follows this story of first impressions, Teresa takes Alicia back to the place from which the *Letters* get their name. From this telling, it is clear that their weekend excursion to Mixquiahuala holds a special place for both them in their repertoire of memories focused on that summer. The story tells of a serene outdoor breakfast scene, the subdued but fierce texture of patriarchy in this remote village, and a hike in which Teresa almost falls into a river. These events form the basis of a private language that Teresa and Alicia construct around the name Mixquiahuala. For this reason, it is not surprising that, despite the fact that the name

Mixquiahuala never again appears in any of the letters, it is a name that encodes everything that is worth saving in their relationship. The name designates, on many levels and orders of signification, the core of their experiences together, what has allowed them to be allies, rivals, and in many ways, incomprehensible to each other. For example, the outdoor breakfast scene, filled with a quiet charm and grace, reflects a moment of shared peace, an existential commodity both women sought in their trip to Mexico. Later in letter three Teresa asks about the lack of this commodity in their lives that summer: "We were filled with vivacity for scooping up life, enjoying it to its fullest. Why was peace of mind so intangible?" (22) Teresa and Alicia measured their lack of peace relative to moments like those which the outdoor breakfast scene represents, aware that this existential commodity was always too fleeting and never enough.

But while Alicia and Teresa experience stretches of peace of mind, at every turn, the forces of patriarchy are there to undermine their peace of mind. In parenthetical discourse, for instance, Teresa reminds Alicia of Nena, the servant who worked in the house in which they stayed. As Teresa describes her, Nena was "(. . . the thirtyish housekeeper indebted to the family for keeping her on after giving birth to a son out of wedlock)" (20). This parenthetical discourse demonstrates what a keen observer of patriarchy Teresa is, and how sensitive she is to the depth of oppression which it inflicts upon the sexuality of all women. Within patriarchal discourse a woman's sexuality is always not her own property but belongs to someone else, her father or her husband, or in the case of Nena, to her employer.

It is the scene containing the hike along the river winding "through the heart of Mixquiahuala" (20) that tells, in subtle ways, just how close Teresa and Alicia grew to each other from the very beginning of the summer. From that scene, the reader begins to see how the two women develop a private language, a code which no one else has access to except themselves. Teresa uses the hike to paint a picture of intimately shared laughter. The story of the hike culminates in a fall that Teresa has from the river's muddy bank, almost landing her in the river below. From her telling, it is clear that Teresa wants to emphasize not so much the cause as the effect of the fall, putting events not in their temporal sequence but in their reverse order. Appearing as the topic of the narration is the state in which Teresa finds herself after the fall: "My tennis shoes were ruined and the edges of my yellow slacks were caked with mud. . . ." Next is the cause of the fall, ". . . when i lost footing. . . ," and last is a comment on the fall and its cause, ". . . would've ended in the river had it not been for a rotted tree trunk that stopped my descent" (20). By topicalizing—putting first what happened last—Teresa foregrounds in the scene a figure of herself displaying her ruined tennis shoes and muddy slacks. For a moment, Teresa is openly defenseless and vulnerable to Alicia, but it does not matter. This figure of Teresa is in definite contrast to the defensive Teresa of the previous narration. In some sense, Teresa's fall reminds them of how North American they are. In particular, Teresa's Indian features and brown complexion do not make her a native woman, nor a part of the landscape. For this reason, Mixquiahuala becomes for both a name and an experience they can use to play with people's predilections to put Teresa in the position of having to explain the color of her skin and ways of speaking: "For *years afterward* you enjoyed telling people that i was from Mixquiahuala. It *explained* the exotic tinge of yellow and red in my complexion, the hint of an accent in my baroque speech, and most of all, the undiscernible origin of my being" [italicization of temporal adverbial and epistemic predicate added] (20).

As a story—myth—of origins, Mixquiahuala is for the two women a humorous way to play with such predilections. When recalling the picture of Teresa in mud-caked slacks holding up her ruined tennis shoes, they know that their private myth explains nothing about her origin. The inherent epistemic mood of the predicate *explained* takes its ironic force from their privately shared knowledge that it has nothing to say about Teresa. A bicultural and bilingual citizen of North America, Teresa is a Chicana who has withstood the effects of an Anglo American ideology that wants to maintain the illusion of a homogeneous culture and society. The implication to be drawn from the use of this predicate is that both women know why the burden of "explanation" invariably falls on Teresa: she is a woman of color and she does not speak with the intonation of Anglo English. It is in this manner that Teresa and Alicia use the name of Mixquiahuala as an intersubjective myth that turns certain annoying effects of patriarchy—people forever asking where she is from—into a humorous way to build cohesion into their lives.

Furthermore, the adverbial phrase—*for years afterward*—serves as an index of the temporal distance separating the time of the story from the time of its telling. In writing that statement, Teresa is not only looking back from her scene of inscription, but she is also shooting forward in narrative time, from the time of their Mixquiahuala weekend into an indefinite span of time in the future. By differentiating these two "projections" of narrative time, it is possible to get a sense of the considerable gap of time that separates the time of the story—their first summer's odyssey—from the time of its telling. Somewhere between these two temporal points the adverbial expression *for years afterwards* not only sustains its full reference but also gradually begins to lose it. This process of atrophy, while probably not coincident with the exact moment at which their relationship enters into its period of silence, would still mark the turn towards that silence in their correspondence. What this interpretation suggests is that letter three is quite possibly one of the last letters of the temporal chain represented by the corpus of the forty letters. This view would further suggest that this letter can provide the temporal vantage point from which to chart paths into Castillo's narrative labyrinth, particularly as one seeks to understand the cause of the rift in the two protagonists' relationship.

We can catch a further glimpse of the plausibility of the interpretation of the temporal structure being expressed in the *Letters* by turning to the narrations in which Teresa retraces for both herself and Alicia the day to day routine of summer school in Mexico. In this segment of the letter in particular, Teresa recalls how she and Alicia would spend their evenings together in their boarding house room engaged in long conversations. Most salient about those conversations for Teresa, in her words, are the moments of shared laughter and private retreat. As she says: "This, above all, *i've* treasured in *having* known you. How you made me laugh behind the closed door, away from critical strangers" [italics mine] (21). With this utterance, Teresa not only expresses the depth of intimacy into which they fell, but with the use of the present perfect aspect—the italicized auxiliaries—she also implicates that their summer's odyssey is an experience that still reaches into her present. The maxim of relevance, which requires an interlocutor to say nothing that disrupts discourse coherence, here suggests the reading that what Teresa has to say about their first summer's odyssey is relevant precisely because what they stored up from that experience is something that is at present no longer in reserve. The experience of shared laughter, of finding retreat in each other has been spent.

How their shared intimacy grew into a vast reserve is also a topic in this segment of the letter, and its articulation serves, again on the maxim of relevance, as a gentle coaxing of Alicia by Teresa to recall how hard they fought to earn that intimacy. Alicia's mystical dream in particular serves as a symbol of just how soon after meeting each other both women began, in their unconscious and waking realities, to work on making the differences between them differences *within* them. To the extent that they interpret the dream for themselves, Teresa and Alicia can transform the patriarchal elements of the dream into a positive eruption of their shared unconscious into their day to day lives. In the dream text, Alicia plays the role of the ocean and her hair the tide reaching the shore upon which Teresa walks. Teresa appears in this scene as a delicate, feminine figure clothed in transparent, flowing garb, carrying next to her bosom some treasured object, all the while being pursued by a host of male predators. Whether one takes some Jungian or Freudian line of analysis, it seems clear from the commentary with which Teresa surrounds the dream that both women do indeed have occasion to delve into its symbolic contents and agree upon what it could mean for their lives. Their shared understanding of the dream becomes something that stays with them long past the time frame of the first summer's odyssey. In this respect, the dream also foretells the stresses they will have to weather if they hope to construct, stated in hyperbole, a single consciousness, as the opening of the letter asserts. And from what we see of the letters and the labyrinth they create, Teresa and Alicia do indeed weather those stresses born of their differences. From letter two, for instance, it is clear that their relationship endures a decade of duress. But this stems largely, as Teresa recounts in that letter, from without their relationship as an effect of patriarchy. In fact, what letter two recounts is how they achieved a single consciousness.

More disturbing in tone and illocutionary force is letter thirty-four. This letter marks the end of the conformist's trajectory and (re)presents a most unlikely end to their relationship. As the successor of the pair (thirty-seven, thirty-four), letter thirty-four forms a thematic chain with letter thirty-seven by virtue of the fact that in the latter Teresa explicitly requests Alicia to be in touch, saying: "Maybe we can plan a visit, a visit to make a new plan. i don't want to ramble, i want to talk with you" (124). Thus, since it is letter thirty-four that follows, it seems safe to deduce that Alicia and Teresa never make the visit and thus never make a new plan. Why Alicia never responds is impossible to know for sure, but perhaps it is not too much to say that she takes Teresa's decision at the end of letter thirty-four to move to Mexico and live happily ever after in fairy-tale-like fashion as a blow to the style of Chicana feminism they worked so hard to construct for themselves.

Why the conformists ending might seem an unlikely end to their relationship has to do with the hypothesis that letter three represents a letter that is close to the end of the temporal chain formed by the forty letters. As such, what Teresa has to say about the way their summer ended indeed contains the anticipatory traces of the various paths their relationship will traverse—their view of each other's ethnic identity and socioeconomic background, their relationship to men and society in general, etc. Teresa puts it rather well when she writes: "Summer came down, clashed hard against us who had ended in resenting each other because of our desperate acts" (23). What the reference of these desperate acts are Teresa does not go into with any great detail, but probably Alicia's "idyllic affair" with the Indian caretaker could be classed among them. What seems inescapable about Teresa's telling is that these two neophyte Chicana feminists are in a certain sense doomed to repeat such desperate acts, following the testimony of letter two, for at least a decade. The telling Teresa offers here, on the maxim of quality (as best you know it, state what is the case), implicates that she and Alicia have not, to a significant extent, let their desperate acts keep them from deepening their love for each other. As Teresa tells Alicia in poetic verse: "Finally we've come to respect out privacy/slip into quiet moments with a cup of tea, a glass/of wine, reflect on the next project. Life is/balanced. Even New York makes sense" (17). By making their differences work for them, they have simultaneously managed to keep the distortions that patriarchy hoisted on each of them from wrecking not only their individual lives, but also their relationship. Given the general illocutionary force of letter two—a literary speech act representing what ground they have gained in their war against patriarchy—it seems unlikely that either woman, after rescuing that ground, would ever sink back into the suffocations of patriarchy.

From the standpoint of the interpretation for letter three that I am proposing—that it is a request to repair broken lines of communication and that it is a letter appearing late in the temporal chain—letter thirty-four is conformist for the precise reason that it wants to interject into the thematic and temporal trajectories a premature ending to the life Alicia and Teresa have shared. Closer to the spectacle of life is letter thirty-eight—the cynic's ending—in which Teresa and Alicia draw away from each other because neither is able to extricate herself from the command of patriarchy. When a rift comes between them because of their problematical relationship to one Vicente das Mortes, one sees the two women falling prey to the forces of patriarchy. In this ending, Alicia's mystical dream becomes a prediction of doom for both of them, if one keeps with the view that dreams are egotistical.[8] But in the face of these endings stands letter three, which, if taken as occupying a fairly late position in the temporal chain of letters, then predates letter one, the close of the quixotic trajectory. Because letter one speaks of beginnings, it holds not only the first position for the onset of a new temporal chain of events but also the premiere position in all temporal chains that one can chart in Castillo's narrative labyrinth. This is the case to the extent that no single letter in the labyrinth displays the deictic markers necessary to ground them in anything like linear time. This strategy does not make the *Letters* devoid of referential power. For the reader who enters the labyrinth in earnest quite the opposite is true; the letters come to have a disturbing and unsettling way of pointing to the specific acts of violence that patriarchy, with a certain interested indifference, inflicts on women. Castillo's triumph in the *Letters* consists in using all the linguistic resources of patriarchal language without bending the knee to them.

It is in the closing narrative syntax of letter three that the reader sees that in yet one more way the text of *The Mixquiahuala Letters* is a weave of politics and art, with neither dimension able to assert privilege over the other: "We begged for the other's visit and again the battle resumed. We needled, stabbed, manipulated, cut and through it all we loved, *driven* to see the other improved in her own reflection" [italics mine] (23).

What this closing affirms, in no uncertain terms, is the reciprocal commitment that Teresa and Alicia have to the survival of their relationship. What they have survived in a decade's time we read about in letter two; that they will continue to survive such oppression letter one guarantees. What licenses this guarantee is nothing less than the irreducible force of difference, which serves no moral code nor favors any one form of life over another. While Teresa and Alicia have been the objects of each other's needlings, stabbings, manipulations, etc. in time they have come to recognize the male face of patriarchy behind the two-way mirror it puts up to disguise itself. It is when they have been both agentive subjects and reciprocal objects of the love they possess that they have reflected an image that is more truly their own. The final predicate of the last clause—*driven*—encodes their roles as both subjects and objects of their will to create a destiny of their own. The grammar of the predicate requiring the thematic roles of agent and patient, the *Letters* reveal that Teresa and Alicia do come to assume these roles in time. In so doing, they reflect the differences between and within them, and because the reciprocal reflection is an occasion for action, change, and greater wholeness, they practice an *espejismo* that holds up an image closer to that of women than to that of a male patriarchal god.

In sum, *The Mixquiahuala Letters* represent a Chicana writer who understands, from her own experience, just how women of color have withstood the oppression of patriarchy in its various cultural manifestations—European, Anglo, Hispanic, Latino, Chicano, etc. Ana Castillo, because she knows how to translate her experience into a complex literary landscape, has presented Anglo and Chicano/a letters with a text that, at once, calls for a vast redefinition of what it means to be an American and calls into question the narrow boundaries that confine the American literary canon.

## Notes

1. All single page number references in the text refer to *The Mixquiahuala Letters*. I take the liberty of abbreviating the title to simply *Letters*. Thanks are due to Ana Castillo for granting me an interview that helped

me tremendously in understanding this labyrinthine work.

2. In his text, Fowler (1986, 1-12) outlines a program for what he calls linguistic criticism, the assumptions of which inform my study of the *Letters* throughout. In this way of reading literary texts, the categories of contemporary linguistics are introduced for the purposes of offering more empirically adequate descriptions of the literary text's language. But not just description is at stake with the deployment of this critical vocabulary. Fowler also insists "that the significance of linguistic criticism in literature is a function of the relationship between textual construction and the social, institutional, and ideological conditions of its production and history" (12). See also his note 2 for another version of linguistic criticism.

3. Tellability, as an analytical term, gets its currency from Pratt's (1977, 136-147) welding together of the sociolinguistic work of William Labov and aspects of literary theory into a linguistic model for the study of literary discourse in general. Labov's work on Black English vernacular focuses on the oral tradition among Blacks living in Harlem, and its main data is the study of narratives of personal experience, commonly called natural narratives, in the linguistic literature. Pratt supplements this sociolinguistic model with this term, tellability, which she ascribes to, "speech acts that include natural narrative, an enormous proportion of conversation, and many if not all literary work." She describes further its defining characteristics thus: "Assertions whose relevance is tellability must represent states of affairs that are held to be unusual, contrary to expectations, or otherwise problematic. . . a speaker is not only reporting but also verbally *displaying* a state of affairs, inviting his addressee(s) to join him in contemplating it, evaluating it, and responding to it" (136). Given Castillo's introductory discourse to her text and the controversy of her narrative technique, I have found this term useful and relevant for the study of the *Letters*.

4. I am here adapting Pratt's exposition (1977, 44) of Labov's formulation of the notion of minimal narrative. Labov defines narrative as "one method of recapitulating past experience by matching a verbal sequence of clauses to the sequence of events which (it is inferred) actually occurred . . . ." And he further defines minimal narrative as "a sequence of two clauses which are *temporally ordered*: that is, a change in their order will result in a change in the temporal sequence of the original semantic interpretation" [italics in Pratt] (44). The adaptation I propose amounts to a generalization of this notion of minimality of temporal sequence. For Castillo's text, my claim is not that the *Letters* do not form temporal chains, but that it is always possible, in principle, to reverse the sequence of any two letters without affecting an original semantic interpretation, and this because it is just the issue of an original semantic interpretation in the first place that is so hard to settle in Castillo's narrative labyrinth.

5. In Ricoeur's (1984, 52-87) analysis of narrative and time, it is plot that

mediates between these two terms, and yields, in a certain sense, the refiguration of the text, where this last process is understood in terms of the text's reception.

6. I rely on Pratt's (1977, chap. 3) exposition of Searle's taxonomy of speech acts.

7. As part of her model of linguistic criticism, Pratt (1977, 125-151) enriches the Labovian model with the philosophical work of H. P. Grice, who has had a great deal of influence in the study of linguistic pragmatics. Pratt gives an exposition Grice's notion of the Cooperative Principle (CP) of communication and its four attendant maxims. The import of the CP is that an interlocutor should make his/her contribution to a discourse "such as it is required, at the stage at which it occurs, by the accepted purpose or direction of the talk exchange..." (129). For purposes of brevity I here give short paraphrases of the maxims: (1) Quantity: be neither over- nor underinformative; (2) Quality: advance statements for which you have evidence; (3) Relation: be relevant; (4) Manner: be brief, clear, and orderly in the presentation of information. For purposes of clarity of exposition, I give other versions of these paraphrases in the main text of my essay. Inferences made on the basis of the CP and its maxims are called implicatures and the maxims are said to implicate the inference itself.

8. See Freud (1965, 301-305, 357-358). It seems clear that Alicia's dream, dreaming, the unconscious and parapsychological phenomena in the *Letters* form a subject unto itself. This reference is only to suggest the need for such studies.

# The Street Scene: Metaphoric Strategies in Two Contemporary Chicana Poets

*María Herrera-Sobek*

> . . . the greatest of all is to be happy in the use of metaphor; for it is this alone which cannot be acquired, and which, consisting in a quick discernment of resemblances, is a certain mark of genius.
> —Aristotle, *Politics and Poetics* (252)

> . . . the issue is no longer the *form* of metaphor as a word—focused figure of speech, nor even just the *sense* of metaphor as a founding of a new semantic pertinence, but the *reference* of the metaphorical statement as the power to 'redescribe' reality. The most fundamental support of this transition from semantics to hermeneutics is to be found in the connection in all discourse between sense, which is its internal organization, and reference, which is its power to refer to a reality outside of language. Accordingly, metaphor presents itself as a strategy of discourse that, while preserving and developing the creative power of language, preserves and develops the *heuristic* power wielded by fiction.
> —Paul Ricoeur, *The Rule of Metaphor* (6)

Chicana writers and their creative oeuvres are evincing great interest in literary scholarship. Various book-length studies analyzing the writings of Chicana authors have been written since 1985 (Sánchez 1985; Herrera-Sobek 1985; Herrera-Sobek and Viramontes 1988; Rebolledo) and the authors themselves continue to produce outstanding poetry and prose collections. The critical works attest to the vigor, productivity, and creativity of these women and to the increasing prominence they are achieving in literary circles.

In this study, I analyze the writings of two Chicana poets: Evangelina Vigil's collection of poems entitled *Thirty An' Seen a Lot* (1982) and Beverly Silva's *The Second St. Poems* (1983). My primary focus centers on the analysis of the metaphoric strategies utilized by the above two writers in the process of structuring their poetic universe. It is my contention that in both authors the street scene is a poetic fount through which these women receive their primary source of inspiration and the principal geographic space from which a great number of their images emanate.

The term "street scene" implies a complex of images associated with the public domain of the city: bars, street language, street people, street happenings, the *pachuco*, the *bato loco*, the bag lady, "winos," and so forth. The street, I propose, serves as a metaphor to represent these Chicanas' "going-out-into-the-world." I further posit that firstly the central axis upon which both Vigil's and Silva's collection of poems revolve is the quest; that is the search for their identity as Chicanas, as women, and as human beings. The metaphor of the street—and all that that metaphor encapsulates for the process of searching out, for self-fulfillment and transformation through exploring the world at large—becomes a perfect vehicle through which the poetic "I" can find expression. Secondly, I posit that both Vigil and Silva articulate through their poetic persona a feeling of being at the crossroads; a feeling of being in between two worlds: the world of the *cantina*, the outside—again a spatial metaphor expressing or encoding a traditionally male domain—and the world of the house, the inside, traditionally connotative of the female domain. The juncture or unifying link between these two extreme poles beckoning the poetic persona of each author is the street, which the poets traverse back and forth, heels clicking to the beat of an inner rhythm that seeks liberation from the multiple shackles imprisoning women: males, tradition, poverty, censorship, social mores, and other restraints imposed by patriarchal society. The poets oscillate between the two domains; they hesitate at each juncture, not ready, or perhaps not willing, to totally embrace one or the other. And it is precisely this oscillation between the two referential signs, house and *cantina*, which creates an unbearable tension and supplies much of the form and content of Vigil's and Silva's poetic universe. The above conceptualization can be graphically depicted thusly:

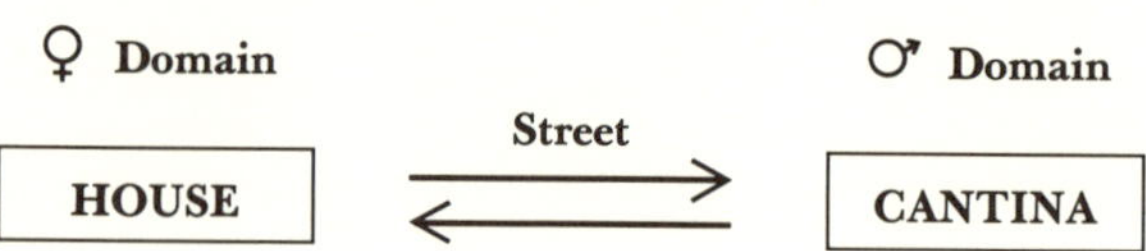

**Thirty An' Seen a Lot**

A close examination of Vigil's *Thirty An' Seen a Lot* immediately informs the reader of the "liberated woman" theme of this anthology. The title itself is a metaphor connoting street-wise knowledge and woman-of-the-world experience. This is not only expressed linguistically by the common idiomatic expression "An' seen a lot," which is metaphorically linked to the meanings cited above, but in addition contains the apostrophe (') which transforms the conjunction "and" into "an'." This phonetically and graphically transports a word in standard English into a dialectal variation of the language. This non-standard variation of English, or slang, is commonly associated with the jargon of "the street."

The photo on the cover of the book reinforces the primacy of the street scene encompassing the poetic contents of the book, for we perceive a smiling young woman (Evangelina) posing in front of a *cantina* inviting the onlooker, by means of body language (fingers curled, thumb extended, pointing in the direction of the "Ladies Welcome" sign, towards the inside of the bar) to join her. Indeed, the photo on the back cover of the book portrays the author again, this time seated on a bar stool at a *cantina* counter, half-smiling, drinking a beer while a slightly puzzled Mexican male looks on. Both photos, read as semiotic signs, metaphorically indicate by means of these visual codes the supposedly liberated status of Evangelina, and by extension of all Chicanas. The inside of the book, however, will present a more complex situation vis-à-vis the current status of these women.

Vigil's collection of poems in *Thirty An' Seen a Lot* falls within the parameters other Chicana poets—e.g. such as Alma Villanueva—have followed; it is in the autobiographical mode or style of writing.[1] The poetic voice, at thirty finds herself at the crossroads of life and is searching for the "correct" route to take in her life's journey. A preoccupation with temporality is denoted by the specific age cited: thirty years. The third decade in a person's life is symbolically rich with biblical connotations: Christ's coming out, His being reborn through baptism; and His being "reborn" through resurrection all at the age of thirty or thereabouts.[2] It is associated with the number three, a number imbued with magical qualities.[3] It is a time conducive to introspection and projection: for both looking back and looking forward. Indeed, her poem "to the personalities in the works by José Montoya and the chucos of the future" posits this fundamental paradox of life: your past is always part of your future:

recall that memory
that keeps calling you back in time
but will show itself:
invisible fiber connected to the past
needled through your ombligo
it pulls you onward
but at the same time
aback

aback
like a bato loco from the barrio
confident stacey adams steps
clicking rhythmically forward
but head swung back some
as if poised to say
"¿qué pajó, ese?
"What's happenin' home"

yes, head swung back some
because string of consciousness
pulls him back in time
although the dude
is really walking forward (55)

Vigil's poetic universe will be characterized by an oscillation between past, present, and future. Here "remembrances of things past" in Vigil will transport her to the image of the house, the central metaphor for women's domain as stated earlier. But in order to remember the past the author needs to enter into a state of solitude. Gaston Bachelard discusses the importance of solitude in providing the proper environmental context in which the felicitous combination of reverie and imagination can properly germinate.

> The cosmic reverie as we shall be studying it is a phenomenon of solitude which has its roots in the soul of the dreamer. It does not need a barren land to take root and grow. A pretext—not a cause—is sufficient for us to enter the "solitary situation," the situation of the dreaming solitude. In this solitude, memories arrange themselves in tableaus. Decor takes precedence over drama. Sad memories take on at

> least the peace of melancholy. . . . Cosmic reveries separate us from project reveries. They situate us in a world. They situate us in a world not in a society. The cosmic reverie possesses a sort of stability. It helps us escape time. It is a state. . . of mind. . . . The task remains for the mind to make systems, to arrange diverse experiences in order to understand the universe. (1971, 14)

Vigil begins her anthology precisely with a poem expressing feelings of solitude, or alienation, a feeling of aloneness in the universe, a feeling best conveyed by the Spanish word *desgano*.[4] Indeed, she utilizes this very word in her poem: "sin ganas en primer lugar." In this specific poem the poetic voice experiences complete alienation from all that surrounds her. Her simile of being

> like a good actress on a stage
> but with no props
> no supporting actors
> no friends in the audience
> and no heart for it all (1)

strips her of all support systems except her own skill at surviving ("good actress"); yet she goes through life's motions without the *joie de vivre* or *élan vital* necessary for complete self actualization and fulfillment.

Immediately, however, in the second poem of this anthology the poetic voice introduces a central metaphor for the Mexican culture which Chicano poets both male and female have appropriated—the image of the grandmother. Vigil associates this image with the private domain or house complex.[5] The alienation and *desgano* that the poetic voice is experiencing in the first poem turns optimistic upon reflecting on the all-knowing image of the Grandmother—a sign encoding the Chicano-Mexican culture. Thus the poetic voice optimistically articulates:

> surely soon I'll come to know
> behold
> that secret
> something that my grandmother knows
> but that I don't
> something so much there
> that I do not appreciate it

I've seen it in her eyes bright
I've sensed it close-up
in her childlike happiness
her appreciation for all
that makes her world

Surely soon I'll come to know (2)

and through the medium of the spoken word projects us into a more optimistic future. The poem that follows, "remolino en mi taza," confirms this optimism and is indeed a poem celebrating the "rich flavor" of the *raza mestiza* metaphorically rendered as the mixture of "thick white cream" with "grandma's strong black coffee."

The image of the grandmother is recalled in "spinning on solid ground"; here for the first time the poetic persona is conjured as one who walks the streets at night uneasily. Paralleling the first poem, the poetic "I" is imbued with a feeling of deep, unfathomable *desgano*. Fortunately this *desgano* anew redirects the imagination to a state of reverie. This reverie, however, will be focused inward toward the innocent, prelapsarian stage of joyous childhood, and will be a predominant characteristic in several of the poems in the collection.

Gaston Bachelard comments regarding the significance of these reveries:

> From poetic reverie, inspired by some great spectacle of the world to childhood reverie, there is a commerce of grandeur. And that is why childhood is at the origin of the greatest landscapes. Our childhood solitudes have given us the primitive immensities. By dreaming on childhood, we return to the lair of reveries, to the reveries which have opened up the world to us. It is reverie which makes us the first inhabitant of the world of solitude. And we inhabit the world better because we inhabit it as the solitary child inhabits images. In the child's reverie the image takes precedent over everything else. Experience comes later. They go against the wind of every reverie of flight. The child sees everything as big and beautiful. The reverie toward childhood returns us to the beauty of the first images. Can the world be as beautiful now? Our adherence to the original beauty was so strong that if our reverie carries us back to our dearest memories, the present world is completely colorless (1971, 102-103)

In "spinning in solid ground" Vigil's poetic persona returns to a simpler, uncomplicated age, encapsulated in the childlike interjection "Golly." This speech act effectively divides the poem into two temporal sectors: the present and the nostalgic preterit. The poem reminisces in the second part:

> I used to have such nice times en los carnavales de San Antonio
> I could pick out my thrills undiscovered
> without consciousness of consequences
> rides were cheaper too
> and gypsies looked like gypsies
> 'cause they were
> and you could not look forward to a scarey walk home
> in the dark, across railroad tracks
> where winos, hobos and tecatos converged
> with the other westsiders (4)

The poet proceeds to code-switch to Spanish; a language connected to the image of the grandmother. Through Spanish she projects the nostalgia even further back in the vectors of time and space. A sense of loss and sadness is conveyed for the missing security and warmth characteristic of the past.

> No, ya no es como antes
> todo ha cambiado
> dice mi abuela
> suspirando
> viendo
> marveling at la transformación
> del centro, del mercado—
> cosas concretas y seguras
> en mi espacio hueco
>
> Jijo. (4)

Poetic closure is achieved through another forceful interjection: *Jijo*. This time the interjection is not associated with the thematic domain of innocence and paradisiacal childhood but with a street slang expletive. The utilization of *jijo*, which is the contracted form of "hijo de la chingada" (son of a whore), underscores the transformation and metamorphosis of the poetic persona from childhood innocence to street savvy. However, by employing the abbreviated, more timid, less explosive, and innocuous form of "hijo de la chingada," the poet is making a statement: the transformation to a completely street-wise woman has not crystallized yet. This is only a timid foreshadowing of the strong street language that is about to appear.

The coming transformation of the poetic persona is further expressed in "they say she dared converse with the full moon," for the poem is a statement depicting the poet as an entity "different" from the rest of society. The association between moon and woman connotes images of witches and magic; of possessing or being in touch with powers beyond normal human experience (Cirlot 1962, 214-217). The very act of daring to converse with the moon indicates a rebellious spirit which is willing to transgress the interdicts, to break the norms and strictures of social conventions. Cirlot expands on the multifaceted symbolism of the moon, noting its association with such lunar goddesses as Ishtar, Hathor, Anaitis, and Arthemis. He further confirms that the ancients were also aware of the "relationship between the moon and the tides, and of the more mysterious connexion between the lunar cycle and of the physiological cycle of woman" (1962, 214). The power of the moon on women is believed to be so great that some tribes (in Greenland for example) have gone so far as to prohibit women to contemplate it for long, for it is believed to incite them to orgies. Cirlot adds that "Another significant aspect of the moon concerns its close association with the night (maternal, enveloping, unconscious, and ambivalent because it is both protective and dangerous) and the pale quality of its light only half-illuminating objects. Because of this, the moon is associated with the imagination and the fancy as the intermediary realm between the self-denial of the spiritual life and the blazing sun of intuition" (1962, 216). The association between moon and madness has been firmly established in literary tradition and etymologically the word "lunacy" (madness) is derived from *luna* (moon). The narrative voice in "they say she dared converse with the full moon" indeed asserts that

> they say she dared converse
> with the full moon
>
> la oscuridad
> de lo hondo del mar

es tan rica
misteriosa

me hace voltear
hacia la luna
y al ver su cara iluminante
redonda
me vuelvo loca (5)

The poetic persona proceeds to discover her sensuous self through a period of self-introspection and poetic incubation in a magnificently sensual poem "night vigil." A kaleidoscope of sensual metaphors permeate the lyrics of this poem. However, complete sexual satisfaction is not achieved in "night vigil." It is nevertheless an introduction to the poem that follows for it is precisely in "transcendence" that the poetic persona is completely initiated into womanhood.

In the poem, "transcendence" can be read both as a metaphoric elaboration of the act of intercourse as well as a more spiritual transcendence. The new-found ecstasy is rendered in a simple and clear language:

my god how
did you do that
to me just
said I'm coming
in and wiped out
all the world just
me and
you my
god (12)

If the poem is read as a paean to sexual intercourse, close examination demonstrates that the male in this particular poem is granted the status of a God. However this status does not last long for immediately in the poem that follows "transcendence" the "God" is demoted into a helpless observer.

my god
look at me what
have I become but
a bundle of nerves

can't even cry no tears
only cold tension
that not even the sun
can penetrate (13)

The devaluation of the male further continues in the juxtaposition of the poems "splendor" and "momma's bosom." In "splendor" the woman holds in the palm of her hand a mysterious and wonderful secret (life)

"I have a surprise!" she'll announce
she will extend delicate palm before your eyes
revealing diamond of music in her hand
its radiance will be dazzling
its beauty illuminating (14)

Contrasted to this exuberant richness and energizing zest for life is the quivering man-child in "momma's bosom" who holds "un centavo" (a penny—synecdoche for money) in the palm of his hand. Derision follows:

¡ u, yu yuy!
¡ válgame dios!
¡ ah, qué muchacho!
¡ ya va comenzar a chillar!
¡ újule, hombre!
no te digo. (15)

The poem begins with a derisive interjection "¡ u, yu yuy!" It proceeds to invoke God in a tone of exasperation "¡válgame dios!" The annoying culprit is the male-child: "¡ah, qué muchacho!" who is ready to explode into sobs: "¡ya va comenzar a chillar!" The tone betrays scorn for the helpless male-child through the infinitive *chillar* which denotes disgust, and conveys a lack of sympathy for the cry-baby. The final, knowing "no te digo" (Didn't I tell you?) emphasizes the superiority of the speaker—momma—a woman.

## The *Cantina* Metaphor

Appropriation of the male domain is finally accomplished in "por la calle Zarzamora." The *cantina* here functions as a metaphor for the privileged space of the male in Chicano culture. In Mexican/ Chicano culture and the other Latin American countries only "bad" girls—namely prostitutes—inhabited the dim-lit tabooed geographic space of the bar. In the *cantina* male socializing, as well as drinking and male-bonding take place and in barrio neighborhoods the *cantinas* are supposed to be strictly for males only. As far as I know, of the major poets only Lorna Dee Cervantes in her poem "Visions of Mexico while at a writing symposium in Port Townsend, Washington" (1981, 45) had thematized the *cantina* scene vis-à-vis women previous to Vigil's poems. Nevertheless, it is Vigil who for the first time consistently invades this male domain, appropriates it and makes it the center of much of her poetry. The following year, Beverly Silva, another Chicana, will likewise invade *cantinas*, dance halls, and bars and transform them into the center of her poetic discourse. Vigil's poem "por la calle Zarzamora" boldly states without any preliminaries

entro a una cantina
y como ciega busco mi lugar
eso es muy importante
luego ordeno una cerveza
y me acomodo (19)

The present indicative of the verb "entrar" = "entro" conveys confidence and a sense of self-assurance, of knowing exactly what one is doing and having a right to do it. The second line however deflates and negates this first assertion of assurance: "y como ciega busco mi lugar," for the word "ciega" connotes a feeling of not knowing what one is doing, of being totally unfamiliar with ones surroundings. Indeed she may feel that she does not rightfully belong there. The poetic I proceeds to describe what she sees:

Allí están sentaos
los batos y señores
on bar stools like pájaros cansados
periqueando y pisteando
y de rato a mi presencia se acostumbran
y siguen con su onda natural (19)

Again the author appropriates another linguistic register traditionally associated with the male domain: street language. The *caló* words batos (dudes), *periqueando* (talking), *pisteando* (drinking), *trosteo* (trust), "bro' " (brother), and *jijo*, are aggressively utilized in the lyrics of her poem. The males in the *cantina* are at first uncomfortable, but gradually become accustomed to a woman's presence in their midst and continue their manly chatter. The tranquility of the bar is again broken by the appearance of two street-wise women. The ensuing scene is typical of a man-picks-up-woman-at-bar routine. However the poem closes with the males ridiculing, albeit secretly, the two "intruding" women. Although we find three women, the poet plus two others, penetrating the dark recesses of the once forbidden *cantina*, access to this male domain is still not completely secured in this particular poem. The blind groping of the poetic persona upon entering the premises and the subsequent ridiculing, and joking at the two anonymous women's expense point to the still unacceptable presence of the feminine element and underscores the newcomer's unwelcomed status in this particular "masculine" space.

The *cantina* motif reappears in poems such as "with a polka in his hand," where the poet again inhabits a "classier" "gringo" bar to have a drink. Here, although the poet finds herself in a potentially hostile space—a gringo bar—she projects an aura of self confidence. This confidence is, surprisingly enough, derived from her Mexican culture, for as she comfortably sits in the bar ordering a drink she observes an old brown, weather-beaten face of a man holding a transistor radio in his hand playing a Mexican polka. This image connects her to her Chicano past where she retrieves the memory of the legendary figure of Gregorio Cortez, the famous Chicano rebel from south Texas (Paredes 1978). Again Vigil does a very "unfeminine" act: "se echa un trago"—she makes a toast to the freedom to retain ones culture and to her innate birthright as an American citizen to have freedom of movement (i.e. to be able to sit in a bar—a male domain—in the United States—a "gringo" domain).

An added male domain appropriated by Vigil, and which like the *cantina* is part of the street scene, is the linguistic domain of the expletive or obscene word. Two poems are worthy of study: "me caes sura, ese, descuéntate" and "para los que piensan con la verga (with due apologies to those who do not)." The tone and tenor of the first poem is set in the title itself. The title of the poem is derived from the Chicano dialect of *caló* or *pachuco* speech and translates into English thusly: "I despise you, man; leave me alone." It proceeds crecendo-like to delineate in the strongest language possible the portrait of the male *chingón* or "supermacho":

eres el tipo
de motherfucker
bien chingón
who likes to throw his weight around
y aventar empujones
y tirar chingazos
and break through doors
bien sangrón
saying con el hocico
"that's tough shit"
bien pesao
el cabrón (46)

The series of expletives and obscene metaphors: motherfucker, *chingón*, *chingazos*, shit and *cabrón* are all strategically combined to paint the portrait of a totally disreputable, repugnant most disgusting image of the Chicano/Mexican macho. In this verbal battle the poet completely demolishes her macho adversary with those linguistic weapons which have traditionally belonged to the male domain. Paralleling Vigil's previous appropriation of the sacrosanct male domain of the *cantina*, the poet defiantly marches forth to invade the linguistic preserve of male expletives. Once more Vigil becomes one of the first Chicana poets to utilize consistently such starkly obscene language throughout her poetry. The second poem cited above "para los hombres que piensan con la verga (with due apologies to those who do not)" reiterates a similar paradigm vis-à-vis the incorporation of obscene language in her lyrics:

lost cause:
ya no queda energía mental
y ni siquiera señas
del sincero deseo
de tratar de aliveanarle la mente
al hombre bien perdido
en el mundo de nalgas y calzones

se trata de viejos repulsivos
tapados con cobijas de asqueroso sexismo
agarrándose los huevos
a las escondidas
with brain cells
displaced/replaced
by sperm cells
concentrating:
pumping away

ya no queda energía mental (47)

Again the structuring of the metaphor "mundo de nalgas y calzones" (which represent the act of coitus) from street language indicates Vigil's complete invasion of this male linguistic domain. The street metaphor "huevos" for testicles and the substitution of the slang "pumping away" for sexual intercourse further underscores Vigil's aggressive stance and stubborn insistence focused on abolishing sexist domains in the sphere of language. The central theme of both poems is sexism and the poetic persona's desire to exterminate it. She most astutely initiates her onslaught on male sexism with the incorporation in her discourse of those specific taboo words traditionally off limits to "nice, sweet, angelic, passive girls." The abrupt introduction of obscene language metaphors forcefully articulates the central statement of the two poems: the Chicana is no longer limited in her verbal repertoire to "pretty" or "sweet-little girl" imagery. She is now free to utilize the full spectrum of poetic discourse previously available only to males.

Vigil's strongest statements in the entire anthology are encoded in the lyrics of the above two poems. However, although the incorporation of traditionally male speech patterns in Vigil's poetry is now complete, the poet will still veer back and forth from the male domain to the female domain, or metaphorically speaking, from the *cantina* to the house. Such poems as in "ser conforme" and "kitchen talk" exemplify this going back to the house, to the comforting space of mother and grandmother whose wisdom and knowledge elicits respect and admiration in the poet.

## The Second St. Poems

Beverly Silva, a Chicana born and raised in East Los Angeles but residing in San Jose when she wrote her anthology, structures poetic discourse through the same three metaphors Evangelina Vigil utilized: house, street, and *cantina*. Vigil and Silva's books were published in 1982 and 1983 respectively. It is not certain whether Silva had read Vigil's poetry and was influenced by it. The author of *The Second St. Poems* had read Lorna Dee Cervantes's poems, as she acknowledges in the poem "Reading Lorna's Poems" (69), and of course Silva's literary background (Master's degree in English literature) provides her with a solid grounding in literature.

If Silva had not read Vigil's poetry, it is indeed surprising that the contents should coincide vis-à-vis the metaphoric strategies utilized in the poems. Silva's poems parallel Vigil's in the tripartite metaphoric structure of the three basic spatial metaphors: the house—or apartment—to be more specific, the street, and the *cantina*. Furthermore, analysis of the poems yield the spatial dialectic of "inside" and "outside." These two concepts are in turn related to the psychological feeling of alienation. Gaston Bachelard points out the importance of the inside-outside dialectic and its relationship to other philosophical systems. He proffers: "Philosophers, when confronted with outside and inside, think in terms of being and non-being. Thus profound metaphysics is rooted in an implicit geometry which—whether we will or no—confers spatiality upon thought. . . ." (1969, 212).

Spatial reality, therefore, becomes a most significant component of Silva's poetry in the structuring of her poetic universe.

## The Street

Beverly Silva's anthology *The Second St. Poems* contains a total of thirty-five entries. As we read the poems we realize that a major street in the city of San José, California,—Second Street—is the main protagonist of her poems and the principal structuring agent. In addition to being the title of the collection, the term "Second Street" appears in nine out of thirty-five poems.

The street for Silva is the linkage that unites her inside world to her outside world. By appropriating the street, "pounding" it so to speak into submission, she can begin to assert herself into the world. Furthermore, by personifying it, naming it, making it her lover and confidant, she seeks to obliterate the abstractness of the world outside and thus humanizes it. Through this process she is able to incorporate the outside world with her inner world. The street (or outside world) eventually becomes less menacing, less threatening for the poetic persona until she manages to conquer it through the magic and power of language: the street becomes a mere line in her poetry, albeit an important one. She states:

Second St.,
with a fierce passion i have claimed you.
With a fierce passion i have named a book of poems for you.
As i stand here
balanced between East and West San José
weighing my life
you hold me.
Like a well used shoe
no longer respectable or stylish
but comfortable as old leather
you hold me.
Like a new lover
deftly withholding pleasure one moment
opening new dimensions of himself the next
you hold me.
i walk the length of your pavement
writing poems. (35)

Second Street is the embodiment of life outside. It embodies the metaphor that perfectly conveys the dangerous, soul-killing, physically endangering world that the poetic voice seeks to tame. Second Street is the universe in miniature at its most violent, at its most spiritually degrading self. In "Always close to death on Second St." she describes life on the street:

there's no way to escape knowledge of mortality
living on Second St.
with only a pane of glass separating you from prostitutes,
dance hall music entering all your windows,
& a mortuary across the street.
Downtown violence is a thing you live with:
all night sirens,
barroom knifings,
once a month eruptions from people on dope or booze
wrecking their apartments.
Poverty and frustration speak out.

Every few months there's a murder,
an unidentified body
the police always link to dope or passion or prostitution. (53)

The poem vividly presents Second Street at its most sordid, degenerate, vice-ridden self. It serves as a magnificent metaphor for the negative side of life, for the struggle, the brutality that often crushes a person's spirit; a side of life too often denied by the more affluent sectors of society and relegated to the "other side of town." The street is nevertheless there, asserting its existence with the finality and insistence of a police siren's wail. Silva is a participant observer of this precarious environment; she is barely one step away from death, both spiritual and physical. And it is only through her long forgotten Mexican culture, from which she now begins to nourish her spirit, that she learns to survive in this hostile space.

The poet acknowledges that Second Street is "not an easy place to live"; knifings, rapes, murders, the constant threat of physical harm are all part of the daily fare. The poet watches from her window, mesmerized by the kaleidoscopic side of life as it unfolds on a Second Street parking lot:

people passing through town slept in their cars
truckers parked for a few days
police had their check points here
lovers met on lunch hours or after work
others came just to drink beer
prostitutes made their connections
old & young men stopped to piss beside the concrete posts
as if no one could see them
the mexican guys from the apartments worked on their cars
usually all day Saturdays
leaving littered beer cans for the Sunday morning recycle collector
page after page of my journal
became filled with these events.
i dreaded evenings when i had to shut the drapes. (65)

## The House

Bachelard (1969, 6) asserts that: ". . . the house shelters daydreaming, the house protects the dreamer, the house allows one to dream in peace." And because the house is the spatial area where these daydreams manifest themselves more readily it becomes a most powerful integrating force for "the thoughts, memories and dreams of mankind" (1969, 6) The great magnetism the house exerts in uniting humankind's thoughts and actions from past, present, and future events resides principally in that propensity for stimulating and providing the proper locus for a person to dream and engage in daydreams. Bachelard insists that:

> Without it, [the house] man could be a dispersed being. It maintains him through the storms of the heavens and through those of life. It is body and soul. It is the human beings first world. Before he is 'Cast into the World,' as claimed by certain hasty metaphysics, man is laid in the cradle of the house. And always, in our daydreams, the house is a large cradle. . . . Being is already a value. Life begins well, it begins enclosed, protected, all warm in the bosom of the house. (1969, 7).

The dialectic [house:universe] parallels the inside outside dialectic explored previously.

The house acquires in Silva that primary valence, or symbol, of being the first human shelter, the original paradise from which humanity was expelled. However, the poetic persona in *The Second St. Poems* has already been evicted from paradise; she is alone pounding the streets, looking for shelter. And here a transformation takes place. Silva the mother becomes Silva the daughter of her own daughter Joy, who is supporting her and sheltering her. The house, a previous symbol of paradise becomes transformed into a semi-nightmare of cockroaches, of cracked peeling paint. It is an inhospitable environment from which Silva dreams of escaping. The poetic voice recounts the nightmare in "The roaches came from everywhere":

> under
> over
> above
> behind
> between
> around
> below
> it was a lesson in prepositions to ponder them.
> Big ones
> small ones

medium sized ones
Families & communities of them invaded our apartment.
. . . . . .
At night they crawled from all the cracks
to cover our walls like some grotesque canvas
painted by a madman. (38)

The metaphor of God the Painter or nature gone mad underscores the absurdity and insanity of the poetic persona's struggle to survive. The cockroaches become a metaphor for the hostile uncaring, inanimate forces that are ever-ready to strike down and engulf the weaker species. The poet embraces the challenge and defiantly, military-like, aggressively stands her ground and angrily strikes back:

My method was attack.
with spray can & poison i'd hit & run.
Joy preferred to crush them
with an old butter knife she kept ready for this purpose
She was slow & meticulous about crunching each one. (38)

The brown cockroaches simultaneously encode two symbols: Mexican poverty and the indomitable will to survive. Scientists have stated in unequivocal terms that the cockroach is the only living entity which is not affected by radioactivity. If mankind manages to exterminate itself with a nuclear bomb the lowly cockroach will inherit the earth.

In the poem, however, the cockroach represents the hostile forces of man and nature and the two women's will to survive in spite of all the odds running against them.

To move wasn't possible,
we had to fight. (38)

Because of the horrible, poverty-stricken, unsanitary environment of the apartments in which she lives, the concept of "house" begins to assume negative connotations. Indeed, for feminist writers the house is no longer perceived as a symbol of security but as a metaphor for prison. It has become a claustrophobic space which enslaves and imprisons women within its four walls. Thus Silva writes "Pain":

is a box.
i'm in a box
& i can't get out of it.

It is a house.
Walls and a roof.
& a solid floor,

but no door. (70)

Nevertheless the poetic persona often finds herself in the confining space of the house looking out into the world through a window. The window becomes a much reiterated motif in the poet's lyrics; it is a locus from which she observes life unfold, paralleling the passive spectator who watches life through the medium of the television tube:

Not because i love literature less
but because i love life more
i'm content to sit here at this window
waiting for the next chapter. (37)

Paradoxically she seems to perceive this passive "watching" of life slide by her window as a more worthwhile activity than reading about life through the medium of literature. Her conceptualization of life, however, is expressed in the medieval metaphor of *vita ex libris* with "chapters" that can be read or experienced as time evolves or passes by.

In the poem "Depression" she reiterates the theme of the passive observer sitting by the window "watching" life go by. The tone, however, is less optimistic and upbeat. The poetic voice realizes that "watching" life, as opposed to experiencing life, is not a fulfilling and satisfying enough experience:

No one calls
i've always been the outgoing one.
i crawl within myself
staring out this window
day after day
waiting to die. (51)

Escape from this self-imposed enclosure then often becomes a necessity. It is this necessity that propels her to sail forth into the throbbing orb of the street in search of a connecting, electrifying spark that may shock her back to the realm of the living.

## The *Cantina*

The *cantina*, on the other hand, will be transformed into the primary locus from where the poetic will derive her energy. She will seek within its warm entrails, in the dark, womb-like recesses of bars and dance halls nourishment for her starved soul. And she will find it. Paralleling Vigil, the *cantina* again become a metaphor for the male-centered Mexican culture. Traditionally tabooed to women as stated earlier, Silva invades the prohibited confines of this space and makes it her own. Paradoxically, it is in this tabooed space that she will connect to her ancestral roots through the brown, comforting, entwining arms of her Mexican lovers. She dances blithely toward her origins in the warm, passionate embrace of the Mexican men she meets there. And it is in this specific space that she will experience the vitality and energy of life. Her earthy campesino lovers will transport her in time and space and will revitalize her weakened and deteriorating psyche.

> when i need conversation
> there's a corner bar filled with characters as interesting
> as any professor.
> when i need love
> there's a next door dance hall filled with romantic men
> as handsome as my young dreams.
> They return me to a world of feelings
> a belief in love and sentiments (37)

The dark macho men fascinate Silva; they are the "salt" and "salsa" that reawaken her to a different more fulfilling way of life; to another dimension of the universe. In the poem "José Luis" she admires her earth-toned campesino boyfriend:

> José Luis.
> The blue silk shirt from Mexico
> extravagantly emphasized by white trousers
> legs spread
> left foot on the bar rail

right hand on his hip
a Coors carefully cupped in the left
elegant in shoulder length black hair
heavy Villa moustache.
All so intenso y serio. (46)

The Mexican campesino men in her life touch a resonant chord in her subconscious, a chord whose vibrations stimulate the desire to fulfill a longtime dream—her dream to visit that brown land of "magia y ensueño." She records this in:

"i went to México, Mi Amor"

to forget you.
i wanted to see Pancho Villa's house
the Noa-Noa club in Juárez
the silver mines so much part of you
& ride the Chihuahua railroad.
But you didn't answer my telegram
so i went to México, Mi Amor (75)

Silva and Vigil have carved out of the topology surrounding them —house-street-cantina—a literary space. The transformation of these spaces through their artistic elaboration yields a metaphoric triad which transcends its geographic specificity and functions as a referential sign encoding and redefining Chicana reality. Every artistic text is inevitably embedded within a historical and ideological context. The analysis of *Thirty An' Seen a Lot* and *The Second St. Poems* demonstrates how these works actualize and concretize through a series of signs the centrifugal forces operating in the contemporary Chicana experience.

The hypersign function of each of these literary texts presents a dynamic vision of the Chicana's struggle to enter into a meaningful, restraint-free dialectic with the world at large. Both the Vigil and the Silva texts can be perceived as manifestos or declarations of independence; they forcefully point to the complete liberation of the Chicana, to a time when she will be free from the outside-imposed bondage of gender.

I would like to thank Professor Jaime Rodríguez, Director of the Mexico/Chicano Program, Juliet MacCannell, Director of the Women's Studies Program, and the Humanities Research and Travel Committee, all from the University of California, Irvine, for the generous grants I received to research and write this article.

## Notes

1. According to Sánchez (1985, 24-25) "Villanueva is a poet who senses her personal development in terms of time. In fact, among the poets discussed in this volume, she is not only the most sequential in presentation but also the only one to write a poetic autobiography, an achievement that makes her unique also among Chicano poets. Well-known male poets like Gary Soto, José Montoya, Tino Villanueva, and Raul Salinas have indeed written personal poems that capture fragments of their lives, but none has written a sustained narrative sequence in lyric form, as Alma Villanueva has done" (p. 24-25). Although both Vigil and Silva write in the autobiographical mode, their concerns are not centered on a search for origins nor are they preoccupied with the mother-daughter dyad as Villanueva seems to be. Vigil and Silva focus their poetic activity more on their present status as women and the dialectic of outside:inside, or the pull exerted by both the public and private domains.
2. "Jesus, when he began his ministry, was about thirty years of age. . . ." (Luke 2:23).
3. Cirlot (1962, 232), states that "Three symbolizes spiritual synthesis, and is the formula for the creation of each of the worlds. It represents the solution of the conflict posed by dualism. It forms a half-circle comprising: birth, zenith and descent. Geometrically it is expressed by three points and by the triangle. It is the harmonic product of the action of unity upon duality. It is the number concerned with basic principles and expresses sufficiency, or the growth of unity within itself."
4. The *Pequeño Larousse Ilustrado*, 1968, defines *desgano* as "*falta de gana o apetito*" and equates it with apathy.
5. Tey Diana Rebolledo (1983) has written an excellent article on the abuelita figure in Chicano literature. See also Wolfgang Binder (1986).

# Webs and Interrogations: Postmodernism, Gender, and Ethnicity in the Poetry of Cervantes and Cisneros

*Elizabeth J. Ordóñez*

> . . . look what they leave
> in the dew. Look
> —Lorna Dee Cervantes, "Spiders"

When one speaks now of poetry or poems, one feels a bit retrograde. Now it has become virtually "de rigeur" to say "texts," and when one speaks of their generation one is bound to consider the discursive web out of which they originate. Creativity has become cultural production, and to speak of its process today is to inevitably invoke the term postmodernism. History seems to demand such a position, for now the transcendental signifier has been crossed out and essentialist notions of good and evil, beautiful and ugly have been effaced. The modernist urn stands before us irreparably cracked, yet in its fissures there emerge designs unclassified by the authoritative curators of the culture. Thanks to theorists like Roland Barthes (1979), the literary work has been released from the signature of the father, and the more open text has been placed into the hands of the collaborative reader—active, conspiratorial, and ever more attentive to the subversive, playful force s/he has agreed to co-produce.

Yet, when the writer or reader of such texts is female, she may find herself uneasy in the ambience of postmodernism's seemingly liberative disruptions. As British critic Patricia Waugh (1989, 3) has found, women writers display an ambivalent relationship to postmodernism, "despite the fact that postmodernism is usually presented as an art of the marginal and the oppositional." Why might this be so? Waugh suggests that one reason for this position is that "postmodernism assumes or even rejects relationships which women have never experienced as subjects in their own right: relationships to the dominant literary and political institutions which legitimate and reproduce the 'master narrative,' for example" (1989, 16). Since woman's cultural work has never occupied the privileged center, she may wonder (as does Shari Benstock about Gertrude Stein) whether to "claim the center for ourselves (taking up the modernist project)" or whether it might be preferable to "redefine the limits of authority by which the center constitutes itself (taking up the post-modernist project)" (Benstock 1987, 12). Or should she, as Benstock has further inquired through Stein, try to do both? Still closer to "home," Diana Rebolledo (1988, 131) has humorously voiced a related dilemma facing the Chicana critic as she confronts the pervasive but often alien authority of current theory: "I would say a typical talk could be summarized in the following way: the speaker begins, 'This paper will focus on the ideology of cultural practice and its modes of signifying.' S/he then spends twenty minutes discussing how the works of whatever theoretical great s/he selects will define, inform and privilege the work s/he is doing. Such names as Jameson, Said, Williams, Hall, Burke and other contemporary 'meros, meros' (mostly male) will be invoked over and over. And whatever the Chicano/a writing or phenomena that was to be discussed is quickly summarized in two minutes."

Waugh's uneasiness, Benstock's musings, and Rebolledo's irreverence remind us of ways feminist readers and writers of differing nationalities and ethnicities have articulated a common double-bind of wishing to authorize their theory and writing, yet not feeling entirely comfortable with the cultural "consagrados," "meros, meros," or theories that seemingly everyone is invoking. On the one hand looms the inevitability of history, but whose history? On the other hand beckons the lure of fashion, but who or what are the models? How do women as writers and readers—especially those of non-dominant ethnicity—negotiate between reasonable (may such an appeal to logic even be invoked?) and unreasonable demands as they seek to articulate their gender and ethnicity? Recalling Benstock's inquiry, is it even a question of either/or?

I have always believed that theory is helpful only insofar as it serves as an opening to specific texts. If it obfuscates them, ignores them, or trivializes them, then, like Rebolledo, I would question its usefulness as an aid to our understanding of a specific body of writing or cultural production. Still, the pervasiveness of theories undermining the hegemony of modernist authority (such as post-structuralism and deconstruction) and the current widespread presence of artistic responses to established cultural authority (i.e. postmodernism), have made current theories impossible to ignore. Ours is unavoidably a reactive as well as an active age, unceasingly drawn toward iconoclasm and the unfixing of traditional, patrilineal, and Western criteria regarding questions of ethics and aesthetics. In short, postmodernism insists upon issues that go well beyond questions of style; indeed the very idea of a postmodern era has come to signify nothing less than a crisis of Western, white, male cultural authority. There is no turning back, then, but how and how far can women as writers of non-hegemonic ethnicity go? Indeed, where are such women located on this landscape?

As Craig Owens (1983, 61) has contritely pointed out, "theories of postmodernism have tended either to neglect or to repress" the feminist voice. Even less audible, we might add, has been the non-Anglo feminist voice. As a corrective for these omissions, considerations of literary production from the perspective of postmodernist theory should include within the reception process a sensitivity not only to the processes of gender construction, but also to ethnicity as a function of cultural positioning. In this way theory may become a useful accomplice; as readers of non-hegemonic texts we can thereby acknowledge postmodernism as a hallmark of contemporary cultural change and diversity, while at the same time remain attentive to its limitations for certain writing sectors of our culture. For these reasons, I would ask us to keep in mind the preceding rhetorical questions and cautionary remarks as in the remainder of this paper I consider aspects of two collections of Chicana poetry—Lorna Dee Cervantes's *Emplumada* and Sandra Cisneros's *My Wicked Wicked Ways*—from the perspective of some suggestive, though sometimes problematical, premises of postmodernist theory.

The following reading seeks to point out specific aspects of these texts that place them within the general postmodernist enterprise. Both collections can be seen to challenge master narratives with the "discourse of others" (Owens 1983); both question dominant cultural codes. Cervantes and Cisneros similarly engage in such postmodernist strategies as repositioning the subject, rereading inherited knowledge, understanding the relationship of knowledge to power, and rejecting logic and heroic mystification as implicitly patriarchal concepts underwriting internalized master narratives.[1] Yet, at the same time that poets engage in rather easily identifiable postmodernist strategies, one senses that they have not altogether abandoned the modernist project; that is, their texts acknowledge the push and pull of literary tradition and its ineluctable seductivity. Perhaps as historical outsiders to that tradition they have less to give up, more to desire. Within the framework of postmodernist theory, then, these poets reveal to us the tension and multiple function of the Chicana postmodernist position: desire, rupture and recomposition; a longing for aesthetic perfection, a participation in the counter-practice of cultural interference, and an engagement in woman-centered synthesis and reinscription.

Cervantes begins her collection by employing memory as a strategy for uncovering the masterplot of violence that has silenced and oppressed both women and men in our culture. As the epigraph to Part I of *Emplumada* suggests, (Consider the power of wrestling your ally [1]), the first group of poems engage themselves in what Foucault (1984, 431) has called "a strategy of struggle." This strategy, as Foucault explains, does not attempt to manipulate or induce actions, but rather reacts to them after the event, introducing points of insubordination as means of escape. Such a confrontational strategy establishes a relationship of power which may, eventually, become a winning strategy (Wallis 1984, 431-432). In "Uncle's First Rabbit," a strategy of confrontation between the narrative perspective of the poet and the male subject (the uncle) has the effect of interrogating not only the masterplot of the hunt as a vehicle for male gender construction and heroism, but as it confronts the "phallacy" of the uncle's entrapment within the terms of that bloody plot, traditional power relations between hunter and the hunted, husband and wife, man and woman are necessarily destabilized. The need for escape from this unrelenting masterplot is underscored through a metaphorical meshing of the "keening" of the pursued rabbit with the "keening" of the battered mourning mother with the wife's slugged "bloodied face." (3, 4). Intense confrontational testimony is thus assembled against this plot of violence that entrapped man and woman into a series of gender circumscribed contracts—the hunt, family violence, war —that all were powerless to escape. Through the alternative power of the "other's" poetic word—painful, poignant—this master narrative is countered and exposed as an inglorious and benumbing agent of destruction.

In "Lots: I" and "Lots: II" rape is remembered in another confrontation with the brute and violent power that threatens to silence women (He told her/shut up and die [8]); but here woman breaks out from silence (She would not be/silent and still. She would live arrogantly,/having wrestled/her death/and won [8]). The poetic voice changes to first person in "Lots: II, Herself," as the subject literally repositions herself (I picked myself up [9]), represents herself through blunt olfactory perception instead of through the idealizing gaze of Western patriarchal art (noticing for the first time my body's stench [9]), and redefines the essence of beauty and preciosity (my used skin glistened/my first diamond [9]). Female speech and integrity is affirmed through this confrontation with, and victory over brute, raw male power.

That power, that force and violence are, however, seemingly everywhere. There appears to be no effective escape nor definitively winning strategy. Canneries render working women dumb with their "can's clamor" (6) ("Cannery Town in August"), stepfathers threaten ("Meeting Mescalito at Oak Hill Cemetery"), grandfathers and fathers attack their women in drunken fury ("Beneath the Shadow of the Freeway"), young wives bleed "in purple blossoms" (18) ("For Virginia Chávez"). Still the Chicana poet affirms other discourses, other voices that oppose the logic (or illogic) of degraded paternal power with other forms of power. Certainly, not all men are raving maniacs: Edward Long "knew a code so secret/they locked it away" (15) ("For Edward Long"), yet he was "father, grandfather" (15) long enough to give the poet her voice. Nuances of that voice even came from poetry we might name "modernist" (the verses of Stevenson [15]). Also, in the midst of more sordid "facts of life," the poet reads her friend Virgina Chávez "the poems of Lord Byron, Donne,/the Brownings: all about love" (17). Even if the "modernist" tastes of the poet prove out of joint with the harshness of reality (explaining the words/before realizing that you knew/all that the kicks in your belly/had to teach you [17]), her "postmodernist" weave of voices still longs to bring some kind of mediatory consolation to the memory of her friend's painful life, and tries to bridge the either/or of two poignantly divergent lives: "my diploma" and "your bookless room" (18).

A source of the desired both/and can be found in "Caribou Girl" "who spoke the cadence/of her own mythology, with the words from books/trailing her lips like shadows" (21). The example of Caribou Girl evokes dreams of a weave of myths: "Quetzalcoátl, Ometeótl, the Great Manitou" (22), and shows that it is possible to find "books that echoed her dream,/a man who dreamt as she" (22). And so the poet, with love for such a figure for "whom everything was sacred" (23), plunges "with her again" (23). What might this enigmatic Native American girl signify for the Chicana searching for her own voice in an irreverent era of interrogation and disruption? Apparently she signifies synthesis, something even more inclusive than syncretism, for Caribou Girl's sacred derives from "her own mythology," not just a blend of set systems. She emerges as a sign for the Native postmodern woman artist whose symbolic system diverges not only from patriarchal belief systems, but from the master sacred texts of the West. To merely disrupt or combine cultural traditions is not enough; she finds herself in the position of reinventing her own myths from non-Western traditions, her re-vision of nature, and books that enunciate the differing stuff of her own dreams.

Which brings us now to one of Cervantes's central metaphors for the mediation of oppositions and the affirmation of her own version of postmodern difference: "the quilts/grandma stitched/from his suits/the patchwork singing/of mockingbirds" (13). In "Meeting Mescalito at Oak Hill Cemetery" and "Beneath the Shadow of the Freeway" the quilt—either the poet's that she "Sewed myself" or the grandmother's—signifies safe haven and comfort from male violence. But Grandma's, especially, is significant as a patchwork made from bits and pieces of the violent grandfather's old clothes. Women salvage the remnants and worn leftovers of even their adversaries, making of those discards something wonderful and new. The grandmother's quilt that sings of a different kind of husband and father (like "mockingbirds" who "don't leave their families/borrachando" [12]), and is made with materials from the abusive father, stands as a metaphor for the kind of postmodern thought observed by Jean Francois Lyotard: "Thinking by means of oppositions does not correspond to the liveliest modes of postmodern knowledge."[2] The quilt, as a trope for blending, combining, and re-creation also metaphorically encodes Owens's perception (1983, 62) of the feminist postmodern voice as "difference without opposition."

There is no escaping these bits and pieces of patriarchal texts that work themselves into the postmodern recompositions of women, and yet their echoes are not confined solely to the elaboration of gender differences. In "Poem for the Young White Man Who Asked me How I, an Intelligent, Well-Read Person Could Believe in the War between Races," the implied presence of a white male reader engenders a response of ethnic difference and the both/and realization "that this is not/my land/and this is my land" (36-37). This political, as well as poetical, conundrum emerges from another instance of implied confrontational strategy, this time between the brown woman poet who knows too much and the white male interlocutor who seeks to suppress such knowledge. No doubt the poet would long to recur to the Utopian land of timeless ("modernist") poetical pursuits (In my land/people write poems about love,/full of nothing but contented childlike syllables./Everyone reads Russian short stories and weeps [35]), and she would like to invoke a land where there is no nationalism, no hunger, no greed. It would be cozy to restore perfection to an idealized urn. Yet though the poet might yearn "to dance on rooftops/to whisper delicate lines about joy" (36), the ivory tower is powerless to muffle the sounds of violence and injustice. They intrude into her text alongside expressions of Utopian desire.

Such a juxtaposition of political anger and aesthetic desire proves inevitable, and I suspect discloses a central characteristic of the postmodern Chicana voice: the inescapable consciousness that to be brown and female in a culture that represses the political and aesthetic consequences of this difference is to long for myths of modernist perfection, yet find oneself poignantly dispossessed of the fulfillment of such desires. This may well constitute a hallmark of postmodernist Chicana representation: the fantasy of beauty and perfection alongside the ugly, painful political reality of the poet whose ethnicity—as well as gender—forcibly repositions her on battle lines that white, patriarchal, modernist systems of representation sought to ignore or deny. Direct, binary opposition indeed may not be the strategy of choice for the post-modernist feminist voice. It may not even be possible. Yet some kind of confrontation with and insubordination of repressive cultural authority is often unavoidable for the Chicana, given her material and political position. (An interesting footnote to this reading is the following recollection of the poet's own introduction to this poem at a public reading I attended in Boulder Colorado: Cervantes explained how these words were penned after the fact, as an outpouring of what she would have liked to say to the young white man's face but finally did not.)

"Barco de refugiados/Refugee Ship," "Poema para los californios muertos," "Oaxaca, 1974," and "Visions of Mexico While at a Writing Symposium in Port Townsend, Washington" all reveal that aspect of the postmodern age (the coexistence of different cultures) that, according to Paul Ricoeur (1965, 278), can prove disconcerting: suddenly "we ourselves are an 'other' among others." The Chicana finds herself "other" both at home (a captive/aboard the refugee ship [41]), and in the place of her ancestors ( Esputa! on this bland pochaseed [44]); the Spanish language is both "my own words" (45) and the words of conquerers of indigenous peoples from whom she also originates (signified by places such as "Michoacán, Tenochtitlán, Oaxaca"). Anywhere she looks she again finds remnants—this time of herself—"antepasados muertos" (42), traces of what she is or might have been. And so in "Visions of Mexico," the Chicana poet attempts to come to terms with her unstable identity and find a means for articulating a typically postmodern consciousness of cultural heterogeneity. From the meadows of Mexico to the seaside of Washington, she represents herself as someone who is and is not the Mexican "women in the adobe," and who is as out of place in the north as a barroom pin-up (her glowing/silk skin, a halo/extending from her golden coiffure [46]) or "two Chicanas" who "hung at their beers" (46). Between indigenous women and sex objects iconographic and living, this Chicana poet traverses time and space and the refractive representations of multiple cultural identities.

Passing from the "epic corrido" to her own need for words (simple black nymphs between white sheets of paper [45, 47]), the poetic voice of "Visions of Mexico" deconstructs myths and stereotypes about México (there are songs in my head I could sing you/songs that could drone away/all the Mariachi bands you thought you ever heard [47]), stealing words, gathering up feathers "for quills" so that she may write the voices of other/s beyond the distortions of media and misconception. In an appropriation of classical-modernist tradition (nymphs), the Chicana poet pares down and reconstructs it (simple, black), making the modernist nymph or traditional muse more like herself—the dark "other"—within a space and time beyond restriction (in the dark when no one can hear me [47]). This is the threshold of postmodernist creation where inherited knowledge and practice are reconceived, and where, ultimately, other kinds of power based on other forms of knowledge are incorporated. As the poet gathers her feathers for quills, the master narratives of both Mexico and North America are challenged with words stolen from both, words weaving a web between two cultures while transforming them both.

The third and final part of *Emplumada* speaks for itself, without epigraph, with only the subtitle of the collection itself. The feathers/quills/pen/word have been gathered through inspiration and struggle. Part III represents the culmination of a process, a gathering up and acquisition of other voices, other powers. Like the hundred robins of "This Morning," the poet will tell things her way; she inhabits a world in which "everything has let go" ("Café Solo"); she redefines beauty, and like the beetle burrows and glows ("Beetles"); she knows that she can not say a word and say everything ("For All You Know"). These initial poems of the collection's last section recapitulate the book's process of redefining the nature of poetry from what we might call a Chicana postmodernist perspective: they reaffirm a tendency to break (selectively) with traditional rules and logical accountability in order to arrive, finally, at other ways of knowing and desiring. These ways, drawn from feminine/feminist and Native American/Chicana sources, return to the truths of body and nature (there's no truth/more simple ["Como lo siento" 56]), affirm mystery and ambiguity (I . . . won't tell him/if it's omens/or ice ["The Body as Braille" 57]), and take us beyond language or the symbolic contract of dominant patriarchal culture (what I want/is an unnamed/thing ["Shells" 62]).

The final poems of *Emplumada* are thus contemplative yet playful, evasions of language as bounded exactitude and affirmations of preverbal indeterminacy (This was hope of a kind,/a bare, prenatal longing and return ["For John on the Cape" 64]). Poem and poet thus reposition themselves as beings and doers beyond strict, univocal cultural codifications. Like hummingbirds that distance themselves from history (we might add "their" Western patriarchal history) and "find peace/in the way they contain the wind/and are gone" ("Emplumada" 66), the oneness with nature and its ways of being and speaking reiterated throughout *Emplumada* may be viewed as a particular postmodernist discursive position. As Chicana and woman, Cervantes questions the modes of representation and being of Western, male culture and arrives at a synthesis or web made up of what the dominant culture may offer of value and beauty along with the ways of seeing, speaking, feeling, and writing of the cultures of Native America and women. The result is something larger, more inclusive, elusive and evocative than either the bounded precision of Western modernism or the skeptical iconoclasm of white, male-gendered postmodernism. As the poet remarks upon seeing the handiwork of her "Spiders": "look what they leave/in the dew. Look" (32).

Sandra Cisneros's *My Wicked Wicked Ways* also structures itself by means of some familiar postmodernist strategies. Its four-part structure—"1200 South/2100 West," "My Wicked Wicked Ways," "Other Countries," and "The Rodrigo Poems"—engages in the following tendencies of postmodernist cultural/aesthetic production: 1) an outward movement away from repressed voices toward a tendency to reposition the subject; 2) a challenging of paternal discourse with its reassessment of inherited knowledge; 3) an appropriation of alternate space and other forms of female power; 4) a challenging of the "master narrative" of love or a provocation of patriarchal concepts of love and poetry about love. Yet Cisneros's collection, too, seems residually reluctant to abandon altogether the bittersweet seductivity of traditional narratives.

As the book's epigraph to Part I (from Gwendolyn Brooks) declares, the introductory poems allow us "a peek at the back" yard. The hidden, the concealed, the repressed are given voice: domestic violence, aging, poverty, mental retardation. Not exactly the stuff of modernist poetry; instead, the articulation of these concerns contributes to a repositioning of the poetic subject, a process that allows the unsaid, "the powerless" to be heard in ways Cisneros has made her goal to record (Cisneros 1987a, 76). Consequently, in Part II the poetic voice humorously and impetuously becomes "the notorious/one" (28), likening herself to her namesake who, in Mexico, "was arrested for audacious crimes/ that began by disobeying fathers" (36). She is "bad" (23), "mad"

(25), "wildness" (29), "a wicked nun" (32), and most importantly, a poet who "reflects on her solitary fate" (35). At this juncture, she has cast herself upon the margins of "His Story" (36); now poised and ready, "she must write poems" beyond the boundaries of inherited, paternal (or familial) discourse (She/Has abandoned the brothers,/the rooms of fathers/and many mothers./ They have left her/to her own device [35]).

And so in Part III, guided by an epigraph from *The Three Marias*, the poet is off to another country, like an exile, for not living up "to the image of her required by the times" (39). In this alternate space she wanders "darkness like a man" (41), finds Ophelia in the Seine, tells a Frenchman he is beautiful to which he replies "beautifully, Mercí" (44), declares herself to one man "not for sale" (45), invites another to Spain (49), becomes a raucously witty Pygmalion before Michelangelo's David, learns about women who "no longer wait/for their Theseus/to rescue" (57), and finally learns to "let go" and "never wash a man's clothes" (60). Wit, spirit, and a love for life execute a simultaneous paying of homage to compelling monuments of culture and a salty irreverence that impels the impish voice of *My Wicked Wicked Ways* toward her ultimate challenge of the master narrative of love, "The Rodrigo Poems."

The corpus of "The Rodrigo Poems" follows a love affair from beginning to end. In the beginning it speaks of the familiar and banal—the waiting wife (he does not come home./This is how the story begins [66])—along with the lure of seemingly insignificant detail, the unexpected sign of sensuality ([you] pull like a magician/from your sleeve—a handkerchief./Red./. . . In a few weeks/ . . . the handkerchief/will have done its harm [67]). The initial poems reveal how small things and acts catch one up in a plot or narrative that is at once bigger and older—and more frightening —than any of its separate events. Yet in the course of this affair, the poetic voice destabilizes the power of this mesmerizing though timeworn narrative and eventually disperses it into a soaring happiness "[que] Tiene que ver con papalotes" (93).

The poetic voice is surprisingly lucid even from the start: she knows the difference between the myth of love, "a narcissistic/ yearning," and love that "is a different/kind/of burning" (69). Her deconstructive savvy knows when "a kiss" is "not a kiss" and how the word "love" may mean "many [different] things" to him and to her (70). She also knows that she is a convenience, a "middle-of-the-week wife" (71), who complies with the expected narrative of the independent, other woman. And in sisterly compassion, she understands the flight of wives from a cruelly speaking husband (her lover), similarly relishing a more tranquil world "without Rodrigo" (73).

But paradox constitutes the central trope of love's master narrative: even this postmodernist lover is still caught—at least temporarily—between the push and pull of lucidity and passionate sensuality, the celebration of bed linen alongside the painful consciousness that man is always "waiting endlessly/for [his] Beatrice" (75). She knows that while he never stops searching for his ideal, she is creating hers in him: "I could shape the myth" (76). Woman complies with the demands of the master narrative, molding the "red clay" of her lover into a patriarchal hero—of mutinies, revolutions, armies—a conquering hero that ravishes his beloved like Bonaparte or Caesar.

Such compliance, however, is short-lived. In the dark, as Rodrigo sheds his "uniform of havoc" (78), he becomes "simply a man/like any other" (78). The exotic, even modernist, trope for revered male lover, "rare white Bengali" (77), is literally divested, undone, and Rodrigo—though still "my Bengali" on the poet's terms—is "no longer white tiger/my rival and keeper" (78). Still, woman's desired subject status (I want to be like you. A who [80]) is not unproblematically acquired; the master narrative's road of trials guards obstacles—for one, the requirements of a romantic script in which suffering means life. Echoing the Spanish romantic poet, Béquer—for whom "padecer" was "vivir"—this poet, too, wants and wants her grief—"each cell must have its fill—and I want more of it" (82). Yet, though modernist and romantic tropes insinuate themselves seductively, irreverence again points to divergence from romanticism's insistence on suffering as closure.

Cisneros finally repositions her subject away from the master narrative's center, reconstituting her body and character metonymically of parts from diverse and far-flung reaches of the globe (Madagascar, the Amazon, Egypt, Bengal, Morroco, Gaugin's Papeete, Andalusia, Pago Pago, Tierra del Fuego, and Quintana Roo [84-85]). This subject's body is thus a veritable sign for postmodernism's "crisis of cultural authority" (Owens 1983, 57); this poetic voice finally chooses not to stake a claim on the centered modernist or romantic subject. So, with lover and beloved demythified, the poetic voice finally performs a similar postmodernist maneuver on the lover's wife: the latter emerges therefore as "no Athena. No Medea./No Adelita nor Malintzín./No Botticelli pearl/nor Carmenesque hands on hips,/A female, like any common female./For a common male" (90-91). Masks, be they classical, romantic or modernist, are all finally removed, and no gendered subject is exempt from this process.

Concluding that she was herself "unbrave" as a lover, this poetic voice presents her text as a project paradoxically designed to participate in at the same time that it questions the power relations inherent in affairs of love. As the poet/lover emerges subdued but wiser from her involvement in the master narrative of love, she offers her playful insights with a gesture that Foucault (1984, 428) might call "a permanent provocation." In spite of the staying power of inherited discourses or narratives that shape the ways in which one experiences and writes about love, this postmodernist Chicana poet refuses to surrender all to those master authorities. Neither, however, does she altogether immobilize them or efface them from her page.

As women and as Chicanas, poets such as Lorna Dee Cervantes and Sandra Cisneros thus negotiate the seductive terrain of cultural codes and master narratives (they desire, destabilize and interrogate such authorities), yet they never cede all to these or any other form of discursive hegemony (They instead weave webs). Their restless, witty agon with the powers of textual and cultural authority discloses, finally, how they can opt for the both-and of the hyphenated cipher and in this way affirm the cultural presence and power of the multiplicitous Chicana poetic text.

## Notes

1. Some of these postmodern feminist critiques are identified by Brian Wallis (1984, xviii).
2. Lyotard (1979, 29), cited by Owens (1983, 62).

# Cognitive Desires: An Allegory of/for Chicana Critics

*Norma Alarcón*

## Introduction

As I write this I cannot help but realize that it is 1992, the year of the quincentenary, marking the "encounter," as the Anglo/Spanish promoters call it, between Europeans and the indigenous in the Americas for whom it is more of an agonistic than celebrative occasion. Thus for those of us who continue to exist on the downside of the "encounter," remembrance is more the commemoration of a deadly collision that continues to kill and produce anger and grief in the context of multinational capitalist "development" and exploitation which carries over into institutions, even academic ones, in ways that we have yet to clarify. In my view, then, the academic allegory of/for Chicana critics refers to that woman of Mexican descent who claims the name Chicana, lives in the United States, may even be a descendant of natives or long-time residents, and most importantly refuses to forget that she is also the descendant of peoples, some of whose names have disappeared, who have been engaged in continous conflict with state and institutional power structures that wish to repress the memory of the unsavory consequences of conquest, colonization, dislocation, discrimination and their historical transformations. Though the allegory is one pertaining to an academic power structure, I would like to make the connection that the consequences of imperialisms and their multiple transformations are not only pertinent to the political economy but cognitive as well, for it is within academic institutions that knowledge production may be "recycled" into narratives that support the national(istic) status quo. Cognitive desire, then, is not just a "hunger of memory" which is subsumed by categories produced elsewhere, but a "hunger of memory" desirous of its own productive intervention in the retrieval and making of cognitive symbols and concepts which would help us apprehend our experience of the political economy in conjunction and even conjugation with jurisprudence, history, ethnography and literary mediation. It is after all the conditions of the political economy, especially in the twentieth century, that have made migrants of many of us. Not just migrant workers in the agribusiness fields, but in many other enterprises of industrial development locally and globally, as well as the migration of peoples from third world areas to the Euro/american terrain.

To tell the tale, then, I will start out with an academic anecdote from the U.S.-Mexican border, a border on the verge of another radical transformation as the groundwork is already being laid out so that the U.S./Mexico Free Trade Agreement may kick into place (Ruiz and Tiano 1987; Fernández-Kelly and García 1988). A ground prepared by the establishment of maquiladora shops starting in the early 1960s when the Chicano Movement (1965-75) was just beginning, and Chicanas were struggling for self-defined positions within it and experiencing exclusion there as well as in the contemporary Women's Movement whose own momentum is simultaneous with all of these events. Is it ironic coincidence that simultaneous with the cry of liberation by Euroamerican women and minority populations in the United States the multinationals began the construction of shops whose workers are primarily women, not only on the U.S.-Mexican border but all over the globe? Certainly for the women working in the maquiladoras under polluted, life-threatening conditions, their quietist and exploited group history dovetails into global shifts in the political economy of the metropolis, which place them in a contradictory double bind between necessity and economic "opportunity;" and given the non-safe working conditions, put them at risk. For me, there is a tenuous connection between women working in the actual border shops, who put their lives at risk, and Chicana critics who work an interstitial zone which is constantly on the move given its structural displacements within the academy. That is, the latter displacements parallel those of the former and remain non-equivalent. Thus, though each lives within different economies of signifying circuits, "we" nevertheless share experiences of dislocation which contribute to cultural productions. Since the emergence of Chicana critics can be traced no further back than about 1965, applying the name retroactively is a retroconstruction of a chosen gene(an)alogy, much like calling Sor Juana Inés de la Cruz a Modern Woman. Thus, the Scenario on the Border that opens up the allegory is a necessary step in the travails of the Chicana critic since it implicates both Mexicans and Angloamericans in the production of meaning for her. Such a critic, who could only take shape through this fabulous construction, is a paradigmatic woman of multiple incarnations. The construction aims to situate the Chicana critic in the locus of "la différend," the site of a conflict, collision or contest opposed to judicial litigation, or (constitutional) law, indeed opposed to anything that presupposes for its interpretation an inherent monological rationality. My contention is that heretofore the Chicana critic has not taken account of her insider/outsider/insider status with respect to multiple discourse structures, some of which cannot easily be translated into each other (Lyotard 1988). To pursue the nexus or intersectionality of the multiple discourse structures that surround the Chicana critic is in a sense to come to terms with the modes through which her disappearance is constantly promoted through the speech of others no matter how unintentional, and against which she struggles through counter- and disidentificatory discourses. In the process one may come to terms on theoretical grounds with how the speech of the bordershop worker may be drowned out, so that one may then ask the purposefully "naive" question 'can the subaltern speak'? (Spivak 1988). The struggle is for histories actual and imaginary that give substance and provide an account of her/their position within culture and the political economy.

### Scenario on the Border: (Dis)Identifying the Players

At a recent conference in the Mexican border city of Tijuana, two women—as it happened, one Angloamerican and the other European—presented, sequentially, Spanish-language written papers on the same work—*Querido Diego te abraza Quiela* by the Mexican-Polish writer Elena Poniatowska. Poniatowska grew up speaking French and Spanish—French as the preferred language of the Polish aristocracy and Spanish as a result of her Mexican upbringing and education. The audience included Poniatowska herself, a handful of Chicanas—some of whom fully understood Spanish, others not—a few Angloamerican scholars who pursue Spanish-language literary studies, and local community women, who fully understoood Spanish but not the interpretive apparatus. The rest of the audience were Mexican women who were literary scholars and intellectuals from the Colegio de México, a co-sponsor of the conference with the Colegio de la Frontera Norte. As you may anticipate, given the diverse social identities and their discursive formations, the potential for crosspurposed misdialogue and misrecognition was rife. I cannot pursue the ramifications for each player, but I will attempt them for Chicanas, most of whom were actually critics or writers. Theoretically the various players could, if they so desired place themselves in the nodal point of "la differend." However, I would guarantee a different outcome for each. It is my intention to be as impartial as possible, especially insofar as the Chicana critic does not have a "word to her name" except the proprietory claim to the term of recent recodification—Chicana (Alarcón 1990). On the other hand, to center the inquiry through the term Chicana already bespeaks bias. As such she is, like most women of color in the United States, a recent arrival on the stage of the Western critical (mostly male) tradition. This is not to say that She does not claim female ancestors; however, they cannot be said to exist at the interstice and intersection of the multiple discourses that give shape to the Modern and Postmodern, which cannot be assumed to be sequential either but to be implicitly or explicitly interreferential.

On the San Diego/Tijuana border, the two speakers presented completely different interpretations of Quiela, the writer of the letters addressed to Diego (Rivera) which represent the fictive textualization of a historically real Russian-born artist's ill-fated romantic attachment to Diego Rivera. The Angloamerican critic interpreted the letters as an instance of the social production of female oppression based on the account given in the text of Quiela's experiences which would ultimately silence her but for Poniatowska's intervention. The European critic interpreted the letters as an instance of the symbolic construction of femininity, a near-perfect sample of a quietist "écriture féminine."[1] The first interpretation was motivated by a sociopolitical desire to demonstrate that Quiela's inequality, overdetermined gender identity and experience are so negative that no sane woman should want to assume such a position, a calculated move to put the romantic in crisis and lead listeners to disidentification with Quiela. The second interpretation was motivated by an aestheticist textual desire to demonstrate Quiela's elegantly constructed pathos, a phallocratic production of femininity and its correlative embodiment. The first interpreter insisted on a heterosexist social referentiality that called for political positions beyond the text while the second insisted on a self-referential (inter)textuality, which nonetheless appealed to the audience to share in the work's aesthetic pathos. The first was firmly embedded in the liberal self/other experiential paradigms of some Angloamerican bourgeois feminist theories which, though still historically interesting, are not complex enough to explain our diverse sociosymbolic formations, positionalities or heterogeneous histories; the second was embedded in French feminist appropriations of crosshatched Derridean/Lacanian deconstructive practices which, though also important theoretical contributions, remain a self-sufficient system, difficult to transpose and map on to sociosymbolic formations outside of the bourgeois Eurocentric intellectual tradition, though the possibility of resonance with the non-European is not necessarily precluded. The "new" feminist "identity politics" of women of color forged through a "politics of cultural difference" that have emerged and developed since World War II require multiple theoretical and paradigmatic conjunctions which only now are beginning to be addressed. However, I will elaborate this below as I return to the allegory of "the" Chicana critic who configures in part such conjunctions/conjugations.

The interpreters, who were clearly fully invested in their respective positions, were unable to negotiate a passage between themselves, though they both had a clear claim to the literary discipline. When both finished the silence in the room was stunning. Since neither the audience nor the presenters were forthcoming with questions or responses, Poniatowska herself was asked to comment on the interpretations of her work. Were those her intentions? Did either or both critics hit upon the meaning of the work? Poniatowska, who is the contemporary champion of the silenced in Mexico, in fact giving voice to a forgotten Russian artist, and who feels that if the sociopolitically oppressed are silenced someone must intervene for them, refused to comment on the grounds that the work in question is too close to her. The work was a vehicle for the exploration and displacement of one of her intimate personas. Since Chicanas had been explicitly invited to the conference with the aim of building bridges with Mexicanas, and one kept waiting for dialogue to take place, I for one wondered how it ever could under the circumstances. Further, if for argument's sake any one was looking for some sort of Mexican social identity and experience in the work, or a Mexican interpretation of it, and she had asked, she would have been taken for a fool. The only things Mexican there were the border, constructed and reconstructed as it rubs against/with the United States; a large portion of the silenced audience who carried Mexican passports in case they wanted to cross to the United States, Chicanas who carried proper identification not so much to enter Mexico as to return to the U.S., and Diego Rivera the recipient of Quiela's letters. That is, texts and cultural productions may cross borders, but some people risk arrest without *señas de identidad* (signs of identity), to quote the title of a Spanish novel published in Franco's Spain. People may be more closely tied whether they want to or not to nationally conferred identities than some texts. The fact that one needs "signs of identity" should tip us off to the requirements of subordination to the nation-state that (non)citizens must comply with and the fact that the inside/outside/inside occupied by Chicanas is not just symbolic but sociopolitical as well regardless of the documentation status since the INS may not wait for it. Racism (or the particular historical constructions of mexicanness) makes her subject to a constant demand for the production (proof) of "ethnic" identity and citizenship in both Mexico and the United States. Placing her in continuous movement from inside/outside/inside. . . as I have stated.

Since the interpreters had given us divergent interpretations of the sociosymbolic formation of femininity based not only on a work widely recognized as Mexican, but based on letters addressed to a Mexican, to ask what any of it had to do with a Mexican identity and experience was to risk being seen as an ignorant déclassé given to excessive referential quibbling and maybe even essentializing, which ironically drew one nearer to the Angloamerican than the European with whom most of the Mexicanas sympathized, apparently because the former was too "aggressive" (read too "anti-men"). And yet there is that documentation required by law burning a hole in one's pocket and the knowledge that the aim of the conference was to clarify the proximity/overlap between Mexicanas and Chicanas through literature, our "medium," though apparently the organizers took the meaning of "magical" mediations as the primary meaning of medium. It became increasingly clear that there was no productive strategy for effecting the avowed goals of the Mexicanas, and frankly it reminded one of the National Women's Studies Association, where the organizers often feel that if you have a "caucus" you are participating. Here, if you had a Chicana literature panel that was participation. For me, however, this particular event marked the collapse of the enterprise. Indeed the major accomplishment was one that most Chicanas already knew of, and that was the marked class differences between us—Mexicanas and Chicanas. Also, it would appear that it was such class differences that might draw Chicanas closer to the Angloamerican who did not deny historical socioreferentiality, thus opening up the possibility of addressing class positions; while the taboo of referentiality in the other interpretive system made it impossible even to speak of Quiela/Poniatowska as entities formed through cultural emblems drawn from a different aesthetic.

Such recognized differences make a difference in the constellation and concatenation of texts and critical tools. As in the case of African American women, as Hortense Spillers notes (1989), Chicanas "maintain no allegiances to a strategic formation of texts," which further draws them to a "logological" (textually eurologocentric) feminist discourse. In fact the Euroamerican "process of aligning with prior acts of the text [is] the subtle component of power that bars. . . women of color as a proper subject of inquiry from the various topics of contemporary feminist discourse." That is, the Euroamerican canon formations demand privileged priority over the inquiries of women of color, a fact which may lead to contradiction, contestation, deconstruction, resistance, disidentification or the production of alternative discursive practices. My claim, however, goes further to include the critical speaker who is positioned by that "subtle component of power" as a nonspeaker (a silent subaltern) because the privileged linguistic practices cannot hear, translate or transcode (with a residue of non-equivalence) what is said.

In any case, the disjunction between purported aims and expectations and the actual events contributed to the increasing gap between Mexicanas and Chicanas, which resulted in our marginalization and silence. We became spectators to a textual performative that claimed to incorporate us. Could it be that such interstices are potential sites for the actual productive and bridging dialogues? In this particular scenario the only speech possible was to remark on the discursive weave which did not afford an opportunity for a positive Chicana intervention. Thus Chicanas were placed in a negative position whereby if they had wanted to speak it would have been to note their exclusion from an event that supposedly included them in the conference's goals, most certainly its title—*Mujer y literatura mexicana y chicana: Culturas en contacto*.[2] In the end, Poniatowska herself intervened by stating that when it came to feminist activism the Mexicanas were "mosquitas muertas" (loosely translated, wallflowers), which angered her countrywomen no end. To this day, she told me recently, some of those who were there do not speak to her.

The exchange between Chicanas and Mexicanas does not appear at this time to be as extensive as one might expect. Bourgeois Mexicanas in general tend to find distasteful an identification with their "prole" kin, who are not "gente decente," the "customary" epithet through which raced-class positions are segregated in Hispanic societies. Few upperclass Latin American women would admit to being a colleague to someone who could have been the household maid but for the grace of a minoritizing education in the United States. And now the woman who could have been their maid talks back, often with a class-inflected speech, and has gone the way of many maids in Latin America, to the maquiladoras scattered all over the continent and not just on the U.S.-Mexican border.

## Speaking in Tongues: Cursing the Academy

Yet most Chicana critics are more likely to come in contact with Angloamerican critics who have learned to pretend to some extent that this is a classless society and where economic conditions heretofore, at least since World War II, have enabled a pretense that now begins to crumble (Davis 1986). Within the Angloamerican context, then, Chicana critics are often subtly but forcefully compelled to choose between the Angloamerican and the European interpreters characterized above. Moreover, it becomes increasingly apparent that there is an implicit "two-class theory" in the practitioners of the approaches, not so much because each is inherently of a different class so much as the fact that the European recognize class divisions and the Angloamerican "bracket" them. It is often the institutionalized prerogative of both the Angloamerican and the European to decide where we belong, which may foreclose almost all possibilities for self-propelled inquiry on the part of Chicanas.

In effect these maneuvers recall the old "add and stir" method that a previous generation of Euroamerican feminists protested and have successfully contested, thus radically changing the "cognitive map" of feminism and Women's Studies. Since each practitioner of the critical discourses in question is more interested in strengthening her position than bridging the disparate discourses, there are no adequate sources to aid the observer/reader in negotiating, not necessarily resolving, their paradoxes and contradictions. Moreover, more often than not our students are taught those positions in isolation from each other! If the Chicanas call for a change of critical discourse so that our text may be included in a more dialogized fashion than is possible within the containing "add and stir" method, we may be told to go to Ethnic Studies.

If there is an Ethnic/Chicano Studies and Chicanas take refuge there we may be compelled to historicize (following a male-head-of-household genealogical story) and sociologize (quantitative empiricism) our text into the "raced masculine model" at the expense of whatever feminist insight we may have had, as there too there is an "add and stir" containment. If there is no Ethnic/Chicano Studies a Chicana may get bounced around between the Spanish and English departments, where she may not be better off than before since at this time it is a toss up as to who can silence most. The tendency of many departments is to neocolonize rather than enable critical thinking on her part, which would mean providing the pedagogical conditions for her speaking intervention and for exercising her interpretive agency. A Chicana critic may be inside studying and teaching, but outside the legitimate curricular mission of the department. If as a feminist she decides to insist on taking refuge in Women's Studies, she may once again be faced with the cited interpreters of the text who are indeed sympathetic to her pathos and her unbelievable oppression. Yes, they'd be happy to take her text but not her, except as a seasonal worker. On the other hand she may be glad to learn that her text is already in the curriculum—feminist sociology, anthropology, or regional history—all of which claim their own "inherent rationality." Her feminist critical voice may be muted, but she is now (through the text) part of a guided international tour.

Indeed, taking the long view since the emergence of Chicana critics in the 1960's, after a decade or more of carrying "our text" around looking for a home for both of them, a Chicana critic may realize that she has become typed in one or both of two ways: 1) she is a minority woman narcissistically obsessed with herself through her text; 2) she is a wonderful resource. To employ some Marxist and Freudian vocabulary for a moment, in the first instance she is being so particularistic as to have no use-value; in the second instance she returns as a sample of the repressed and oppressed, and her use-value is theoretically reinstated. Thus in the first instance she is erased from the scene even as her text accrues exchange value because pluralism and diversity are more simply satisfied with texts than with actual people. Since her text has acquired exchange value through the 1970s, in the 1980s another generation of Chicana critics emerges even as the previous ones have disappeared. In the 1990s the successors of those from the 1970s and 1980s plus a new crop of writers are now often seasonally employed, joining the ranks of migrant/segmented, albeit, intellectual labor.

Aside from the fact that the successors have acquired a great deal more book knowledge, we may well wonder how our lot has changed from that of our parents or grandparents who actually were migrant field or segmented manufacturing laborers. Successors should not completely despair though, for at this juncture we have also acquired many kin in the Third World, where intellectuals travel around various schools/universities in order to make a living. This is not so much a misery loves company interpretation as perhaps a reminder that within the U.S. we are viewed in similar fashion to Third World intellectuals, inside/outside/inside, and it is worthwhile to investigate the ground of such views. Yet I do not speak of just any Third World intellectuals as my discussion of Mexicanas should have demonstrated, but a genealogy of writers and thinkers who have been or are engaged in contestatory inquiry rather than sheer mimicry, though the latter should be identified as well. The Chicana critic is now and perhaps has always been positioned as a Third World intellectual, as are Mexicanas, and it was being inside the U.S. which has led her to (mis)recognize the position. That is, if upperclass Mexicanas favor "quietist" European interpretive theories over Angloamerican ones, which may align them away from Chicanas; through her status in the U.S. academy, the Chicana critic is repositioned as "Third World" intellectual, thus realigning her from another angle with the Mexicanas! In other words, boundary crossing has been largely a mental exercise because our "señas de identidad" are inappropriately embodied; that is, the very rage at our embodied history as Chicanas can find no adequate "inherently rational" (monological), in Spillers' terms "logological," discourse with which to sweep up the letters of her name. Moreover the social contradictions at work cannot be easily overcome through symbolic representation at conferences.

If a Chicana critic has had time to meditate about her lot, she now realizes that the only thing she might have had was her version of the (socio)text and not the text itself. It is plain to see, if she is still on the fringes of the academy, that the text she thought was hers may be claimed by everyone. Thus, without having read Saussure, Derrida, Foucault, Lacan, or even Marx, she has discovered that the text/signifier is a commodity, and almost from the beginning she was a "signifying problem" rather than a participant of the "political economy of the signifier." If for some bizarre reason she still harbors an attachment to her text, she now keeps it a secret lest she once again show her déclassé status by identifying too closely with it—you, so the accusation went last time she mentioned her attachment, are essentializing as the version of the text you've hung onto demonstrates. Essentializing is back, however, as the new journal *Differences* (1989) proclaims, so she can essentialize again but she better watch her mouth, for it is only permissible as a rhetorical strategy. In fact, of course, many of us are déclassé but it's best not to show it, except of course theoretically.

My no-win narrative of/for Chicana critics and our text is what Bateson called the double-bind (1972). Since the term has been popularized, it is hard to remember that it is the kind of bind that actually produces psychosis. Most people, as Bateson notes, will do anything to escape the double-bind, or they risk psychosis, at which point psychoanalysis is of no use whatsoever. His solution for escaping the double-bind is to proceed to a higher epistemological/metanarrative ground; however, I think that one must discern and unravel the double-binds that cross our path, since our path is culturally, politically and economically located such that we live out the double-binding "differend" effect, and such junctures help us identify contradictory practices that require transformation. Moreover, there is no "talk cure" for psychosis. By the time a person is indeed psychotic a protective wall has been erected that no one can talk themselves through. Neither the one "inside" nor the one "outside." Except that in the United States it is very difficult to tell what's inside and what's outside because we all share the same political boundary rights, or so we are told. Here again, we are in good company. Because of colonialism and the multinationals' international division of labor a lot of the Third World cannot tell what's inside and what's outside either, as selected discourses, processes and procedures cross borders with capitalist bureaucratic structures. As the Chicana poet Lorna D. Cervantes has remarked in conversation, criticism is not enough to assist us out of a critical situation, yet it is often necessary to its clarification.

Survivalists have had at least three options. The first is the Richard Rodríguez option, whereby one can affirm that "The child who learns to read about his nonliterate ancestors necessarily separates himself from their way of life" (1988, 169). Many people experience this as an incontrovertible force that calls for abandonment, as obviously he did. Today, paradoxically, he finds himself writing about the successor ancestors and makes his living writing about "los pobres." They are, however, now at a safe distance as some reductive version of the nonliterate other. Thus, he preserves his psychic well-being by denying his metonymic relationship to the others while simultaneously affirming it through his brand of journalistic transliterations, and offering us an oversimplified but coherent story. The second is the orthodox Marxist option, where we could join the generic class struggle and change the subject or forget the subject as well as forget the raced cultural history of the group. This version of the déclassé has invited us to view the "marginalized" as some monolith without any clue with regard to the social formation or the conditions of our existence nor recognition of our protestations along the way. The third is the resource option already mentioned, except that in the late 80's and probably in the decade ahead, some may obtain, as a result of the success of our differential text and pluralism, a non-migratory position, albeit segmented. (The "segmentation" could be turned into a less fractured account if the academy in general were supportive of (feminist) cultural studies; however, the disciplined departmental investment continues to dominate.)

If past generations of Chicana critics still desire to stage a comeback, we may discover that our "essentializing" obsolescence has returned under a new market commodified value which has opened up what Trinh T. Minh-ha calls "planned authenticity." She explains, "as a product of hegemony and a remarkable counterpart of universal standardization, it constitutes an efficacious means of silencing the cry of racial oppression." That is to say, the minoritized are granted voice as long as they speak as "authenticators" of cultural experiences without pursuing the dialectical reconfiguration of knowledge production vis-à-vis the "other" (dominant). Angloeuropeans now tell us, "We no longer wish to erase your difference. We demand, on the contrary, that you remember and assert it. At least, to a certain extent" (1989, 82). What extent? Here again, the Chicana critic is on dangerous ground. How much difference is enough? Let's say, she decides to risk, and in the parlance of today take the "window of opportunity" that has opened up to her. Since conferences today are often clearly staged events, perhaps even "minoritizing" spectacles, commodified shows, our older Chicana critic may coincide in the same panel with her younger "sister"; the younger critic unlike herself, has been schooled in representation, thematization of othering and textual difference focusing on the constructed nature of identity while the older critic may continue to "essentialize" social difference. In a sense we are back in Tijuana, though our critics are no longer Angloamerican or European, they are us and we find ourselves unable to speak with each other even in theory!

## Moving on: Subjects-in-process

The perils of this fabulous Chicana critic are endless because, as Cornel West would say (1985), a minoritized intellectual who tries to work with and on the same terms as the dominant/dominating is always on the defensive or, I would add, such an intellectual may already be bidding to occupy a dominant/dominating pose. In fact, our relationship to the hegemonic political economy, institutions, and the symbolic order has always been assymetrical though we are purportedly assured juridical symmetry, i.e. equality. However, as Rosaura Sánchez points out (1990), the terms of the boundaries can be reduced or extended to include us or exclude us by processes and manipulations beyond our control. At this juncture we all discover, as Sánchez suggests that we do not possess much of our identity, difference or experience because some of these are fixed elsewhere; that is, they are not as self-determined as one may pretend, but fixed by political and economic agendas and stereotyping public policies as well as by texts. Resistance through self-determined identity formations, in effect, is a powerful force often doused by official (legalistic) maneuvers, commodifying discourses, and the mass media which keep themselves busy producing, erasing, modifying and transcoding identities. Precisely because there is a continous drive for hegemonic containment towards a stasis that assures its control, resistance movements cannot afford to let up the pressure. If some of this sounds familiar to theory buffs, I want to emphasize that most of us learn this "in the flesh," as social movements continually testify. It is for this reason, for example, that the Chicana poet Lorna D. Cervantes can say that (proto)deconstruction is the social *modus operandi*—not just the textual theory—of the politically marginalized/excluded, which, I would add, generates the "politics of difference" as initially sketched out by Audre Lorde (1981).

The desire for critical agency on the part of Chicana critics and writers presupposes subjects-in-process who construct provisional (self-determining) "identities"[3] that subsume a network of discursive and signifying practices and experiences imbricated in the historical *and* imaginary shifting national borders of Mexico and the United States. A subject-insertion into such a geographical economy and politics presupposes not only specific historical sociosymbolic texts but a situated contemporaneous horizon of meanings and intentions that swerve away from those produced and enunciated by Euroamericans and Europeans especially when the latter produce hegemonic structures and discourses of containment. Identity formations through differentially theorized experience—in this instance through the term Chicana, thus signalling a historically raced/gendered/class position forged through the interstices of two nation-states—proposes a subject-in-process, desirous of self-determination yet is "traversed through and through the world and by others. . . . It is the active and lucid agency that constantly reorganizes its contents, through the help of these same contents, that produces by means of a material and in relation to needs and ideas, all of which are themselves mixtures of what it has already found there before it and what it has produced itself" (Castoriadis 1987, 106). Through the speaking critical subject-in-process cultural production reintroduces what was there before in new and dynamic combinatory transculturations. A bi- or multiethnicized, raced and gendered subject-in-process may be called upon to take up diverse subject positions which cannot be "unified" without double-binds and contradictions. Indeed what binds the subject positions together is precisely the difference from the perceived hegemony. The contradictions between subject positions move the subject to recognize, reorganize, reconstruct and exploit difference through political resistance and cultural productions, and to see herself "in-process."[4] It is not a matter of doing away with "the discourse of the other" (whom/whatever the other, hegemonic or not, is) "because the other is in each case present in the activity that eliminates [it]" (Castoriadis 1987, 107). The traces of a process of elimination (however unintended) may construct the subject as much as the efforts to incorporate. A critical subject-in-process who reorganizes "contents" upon the demands of the contingent historicopolitical moment may discover that it is in the inaugural transitional moment from being traversed to reconfiguration that the political intention as well as the combinatory transculturating takes place. Through such "moments," one can discover diverse cultural narrative formations, translations, and transcodifications which generate texts which are "hybrid" or "syncretic," and far from wanting to remain at rest in that taxonomy make a bid for new discourse formations bringing into view new subjects-in-process. In Gloria Anzaldúa's terms these are the "borderlands" (1987) through which the border "theory circuits" of geopolitics and critical allegories find resonance but the zones of figurations and conceptualizations remain non-equivalent. That is, the very contingent currents through which the geopolitical subject-in-process is dislocated, forced into (im)migration, will retain an irreducible difference that refuses to neatly correspond to the criticodiscursive dislocated subject-in-process.

It is my hope that through the writing of this essay, I have presented to the reader an exemplum, a practice, and a theory of the speaking subject-in-process, who in this instance stands-in as a Chicana critic positioned in the interstice between nation-states.

## Notes

1. By citing Moi I do not mean to endorse her typology vis-a-vis the Angloamericans and the French, let alone her characterization of lesbians and U.S. women of color; rather, I refer the reader to a readily available bibliography. See Moi (1985).

2. For the most recent anthology printed as a result of these conferences see López-González, Malagamba and Urrutia (1990).

3. Commenting on the shift that the notion of identity has undergone in women's discourses, Trinh T. Minh-ha claims that the shift does not lead to "a theory of female identity. . ." but rather "to identity as points of re-departure of the critical processes by which I have come to understand how the personal—the ethnic me, the female me—is political." (1989, 104).

4. The notion subject-in-process (on-trial/in-question) was first introduced by Julia Kristeva (1980a) to refer to the double identitarian status of the speaking subject vis-a-vis the law on the one hand and on the other the transformative and unsettling movements she undergoes in writing, in culture, as agent vis-à-vis her place in the symbolic order. See for example Roudiez (1980).

# "And you know what I have to say isn't always pleasant": Translating the Unspoken Word in Cisneros' *Woman Hollering Creek*

*Katherine Rios*

> Never marry a Mexican, my ma said once and always. She said this because of my father. She said this though she was Mexican too. But she was born here in the U.S., and he was born there, and it's not the same, you know.
> —Sandra Cisneros, *Woman Hollering Creek*

With this provocative statement, Sandra Cisneros begins "Never Marry a Mexican,"[1] a narrative that probes the ideological constructs of the "real" Mexican (and by extension, the "real native" and the "real woman") and challenges received definitions of cultural authenticity. Conceivably Cisneros could be under fire from some readers who might not appreciate her critique, dismissing it (if only by its title) as a stereotypical "American/Gabacho/Pocho's" ("malinchista's"?) denigration of Mexican culture, refusing Cherríe Moraga's insight that "to be critical of one's culture is not to betray that culture" (1983, 108).

A more useful way to understand Cisneros' work[2] would be to look at it as "a tongue-in-cheek critique," directed not (as it seems) to the general U.S. audience that often doesn't perceive differences between groups of people of color (let alone differences within a subgroup perceived as monolithic—"Mexicans") but to an audience that constantly struggles with parameters of self-definition, with identity in a border which doesn't always correspond to a physical location or geographical strip of land. Shared borders of specific material conditions including culture, economics, ideology, and language make up the "borderlands" that Gloria Anzaldúa thoroughly examines in *Borderlands/La Frontera: The New*

*Mestiza* (1987), engendering what Sonia Saldívar-Hull describes as "a feminism that exists in a borderland not limited to geographic space, a feminism that resides in a space not acknowledged by hegemonic culture" (1991, 211).

If borders offer the "invitation to cross over" (Alarcón 1989a, 86-87) *Woman Hollering Creek* offers a collection of stories about "crossing over" in all its manifestations: across geographical borders and borders of culture, class and color; through language and writing; and even across theoretical borders, braving the "crossfire" between hegemonic theoretical discourses. Cisneros explores how these "crossings" or traversals impact identity, authenticity, and the construction of subjectivity in a variety of complex and highly competing ways. Hers is a self-reflexive, self-critical analysis of the utterly transgressive nature of "crossing over" even as it is a distressingly routine way of life for border people—not just people located in or on a physical, geographical border, but as Anzaldúa puts it, those who are the cultural outcasts (38).

Such crossings require risky negotiations. As Alvina Quintana notes, "The Chicana writer is. . .engaged in mediating and negotiating between two cultural systems" so that "Chicana literature functions as a bold cultural intervention, which ironically enough resembles what we have come to respect as interpretive or experimental ethnography" (1991, 74-75). While Quintana's reference applies to the author's use of her characters as ethnographers, or the Chicana critic who occupies an intermediary role in discursive practices,[3] I extend the analogy to examine how Cisneros' work discloses the self-consciousness of the Chicana's betrayal and transgression as she attempts to interpret, translate, and cross cultures.

In this context, the comment "Who would've guessed, after all this time, it is me who will remember when everything else is forgotten, you who took with you to your stone bed something irretrievable, without a name" (Cisneros, "Tepayac," 23) gains a different valence; the "me" is the transgressive one who crossed over, who supposedly betrayed her people by interpreting myths and icons and telling stories.

As the ethnographer or translator faced with analytical discourses which lend authority to the "enigma" of alterity: the Other, the Mexican, the Native, the Woman, and the exemplary case of the native woman who traverses all those subject positions or identities, she can only insist that there is no essential, authentic identity with secrets to reveal. There is no "real" Mexican, no "real" native, no "real" woman; no pure identity uncontaminated by crossing over to *el otro lado* and fraternizing or collaborating with the "enemy." There are no secrets—but Cisneros tells them. The deliberate contradiction of this statement reveals the dislocated, non-linear, and ambiguous stance that Chicana critics must take as a strategy of self-definition that neither accepts nor denies, but unsettles, displaces and restates the question, like Gayatri Spivak's question: "What does this mean?" (1988, 297). In "Never Marry a Mexican," the Mexican narrator Clemencia recounts two major betrayals in her life: her mother's adultery and subsequent marriage to a white man, by which Clemencia is effectively disinherited; and her rejection by Drew, her lover and art teacher, an older white man who leaves her after his white wife bears their child. Clemencia also reveals transgressions of her own, including her many liaisons with married men and more importantly, the secret affair she maintains with Drew's now-teenage son.

For the Chicana reader, the events and characters of "Never Marry a Mexican" can't help but evoke comparison with the cultural-historical Malinche myth, Malinche[4] being the "real—life" native woman who assisted Cortés by translating for him, enabling his victory over the Aztecs and thereby mobilizing Spain's colonization of Mexico. Certainly there are enough textual references in "Never Marry..." to merit a reading of the story as a reconstruction and revision of the Malinche story, most obviously as Clemencia, the Mexican[5] narrator and Drew, her Anglo lover, playfully pose as the historical characters:

> Drew, remember when you used to call me your Malinalli? It was a joke, a private game between us, because you looked like a Cortez... My skin dark against yours... My Malinalli, Malinche, my courtesan, you said... (74)

The Malinche myth is so pervasive that one critic, Emma Pérez, claims the "metaphor cuts to the core of every Chicana," and limits her explanation to a footnote: "I will not reiterate this history, I assume most already know it...ask any Chicana about Paz's *chingada*" (1991, 167, 183). Malinche has become an icon of Chicana identity (or misidentification), sometimes even referred to as a "prototype" (Candelaria 1980). In fact, when I mentioned I was reading this story as a revision of the Malinche myth, a Chicana friend countered, "Is there any *other* way to read the story?"[6]

Of course there are many ways to read the story, including ways that might ignore its cultural specificity and its historical implications in self-interested projects presenting other theoretical perspectives—non-culturally specific feminist readings, for example. On the other hand, a feminist-materialist reading could be equally prohibitive, limiting the possibility of reading silence as I read it in Cisneros' work.

A cultural-historical reading is crucial because Cisneros recuperates the Malinche/Guadalupe/Llorona triad—the three icons that supposedly structure the psychic and material basis of Chicana identity—throughout her stories. Because, according to Anzaldúa, "ambiguity surrounds the symbols of these three 'Mothers' and 'mediators' " (30-31), an interpretation of "Never Marry a Mexican" demands an intertextual reading of other stories in her collection which would interplay with it, or even contest it; scraping up against it like the festering "scab" where "the Third World grates against the first and bleeds" (Anzaldúa, 3). Throughout her stories, Cisneros incorporates narrative reversals and scrutinizes ideological slippages in the construction of these "mothers," challenging and demystifying authenticity through revisions of icons, representations, and myths. She launches a critique that is as multidimensional as the positions its author—and other Chicanas—daily occupy.

Using her tongue-in-cheek approach in another story, "*Bien* Pretty," Cisneros perceives "authenticity" as determined by whether one speaks Spanish and when ("When Flavio accidentally hammered his thumb, he never yelled 'Ouch!' he said 'Ay!' The true test of a native Spanish speaker" [153]),[7] or dresses in ethnic clothing (like a "native"). Other signals of cultural authenticity hinge on whether one hangs Frida's paintings or displays Mexican pottery. Even the manner in which one walks (like Ixtacihuatl, the Indian princess turned goddess) indicates an authenticity modeled on the "royal" forebears rather than their slaves or the native workers who fashion the "ethnic" pottery, metal-work and weavings that are accumulated as signs of cultural identification (139-140).

Lupe's (the protagonist's) inventory of cultural artifacts (which are limited not only to the "ethnic" but also to "*calidad*"—quality —a metaphor for "authenticity"?) in her borrowed house is a sardonic critique of the appropriation of culture through exotica. But it is also a devastating critique of the position of the Third World subject in the U.S., a subject whose fetishization of the "native" or ethnic to recuperate identity marks her inscription and indoctrination in a capitalist society that makes her complicit in the ideology of capitalist consumerism. Cisneros explores how "culture" is constructed as a commodity attainable by the accumulation of "signs" of authenticity, but the problem of authenticity demands more than a cursory class analysis.

## Translating the Knot of Race, Class, and Gender

When (if) hegemonic theorists engage the oft-stated nexus of race, class, and gender, the categories are generally approached in isolation and effectively treated as static. For example, race is examined in relation to gender, gender in relation to class, and so on. Perhaps we need a three-dimensional model to approach the interrelationships of these categories in a way that isn't limited to foregrounding (and thereby prioritizing) any one category. "Real" material, historical conditions reveal the integral interplay and movement of these categories beyond boundaries and into dizzying configurations, as we see when Clemencia attempts to explain her mother's advice against marrying a Mexican:[8]

> I guess she did it to spare me and Ximena the pain she went through . . . Having had to put up with all the grief a Mexican family can put on a girl because she was from *el otro lado*, the other side, and my father had married down by marrying her. If he had married a white woman from *el otro lado*, that would've been different. That would've been marrying up, even if the white girl was poor. But what could be more ridiculous than a Mexican girl who couldn't even speak Spanish, who didn't know enough to set a separate plate for each course at dinner, nor how to fold cloth napkins, nor how to set the silverware. (Cisneros, "Never Marry a Mexican," 69)

How does one begin to unravel a passage like this, so simply phrased and yet so laden with the complexities and shifts of multipositionality? Perhaps a way to begin is to look at how one writes such positionality.

Using reversals as a strategy of unsettling discourses, Cisneros' analysis pivots between nationality, gender roles, tradition, class, status, race, and language. For example, defining the U.S. as "*el otro lado*" rules the U.S. the "Other," designating another Subject. In this instance—instant—Cisneros re-locates the underclass in the U.S., upsetting the prevailing description of Mexico as Third World. She acknowledges Mexican class divisions and refuses the ideology of a monolithic Mexican identity, thereby refusing to romanticize the Mexican as the "indigenous, native" subject of the Third World. At the same time, her move doesn't rule out ethnocentrism on the part of Mexicans; that is, some Mexican nationals' disdain for the Mexican American in the U.S. as unauthentic and contaminated more by their association with "gringos" than by capitalism and class divisions. She acknowledges class hierarchies not strictly as a function of economics, but also of race or color consciousness. Entangled in this problematic is the privileging of the white woman over the brown native or indigenous woman and the contradiction inherent in the ambivalent desire for the status gained by marrying a white woman. Finally, she notes impositions of authenticity per language, foregrounding the question of what Anzaldúa calls "language inadequacy" and "linguistic terrorism" (58) in the example of Clemencia's mother, who most likely speaks an imperfect Spanish rather than no Spanish at all.[9] Cisneros' reversals of language involve code-switching, often leaving the Spanish untranslated. Subject-position determines which language is italicized as "Other," emphasizing free play and multipositionality. In this way, Cisneros' use of code-switching is not just an indication of "bilinguality" but of multiple positionality.

The passage, a scathing critique of cultural discourses of authenticity and their attendant demands, expectations, and exclusions thus draws attention to what is already sorely obvious to many; that is, the problem of location. Locating the critique and the shifts in positionality is next to impossible even momentarily, because the object of critique is never static. As Cisneros deconstructs this ideology of cultural identity (whose binary poles are not individually pure, nor inviolable) as a kind of hegemony in the face of a resisting hybridity which is no longer only the hybridity of white/Spanish and indigenous/Mexican, but "American" in combination with those identities, she attacks the question of identity itself. In her recognition of the materiality of subject positions, Cisneros refuses to see subjectivity merely as an abstraction or a privilege of intellectuals.

With these complications in mind, it may come as a surprise that Cisneros' work should be so intensely pleasurable to read. It is precisely because of the cultural prohibitions delineated through the Malinche myth that the subversions of "Never Marry a Mexican" satisfy a desire for transgression and the expression of repressed rage.

At a recent Chicano art exhibit, Cherríe Moraga commented: "what was missing was the rage and vengeance of women,"[10] recalling Anzaldúa's observation: "I have internalized rage and contempt, one part of the self using defense strategies against another part of the self (the object of contempt)" (45).

The desire for a self-affirming model or narrative, as well as evidence of women's resistance and power, is sometimes expressed in the form of aggression or violence:

> I wanted you bare-breasted, snakes in your hands. I wanted you leaping and somersaulting the backs of bulls. I wanted you swallowing raw hearts and rattling volcanic ash. I wasn't going to be my mother or my grandma. All that self-sacrifice, all that silent suffering. Hell no. Not here. Not me. (Cisneros, "Little Miracles, Kept Promises," 127)

Cisneros, while recognizing the futility and misdirection of that violence doesn't repress it, but acknowledges and writes it.[11] Clemencia is silent and impassive, like Guadalupe. Yet that silence is not inspired by "self-sacrifice"—far from it. She is, in fact, "swallowing raw hearts" and "bare-breasted," invoking both the native as the Mexica/Aztec and the classic image of the Amazon in a kind of revision of ritualistic sacrifice that actually rejects the "native."

Many revisionists interpret Malinche's vengeance as rage directed against the mother who sold her into slavery, her captors, and finally, if only metaphorically, her son by Cortés, the first Mexican and the figurative ancestor of all Mexicans. In a sense, Cisneros rewrites the rage and translates the vengeance. The vengeance in Cisneros' version of the myth is rewritten in Clemencia and directed against Drew (the figurative Cortés) *and* his white wife, through Clemencia's relationship with their son.

Clemencia's unapologetic confession reveals her desire for Drew, a white man, and her indifference to brown men; her vengeful, strategic sexuality as demonstrated through her seductions of married men and her almost-incestuous manipulation of Drew's teenage son; and a spite exploding into rage. She demonstrates a dissociation from and disdain for other women (including other women of color), a rejection of a working class identity ("I'm amphibious... I'm a person who doesn't belong to any class" [71]) and her ready "prostitution" as a translator of travel brochures and an unwilling teacher. Finally, she rejects any possible semblance of "family" or maternity (she "can't stand kids" [71], and figuratively throws "the baby"—Megan's toy—into the creek, in a foreshadowing of her relationship with Megan's son); she even rejects her own mother ("Like I never even had one" [73]).

This inversion of Paz's passive Malinche ("a heap of bones, blood and dust," the raped one, *La Chingada* [Paz 1961, 85]) to an aggressive one (like that Pérez describes as a "maleness...constructed to be competitive, maniacal, and violent" [164-165]) is more like Paz's conception of the *Chingón*, the agent of that which is "cruel: it stings, wounds, gashes, stains. And it provokes a bitter, resentful satisfaction" (77).

Paz's *Chingón* reverberates in Clemencia's confession: "It's given me a bit of crazy joy to be able to kill those women like that ... To know I've had their husbands when they were anchored in blue hospital rooms, their guts yanked inside out..." (77) and recalls Moraga's musing: "what, indeed, must my body look like if I were both the *Chingada* and the *Chingón*?" (1983, 120-121). Can we read Clemencia's perverse delight in her seductions of Drew's son and other women's husbands while the women themselves are giving birth or still feeling their "ass stitches" (77) as a kind of psychic rape? If so, whose? Her relationship with Drew's son is, as Moraga says: "sex turned manipulation, control—which ravages the psyche rather than satisfy the yearning body and heart" (Moraga 1983, 137). Obsessed with plans for revenge, and knowing that Drew admires her eyes, Clemencia thinks: "after you left, I wanted to scoop them out with a spoon, place them on a plate ...food for the blackbirds" (75). In the context of her "incestuous" relationship with her pseudo-son, this fantasy might be read as an Oedipal reversal whereby a "knowing" Jocasta blinds herself. But it is not guilt that inspires Clemencia, but rather, spite: "like cutting off one's nose to spite one's face"—a vengeance that is ultimately self-destructive, that is "eating away" at her, consuming her. If, as Tey Diana Rebolledo says, "Women are so silenced that they are only left to speak with 'their eyes,' "[12] the implications of self-silencing are further emphasized by the violence of the *artist's* loss of her eyes. Clemencia's appropriation of violence as agency is thus not a solution, but self-destructive. Instead of an avenue to self-affirmation, it is merely an appropriation of a patriarchal power which feminists continuously attempt to render impotent. Yet, like the unfinished business of "difference," rage has yet to be spoken, written, and heard.

But Cisneros also moves beyond the pain and rage, that is, "pain or rage" as the only options or possibilities of interpretation. Like Anzaldúa, Cisneros "write[s] the myths she want[s] to become."[13] In the story "Woman Hollering Creek," for example, the La Llorona myth is rewritten when the cry is reinterpreted as a gleeful "hoot" or a "holler like Tarzan" (56).[14] And in "Little Miracles, Promises Kept" Rosario reinterprets Guadalupe's "silent suffering" as "power" and "strength" (127-128).

Moving beyond the critique of the "native," Cisneros plunges into another trajectory, forging an attack on stereotypes of "woman" and the authenticity of the "real woman":

> [I]n my dreams I'm slapping the heroine to her senses, because I want them to be women who make things happen, not women who things happen to. Not loves that are *tormentosos*. Not men powerful and passionate versus women either volatile or evil, or sweet and resigned. But women. Real women. The ones I've loved all my life. *If you don't like it* lárgate, *honey*. Those women. The ones I've known everywhere except on TV, in books and magazines. *Las girlfriends. Las comadres.* Our mamas and *tías*. Passionate and powerful, tender and volatile, brave. And, above all, fierce. ("*Bien* Pretty," 161)

Lupe (like Cisneros?) watches for "real [live] women" as opposed to the representations of the magazine heroines or women in the *telenovelas*. The "real woman" is located somewhere in the border, boundary, in-between but yet not Anzaldúa's essentialized woman, the "new mestiza." Rather than pushing the limits of "newer gender identities" (Alarcón 1989, 82), Cisneros seems to be questioning the "stalled" conditions of raced-ethnic gender identities that have been routinely excluded from hegemonic discourses or obscured under the guise of dominant feminist identity politics:

> Crossings over by "choice" or by force become sporadic individual arrangements that do not necessarily change the status of Indian women or women of color... The realization that the "invitation" to cross over, when it is extended, does not ameliorate the lot of women of color in general has led, in the eighties, to a feminist literature by Chicanas and women of color which demonstrates that, despite some shared perspectives, boundaries exist and continue to exist, thus accounting for differential experiences that cannot be contained under the sign of a universal woman or women. (Alarcón 1989a, 86-87)

Ironically, Clemencia doesn't "know" that she is a "native" until Drew rejects her. She ignores the reasons he offers (age difference and "responsibilities") and focuses on the *real* reason as she recalls their conversation:

> Besides, he could never marry me. You didn't think....? *Never marry a Mexican. Never marry a Mexican*... No, of course not. I see. I see. (Cisneros, "Never Marry," 80)

Clemencia's ideology—"never marry a Mexican"—turns back on her, unsettling and disrupting her definition of self and her self-referentiality when she realizes that to Drew, she is a Mexican. In this way Clemencia may be seen as positioned like "the Chicana intellectual," who, Alarcón notes, "is now and has always been a *Third World* intellectual...it was being inside the U.S. [*el otro lado*] which has given her the wrong impression" (Alarcón 1991, 6, emphasis mine). Clemencia's language inadequacy: "But that's—how do you say it?—water under the damn? I can't ever get the sayings right even though I was born in this country"[15] points to her misinterpretations of positionality.

When Drew rejects Clemencia, cultural readings of denigration and scorn for The Cross-Over (the *Vendida* or "Sell-out") are proved correct. It seems the ultimate betrayal is not the loss of the lover, but the proof of a misalliance,[16] Clemencia's mistake, her mis-positioning, her misinterpretation of "power" or "privilege." The possibility of "crossing" by repositioning (or rejecting) one's class or cultural identity is exploded and at the same time, brings the power differential back to race and gender.[17]

This devastating miscalculation is also at the root of the Chicana critic's anxiety in searching for a theory that "fits." She must be wary of a theory's seductive qualities, for fear that it ultimately might not "work," that it won't affect material practices or conditions. The Chicana critic must also be conscious of her limited "use-value" in theoretical circles that call for the voice of the woman of color. In Malinche's case, Alarcón notes that "once her usefulness is over she is silenced and disappears from the record" (1989, 86). Perhaps we can understand this as a warning to the Chicana critic (read *translator*) or the woman of color who speaks as a critic.

Spivak's insistent question, "Can the subaltern (as woman) speak?" is posed as a way of getting at the intricacies of economy, power, and the discourses that encode us (1988, 296). But because there is no "unmediated" space from which the woman of color can speak, speech demands an unwilling participation in both equally controlling, dominant ideological discourses. The critic finds she must engage both binaries (albeit unwillingly, as there is no recourse), if only to deny them (307). An example of this problematic may be read in the mythical Malinche, always already the aggressive colluder or the passive victim, affording no in-between "border" identity. Because reversals are not a solution, Spivak asserts it is more effective "to displace (not merely deny)" cultural markers (308). Spivak's suggestion of "seeking to learn to speak to (rather than listen to or speak for) the historically muted subject of the subaltern woman" (I would rephrase that to "speak *with*") assumes that the subaltern wishes to speak *to (or with) us* (295). Her suggestion is not to be interpreted as effectively bypassing the necessity of first *listening* to—a step not yet accomplished, "unfinished business" as evidenced by the insistence of repetition as the necessity to say the same thing over and over. But how does one speak to or with the woman of color, in this instance, the Chicana, if, as Moraga claims, "we speak in secret code"?[18] To interpret that code, one might consider Luce Irigaray's proposal of difference in the girl's entry into language, a process "*producing a space*, a *track*, a river, a dance, a rhythm, a song" (1989, 133, emphasis mine).

This "track" is reproduced when, in his house for their last rendezvous, Drew tells Clemencia their relationship is over. She remembers how she then

> went around the house and left a trail of [gummy bears] in places I was sure *she* would find them. One in her lucite makeup organizer. One stuffed inside each bottle of nail polish. I untwisted the expensive lipsticks to their full length and smushed a bear on the top before recapping them . . . (81)

Leaving this "trail" of gummy bears[19] (or "tracks," which recalls Alarcón's 1990 essay "In the Tracks of 'the' Native Woman") is a semiotics the white woman can readily understand on one level as saying "I was here. I exist. I leave my mark." In this way, it is Clemencia's proclamation of subjectivity, her signature, by which she insists on her "presence" just as silence insists on a presence rather than "absence" or "lack." Clemencia's action is an inefficient form of "speech," perhaps, but a readable one.[20] A parallel passage in the story "Woman Hollering Creek" describes the Mexican Cleófila who upon "coming home from the hospital with her new son [and] her husband" finds (reads?)

> A washed cup set back on the shelf wrong-side-up. Her lipstick, and body talc, and hairbrush all arranged in the bathroom a different way . . . Smudged fingerprint on the door. Crushed cigarette in a glass. (50)

Even these subtle signs leave her with "A doubt. Slender as a hair . . . Wrinkle in the brain crumpling to a crease," yet another clue to motivate her to leave her husband ("Woman Hollering," 50). But Clemencia's gummy bear tracks, by virtue of their placement, are anything but subtle. Perhaps this is the only way Clemencia can speak, because Megan (Drew's wife) refuses to recognize her existence. When Clemencia calls Drew in the middle of the night, for example, Megan answers the phone politely, refusing to allow Clemencia to intrude on her world, pretending that nothing is amiss by not acknowledging Clemencia as a competitor.

The role of white women as those who "oversee the dilemma" (Pérez, 169) and in certain critical ways, avoid engaging in it, is coded here in the wife's refusal of recognition. Megan's refusal to "listen" and Clemencia's insistence on being "heard" is analogous to the woman of color's insistent disruption of the dominant feminist's vision of a unified feminist project that attempts to incorporate women of color under the all-encompassing sign of "Woman." The trespassing or invasion of Megan's privacy indicates borders or boundaries between women do in fact exist. Clemencia's act underscores the presence and difference of a "raced" gender, which rejects appropriation or assimilation. Cisneros insists on difference, inverting and unsettling the exoticization or curiosity usually directed at the "native" as Clemencia finds herself inexplicably, irresistibly "curious" about Megan. She examines Megan's things as if to discover her secret, reiterating Clarice Lispector's words: "I fall silent. Because I don't know what my secret is. Tell me yours, teach me about the secret of each one of us" (Lispector 1981, 53).

In the context of feminist discourse and relations, the gummy bears imply an irreverent, aggressive sign of resistance in that, in speaking with the white woman (dominant feminist) we (women of color) will choose our moment to speak, as well as our mode of speech. Admittedly, it may not be a premeditated "speech"; Clemencia, for example, "speaks" on impulse, with the "tools" she has handy, in a sort of bricolage. But this only emphasizes that our theoretical discourse will be on our own terms, even as we stand at borderline odds (in the crossfire) with both hegemonic cultural nationalist and dominant feminist theories.

Although they've both been betrayed by Drew, Clemencia's disaffiliation with the white woman is based on race—the difference "of color" that Megan cannot cross over, even with cosmetic attempts. Therefore, her cosmetics are an appropriate object of attack and contamination. Clemencia takes her revenge by intruding on the intimacy of Megan's things, contaminating (like Paz's "stain") the toiletries and personal items related to beauty and the construction of femininity, specifically "white" beauty. Color or "race" (not nationality, because Clemencia, like her mother, is a U.S. "native") is the difference between them. As Clemencia says, "If she was a brown woman like me, I might've had a harder time living with myself, but since she's not, I don't care . . . I don't care about his wife. She's not *my* sister."[21]

But Cisneros is not ignoring the differences between brown women at the expense of white women. Both women avoid asking: "who am I exploiting?" (Pérez, 173) for Clemencia carelessly exploits the Mexican maid who might be blamed for the gummy bears and actively attempts to "exploit" her lovers' wives. The difference between women of color in also indicated in a more problematic way in "Woman Hollering Creek," in which Cisneros reverses La Llorona's holler of "pain or rage" to Felice's "hoot," a "holler like Tarzan" (56). That is to say, the woman hollers for joy, announcing her conquest, power or reign—again reminding us of Cortés, or Paz's *chingón*.

Or does Felice holler to announce her rescue? After all, the feminist Chicana[22] Felice "rescues" Cleófilas (the Third World woman) from her husband (the Third World man). This scenario is uncomfortably like Spivak's critique of "white men saving brown women from brown men" (297), except that in this instance it is the *brown woman* saving the brown woman from the brown man. As Felice's friend Graciela says, "If we don't help her, who will?" (53). But the adjective "brown" is itself nuanced, marked by differences of culture, nationality, class,[23] language,[24] and sexual preference.[25]

The dynamics between Cleófilas and Felice might be read as Cisneros' delineation of difference between marginalized women of color in the "First World" and "Third World" women of color; underscoring an awareness of privilege as relative, however limited it may be; and questioning the limits of a global feminism with supposedly common goals. In this way, Cisneros challenges the perceived seamlessness of a Third World identity, exploding the assumptions of identity politics.

For what else are we to make of the fact that Cisneros engages the name "Chicano" only once in the entire collection of stories?[26] "To date most writers and scholars of Mexican descent refuse to give up the term Chicana," Alarcón notes, a term which "in body and mind, has become a critical site of political, ideological and discursive struggle through which the notion of 'definitiveness' and hegemonic tendencies are placed in question" (Alarcón 1990, 248-9). But there's no self-referentiality to the term "Chicana" in Cisneros' stories, though we as readers could probably confer the term to name some of the characters. Clemencia's self-referentiality, for example, is only implied when she says "a Mexican woman [like me] would never do that" (Cisneros, 77). And in "*Bien* Pretty," when Flavio insists that Lupe is "American," not "Mexican," the possibility of a "Chicana" identity doesn't even come into question (149).

It appears that Cisneros deliberately drops the name "Chicana," which requires her to revert to the much more ambiguous (and ungendered) name of "Mexican." The emphasis shifts so that "among ourselves," as Anzaldúa explains, "we say *nosotros los mexicanos* (by *mexicanos* we do not mean citizens of Mexico; we do not mean a national identity, but a racial one)" (62). Cisneros in effect engages a self-referentiality in terms of "race" rather than nationality, class, or identity politics, refusing to privilege the Chicana as "knowing" subject through a seemingly fixed political identity. This enables her to make it clear that there are differences within the supposedly monolithic group that names itself "Chicanos/Chicanas," let alone within the more inclusive group that calls itself "Mexican." At the same time, she questions the concept of self-referentiality as a solution, reminding us once again that there is no pure, authentic, self-referentiality.

And so Cisneros' opening statement, "Never Marry a Mexican" can be read as a strategy, enabling her to shift the terms of the debate to examine the multiplicity and ambiguity of identity and subject positioning, and more specifically, to highlight gender in conjunction with racial difference *over and against* class difference and national identities or affiliations.

## "Silenced Before She Even Finds Words to Name It"[27]

What is it that Clemencia wishes to speak? And to whom is she speaking? That she never speaks aloud or with an interlocutor, save for only two words in the entire story ("Hello, Megan" 79) raises the question of "voice consciousness" in her narrative (Spivak, 297). What kind of "testimony" is it that is neither written nor spoken, but all introspective, interior, and unarticulated?[28] Is Clemencia silent because "there are no words to say it"? (Trinh Minh-ha 1989, 27).[29] Or, given Moraga's comments that the "sources of oppression form not only our radicalism, but also our pain... Therefore, they are often the places we feel we must protect unexamined at all costs" (Moraga 1983, 134), is Clemencia's silence a strategy of self-defense? Or is it a strategy of resistance, since Clemencia's silence, unlike her art, is *not* available for ready consumption?

The image of the elegantly articulate, polyglot Malinche (which is translated to silence in Paz's conception of her) is reinscribed as

Clemencia thinks of Drew: "With you I'm useless with words. As if somehow I had to learn to speak all over again, as if the words I needed hadn't been invented yet" (Cisneros, 78). Some things, as Lispector tells us, are untranslatable: "There are so many things to say that I don't know how to say. The words aren't there. But I refuse to invent new ones: the ones that already exist should say what can be said and what is forbidden" (20-12). Is this untranslatability a language inadequacy or is it an example of indeterminacy? Clemencia wonders:

> Why is it always worse at night, when I have such an urge to communicate and no language with which to form the words? Only colors. Pictures. And you know what I have to say isn't always pleasant. (Cisneros, 83)

As a translator and teacher, it seems it is not language that Clemencia is lacking. Is it the "native's knowledge" that can't be articulated or translated?

Alarcón reminds us that "notwithstanding her famed translating abilities, Malintzin has left us no recorded voice because she was illiterate" (1989, 74). Malinche's illiteracy is reiterated in Clemencia's comment about making love with Drew: "You ache and tug. You *rip* my skin" (Cisneros, 78, emphasis mine). To "rip" her skin resonates of the *chingón's* violence, yet it seems an odd idea, implying that it is only the surface (not "the core," and not a "rape") that rips. And if it is only the surface that rips, like ripping paper, that leaves Clemencia (like Malinche and the Chicana critic) "a signifying problem" (Alarcón 1991, 6). But the problem in these readings of Clemencia's silence is that she can thus be figured as the stereotypical native Other. She's a threat, suspected of harboring smoldering thoughts behind a mask of dissemblance; feared by those whites who cannot "read" her silence. She has a "secret" identity, for as Paz says:

> The Mexican is not an essence but a history. Neither ontology nor psychology. I was and am intrigued not so much by "the national character" as by what that character conceals: by *what is behind the mask*. (1972, vii, emphasis mine).

Equally problematic, in the discourse of "resistance" Barbara Harlow asserts that "the use of language is crucial, both as challenge to the antagonist and in redefining the identity of the protagonist" (1987, 55). In this way, then, "there is no place from which the sexed subaltern subject can speak" (Spivak, 307), for she is caught between discourses. Even her silence is co-opted into discourses of alterity or a "lack" of (a *proper*) resistance.

## "Never Marry a Mexican"

In the context of competing discourses of a vanguard cultural nationalism which resists feminist critique and a hegemonic postmodernism which argues against national identities toward an ungendered subjectivity and global solidarity, one might think there couldn't possibly be a more volatile statement. But "never marry a Mexican" is not idiosyncratic; in fact, it could be read as a trope to explore the identity and subject positioning of the person of Mexican descent.

"Never marry a Mexican man. They make you suffer." That's her mother's advice, recalls Rose Del Castillo Guilbault, who has written for the *San Francisco Examiner* under the header "Hispanic, U.S.A."

Del Castillo Guilbault talks about her "female cousins [who] had to get up early to make breakfast for themselves and their brothers, clean up after them, iron their clothes, make their beds and anything else included in their gender-based role,"[30] echoing Cherríe Moraga's accounts of serving her brother and his friends (1983, 90-91). But, she continues:

> It wasn't just the gender-related jobs that troubled me; the darker, more difficult roles Latin women had to play were far more disturbing . . . The aunts [but not her mother?] believed they had to close their eyes to affairs, all-night drinking binges and bouts of unemployment due to stubborn male egos. (Del Castillo Guilbault, 2)

She compares one of her aunts to La Llorona, and notes that later, when this aunt leaves her husband, the family refers to her as "a Malinche" (2).

In her collection of poems, *My Father Was a Toltec*, Ana Castillo offers the framework for understanding the cultural inscription of the "real woman" as the subservient, silent wife and mother. "He" wears silk suits ("*calidad*") which she pays for. "She" washes and irons his clothing, silently, uncomplainingly:

> That's why he married her, a Mexican
> woman, like his mother, not like
> they were in Chicago, not like
> the one he was going out to meet ("Saturdays," 6)

Who is "the one he is going out to meet"; what makes her Other? Is she white? Or is it that she is not a "real" Mexican?

And in the poem "Wyoming Crossing Thoughts" Castillo forcefully expresses a rejection of the Mexican woman's role:

> i will never
> in my life
> marry
> a Mexican man,
> utter
> with deep devotion
> "Si, mi señor." (38)

The speaker, realizing that her survival and empowerment depends upon her rejection of the "Mexican man" and the refiguration of her desire for him, she concludes:

> i will . . .
> drive an obsidian blade
> through his heart
> lick up the blood. (39)

Castillo's poem is a juxtaposition of the passive subject of violence, the wife/mother's self-sacrifice, the Guadalupe's impotent vision of her "son's" sacrifice, with the violent, aggressive action of the Other (slave, captive, victim) refigured as the Mexican man. This recodification of a passive event to an active one also recodes the basis of interpretation so that the act becomes self-defense, not through revenge, but through the effort to appropriate and incorporate knowledge.

Castillo refigures the sacrifice in "Ixtachihuatl Died in Vain":

> It is you
> I share my son with
> to whom I offer up
> his palpitating heart

so that you may breathe,
and replenish yourself,
you alone, whom I forgive. (34)

Castillo thus historicizes, contextualizes and reconfigures women's self-sacrifice.

In Alma Villanueva's collection of poems, "*legacies and bastard roses*" (1977; 1982) the Chicana narrator's mother recalls:

My family
always
said, "marry a good Mexican
boy"—
but the sun on a
gringo's hair makes me
worship
them (63)

And in *Mother, May I?* (1978), Villanueva relates the story of a pregnant (Mexican?) teenager whose white boyfriend says:

—I can't marry you. they
won't let me. they
say,
she'll have 12 more
kids in 10 years, you
know these people.
they
say
NO.— (22)

*Never marry a Mexican*. . . The young woman continues:

. . . my mother
keeps me,
—we women stick together. —she
tells the clinic secretary
—*she* didn't want to marry *him*.— (22-23)

This attempt at another way to read the story, once again through a reversal, offers a doesn't quite succeed as a revisionary account, though it does succeed as a model of reaffiliation.

If, as Castillo says of Chicanas: "We are Ixtacihuatls,/ sleeping, snowcapped volcanoes/ buried alive in myths" ("Ixtacihuatl Died in Vain," 34) perhaps the question "Is there any other way to read this story?" should be restated as "Is there any other way to write (or speak) this story?"

Clemencia's paintings may be seen as a kind of "writing," speech, and empowerment: "I paint and repaint you as I see fit . . . After all these years. . . I've been waiting. Making the world look at you from my eyes. And if that's not power, what is?" (75).[31] But if painting is her medium, Drew has the capacity to disarm her, as when she feels her painter's hand as a clumsy "paw" (79). She has the power to envision and to create revisions, but without speech, she cannot translate. Telling her story is like Lispector's recognition: "I write in signs that are more gesture than voice. All this is what I used to paint, probing into the intimate nature of things. But now the time has come to stop painting in order for me to remake myself, I remake myself in these lines. I have a voice" (Lispector, 16). And yet, Lispector says: "It's so curious to have exchanged paints for this strange thing that is the word" (15).

The "real" act of resistance is in the (re)telling of this story, the transgressions as resistance to cultural restrictions, prescriptions, the socio-historical Malinche narrative, the national allegory which all Chicanas "know," even if they do not know who Paz is, by virtue of the epithet, *malinchista*. The real transgression, despite criticism leveled against her "deprecation of the Mexican," is Cisneros' revision of the Malinche myth to reveal a secret: silence is not passive, not compliant, not complicit, but strategic. Clemencia's silence is as strategic as her seduction of Drew's son. She remains silent only because she's waiting for the most effective moment to reveal itself, to speak or disclose her transgression—her rage and vengeance: "I have the patience of eternity. Rub his belly. Stroke him. Before I snap my teeth" (Cisneros, 82).

And in this lies the problem with Cisneros' revision: she's caught in a bind (border, crossfire) between telling and denying there is anything to tell. Precisely because Clemencia does have something to say, it would seem Cisneros assists in the project of essentializing the native Other (specifically, the native woman) as a mysterious repository of knowledge. The problem is, the "real" Malinche *was* a "repository of knowledge," she *was* a dangerous woman because she had access to both modes of discourse, the

Spanish and the native. Cisneros' bind is only relieved by the fact that Clemencia does "tell," but isn't heard because she has no interlocutor save her own imagination. There are no secrets, but we will never know what the historical, "real" Malintzin really thought; we can only imagine—or fantasize. The tension between "knowing" and the claim of not having "secrets" can only be resolved in the redefinition of "knowledge" and "secrets" from the Other's perspective, a redefinition that would insist: "It's not a defamatory secret. It's simply that, secret" (Lispector, 53).

There are no secrets to tell, yet that you believe there are affords us a position of strength, resistance, power, and refusal, as well as the potential for identity, community, and coalition. In trying to reconcile our desires to be understood but not be forced to speak, we leave it open, ambiguous: "We don't prescribe" (Cisneros, "*Bien* Pretty," 159). Cisneros' revision doesn't resolve questions of identity; rather, it exposes contradictions, making differences more visible in culturally specific configurations.

> *Urracas*. Grackles. *Urracas*. Different ways of looking at the same bird . . . That roll of the *r* making all the difference. (164)

## Notes

1. Sandra Cisneros, "Never Marry a Mexican," in *Woman Hollering Creek*. All subsequent references to Cisneros refer to this title, unless otherwise stated in the text.
2. Despite her critiques, it is obvious from her writings that Cisneros, a self-identified Chicana feminist, celebrates Mexican culture.
3. In "Ana Castillo's *The Mixquiahuala Letters*: The Novelist as Ethnographer," Alvina Quintana states, "Chicanas find themselves resisting not one but two oppositional discourses which deny them visibility." She names these the "Anglo feminist or traditional Chicano ideologies" (258-259).
4. Among others, La Malinche's many names include: Malinal, Malinalli, Malintzin, Doña María, and (metaphorically) La Chingada.
5. Clemencia implicitly refers to herself as "Mexican," like her father, although both she and her mother were born in the United States.
6. Thanks to Yolanda Flores for posing this question.
7. "To make love in Spanish" is the other "natural" example of language, one that suggests Irigaray's conceptions of originary and preoedipal language. Both Flavio and Drew speak to Lupe and Clemencia in "their" (Flavio's, Clemenica's) language—Spanish—when they make

love. In *Loving in the War Years*, Moraga also remarks upon the significance of this use of language: "Mi amiga says to me, she could never go back to not fucking in Spanish" (142).

8. Of course, Clemencia is not a "real, live" woman, only a character. But the experience described is brutally real.

9. That she "couldn't even speak Spanish" (Cisneros, 69) shouldn't be read literally, but rather, in light of the general complaint laughingly mimicked by Ellie Hernández at the 1991 MALCS conference in Laredo, Texas, 2 August: "¡Mira como muestren nuestra idioma!"

10. Cherríe Moraga, "La fuerza feminina; las artistas de Aztlan," paper presented at "Cara a Cara: A Symposium on Current Debates in Chicano Culture," Fort Mason Theatre, San Francisco, California, 20 July 1991.

11. Moments of revenge are extolled as a way of wresting power, if only fleetingly, and if only inefficiently or ineffectively.

12. In "The Politics of Poetics: Or: What Am I, A Critic, Doing in This Text Anyhow?," Tey Diana Rebolledo refers to a passage about Malinche in Margarita Cota-Cárdena's *Puppet*.

13. "I write the myths in me, the myths I am, the myths I want to become," Gloria Anzaldúa (1987, 71).

14. Cisneros' "holler" and Ana Castillo's revisions of self-sacrifice deliberately rewrite Paz's "image of the howl that ends all our songs and possesses the same ambiguous resonance: an angry joy, a destructive affirmation ripping open the breast and consuming itself" (1961, 75).

15. Cisneros (73). This "mistake" is only perceived through a misspelling —suggesting Clemencia's *writing* error.

16. This misalliance and its effects are echoes of the historical circumstances of the conquest. Paz points out "the tragic confusions these errors created: "the Spaniards' Indian allies hoped that the fall of México-Tenochtilán would put an end to the interregnum, the usurpation, and their own vassalage," and surmises: "Perhaps their horrible disillusionment was the cause of their centuries-long passivity," (1972, 102).

17. Drew (the Anglo-American) sees Clemencia as a "Mexican," while Flavio (the "native" Mexican in "*Bien* Pretty") sees Lupe as an "American." Neither Mexican nor American, but definitely not "white," Clemencia and Lupe are forced to reposition themselves.

18. Moraga (1983, vi). Similarly, in "Sign," Melanie Kaye/Kantrowitz writes: "My fingers/move sly against your palm/Like women everywhere, we speak in code" (1980, 85). Quoted in Anzaldúa (1987, 59).

19. This isn't the full extent of Clemencia's trail; I leave the more delicious details for the reader to discover.

20. I am not suggesting these semiotics represent writing, but rather, that they indicate the resistance to being silenced. Clemencia's silence is effectively disruptive; we can assume her "tracks" disrupt the harmony of

Drew's home.

21. Cisneros (76, 73). Though she's talking about filiation rather than affiliation, it seems Clemencia disaffiliates herself from both brown and white women, since she also claims she is "not like Ximena," her "real" sister.

22. This is my imposition of an identity, as Felice's identity is unspecified in the story.

23. The vexed relationship of the "real Mexican" to a class identity is especially complicated in "Never Marry a Mexican." For Clemencia, Mexicans are "the men clearing off the tables or chopping meat behind the butcher counter or driving the bus...not [really] men" (69); Drew's cleaning woman; her sister Ximena, whose husband abandoned her and their children; and her mother, who married her (middle class) father and "never said why" (71).

24. For example, Felice uses code-switching as she speaks to Cleófilas in "a Spanish pocked with English" (55). But her "language inadequacy" is signaled by her inability to recognize Cleófila's name, since Graciela has to spell it out for her.

25. Sonia Saldívar-Hull's intriguing reading of Felice as a Chicana lesbian complicates my reading of the "brown woman saving the brown woman from the brown man" by shifting the "difference" to the difference of sexual preference. My critique is based on the difference between brown women in the "First World" and brown women in the "Third World." I am not addressing the dynamics expressed by Moraga when she says: "My mother was a heterosexual/I couldn't save her" (1986, 14). Saldívar-Hull, paper presented at the MALCS Chicana/Latina Summer Research Institute, Laredo, Texas, 2 August 1991.

26. Cisneros uses the term "Chicanos" in reference to men in "Little Miracles, Kept Promises" (116).

27. Trinh (1989, 27).

28. In this way, Clemencia is more like Guadalupe than Malinche, which raises the possibility of subversion in the figure of Guadalupe.

29. Trinh says, "Silenced before she even finds the words to name it" (1989, 27); while Anzaldúa expresses the need for "a space for...ethnic mestizas who have been silenced before uttering a word, or, having spoken, have not yet been heard" (1990, xvii).

30. Rose Del Castillo Guilbault, "Women's Cross to Bear," *San Francisco Examiner* 2 June 1991: 2. Here it's important to know that her cousins were living in Mexico while she and her family were living in the United States, according to another of her accounts of "being Mexican."

31. Clemencia's paintings of Drew may be thought of as an attempt to speak the unspeakable, that is, pain. In this way, she is reminiscent of Frida Kahlo, who painted her pain on her body, painting and repainting "Diego On My Mind."

# Sheila Ortiz Taylor's *Faultline*: A Third-Woman Utopia

*Juan Bruce-Novoa*

> . . . in social, sexual, and symbolic experiences, being a woman has always provided a means to another end, to become something else: a subject-in-the-making, a subject on trial.
> —Julia Kristeva, "Oscillation between Power and Denial"

Sheila Ortiz Taylor (b. 1939), originally from Los Angeles, has authored two novels: *Faultline* (1982), and *Spring Forward/Fall Back* (1985), plus a poetry collection, *Slow Dancing at Miss Polly's* (1989), all three released by The Naiad Press, a prestigious lesbian publisher. Her work has achieved international success, with *Faultline* appearing in German and Italian translations and a separate British edition. Thus, she represents those U.S. writers of Mexican heritage who have been producing literature for some years now without coming to the attention of Chicano readers or critics. Unlike writers whom the Chicano reading community watches develop in a public or communal space of interaction, sometimes knowing of their writings even before they have published a page, these other authors burst into our consciousness with a record of achievement deserving investigation. That Ortiz Taylor has attracted little attention from Chicano critics is probably due to the lack of overt ethnic identification in her work, and to the tendency in criticism—ours differs very little in this—to impose mutually exclusively categories into which authors and books are distributed according. Yet, like other authors who do not actively affiliate with the group (i.e.: Laurence Gonzales, Ernest Brawley, Cecile Pineda), Ortiz Taylor can be included as a Chicana by reason of her familial heritage.

Though their writing differs considerably in style, thematics, and tone, comparisons can be drawn to that master of male homosexual hustlers' writing, John Rechy, who has not always been accepted within Chicano circles, despite his indisputable Chicano roots and the inclusion of Chicano protagonists and characters in almost every one of his novels. As I have mentioned elsewhere (1986), although Ortiz Taylor has expressed no desire to enter the Chicano canon, one of the aims of Chicano criticism must be to identify authors and incorporate their works into a corpus, thus expanding our literature to more accurately represent all elements of our culture, even those which some, for whatever reason, might wish to ignore or exclude. It is with that goal in mind that I offer the following study of Ortiz Taylor's first novel.[1]

As a lesbian writer, Ortiz Taylor is no stranger to the judgmental rhetoric of exclusion. She knows well the impression that society in general holds of homosexuals and specifically, lesbians, one based on preconceived values of normalcy, morality, and the heterosexual character of the family. However, instead of attacking these prejudices directly, which could radicalize readers into polarized camps, Ortiz Taylor chooses another tactic, that of apparently empowering readers with decisive authority and appealing to their sense of, if not fair play, at least of playfulness. *Faultline* is constructed to engage the reader as the judge, jury member, or simultaneously both in the person of society's appointed representative—like the case worker from a government agency, who, as we come to understand in later chapters, must decide whether the female protagonist is a fit guardian of her own children or if she should be excluded, ostracized from the family and society as a criminal. In terms of the writer's project, the reader has the authority to judge the novelist by deciding whether she has been a fit progenitor and nurturer of her creation. To achieve this end, she must bring about the suspension of prejudice to produce the condition of free-thinking which, in turn, would allow an individual to judge the situation on the basis of its merits. In a sense, she is appealing to a fundamental ideal of this country's legal tradition, the right to a fair and unbiased trial.

The novel begins with a chapter title "A Word From the Defendant," in which Arden Benbow proclaims, in first person, "I realize that my three hundred rabbits are the most serious piece of material evidence against me" (1). We are confronted by the apparently clear situation of a trial, an interrogation, within which the first statement comes from the accused who speaks in her own defense. Later we must analyze further to what purpose this strategy is used, but for now it suffices to see that the author inscribes the reader's role as that of an interested party with the power to make a judgment on the believability of the text, one which may condemn or vindicate the protagonist. But before going on to discuss in more detail Arden's opening defense statement, let us pass on to what can be called the intertext or context of accusation, the pre-text of pre-judgment Arden addresses in the form of the reader/social worker/judge/mainstream code of signification.

Chapter two presents the next in the series of voices summoned to testify about Arden Benbow, the accuser. Fittingly, the voice of opposition assumes the position of an enemy of the uncontrolled fertility Benbow attributes to herself as the primary symbol of her encounter with the reader. Arden's exhusband is named Malthus, a reference to Thomas Robert Malthus (1766-1834), the English economist and demographer, author of *An Essay on the Principal of Population as it Affects the Future of Society, with Remarks on the Speculations of Mr. Godwin, M. Condorcet, and Other Writers*, in which he posited his pessimistic view that population growth will always tend to surpass food supply and therefore social well-being and order is impossible without stern and harsh limits on reproduction. True to his namesake, the ex-husband expounds Malthusian social morality, believing that the human species must be strictly controlled lest it multiply beyond its means and self-destruct. According to this theory, moral restraints are inherent in the traditional family and social structure; a lack of respect for these supposedly sacrosanct units are considered violations of this natural order that automatically sets into action a system of checks that manifests itself in the form of evils, such as poverty, famine, disease, etc.

As the would-be authoritative representative of mainstream society, Malthus bespeaks traditional dichotomous, bipolar moral logic. "Lesbianism and motherhood are at war" (8), he declares categorically, as if it were an ontological given. The basis for his position is that a lesbian who has children "will lack the tenderest instinct of a real, or we might say, of a social mother, and will quite simply lack both the ability and the desire to make her own needs subservient to those of the child and his environment" (7). As is befitting in Ortiz Taylor's openly allegorical tone, Malthus is stereotypical in his biases, incarnating what Adrienne Rich has described as the male's compensation for his fear of women's creative and transformative power through the channeling of that power into a system of production in which he occupies the position of entrepreneur, owner, and director, and branding any woman who does not conform a social deviant. Rich states what could well be the basis of Malthus's characterization of social mothers: "Maternal altruism is the one quality universally approved and supported in women" (1976, 212). That Malthus's ideal child is male—"his environment"—should surprise no one, for the lesbian mother threatens, most of all, the status of the male, thus, according to the patriarchal spokesman, placing society itself in danger. In other words, Malthus believes that Arden, or any woman, should sacrifice herself for the good of men.

This hostile witness, chosen to represent the patriarchal position, as well as the plaintiff in the custody case the reader gradually realizes s/he is involved in as investigator and judge, significantly begins his argument by appealing to a traditional system of order and logic, rhetoric: "Any thinking person will agree that the term *lesbian mother* is oxymoronic" (7). Malthus counts on the reader's acceptance of a set of rational categories based on the opposition of terms. We could say that he not only affirms, but utilizes—even in his speech patterns—the traditional bipolarity of differences common to Western thought, splitting experience into separate, mutually exclusive dichotomies. Malthus leaves nothing to discuss, eliminating the middle ground of compromise: the positive and negative value attributed to the poles are clear. His opposition, as he patronizingly states, is not to homosexuals—"Understand I have nothing against homosexuals. Certainly they have enough misfortune in their lives without our mockery. Tormented creatures!" (8)—but to his ex-wife's refusal to respect society's system of logic. Instead of leaving two opposed terms separate and distant by choosing one and only one, she insists on juxtaposing and even combining them, thus threatening to introduce chaos into the system. Faced with the subversion of the rules of his system, Malthus, the self-appointed guardian of order, feels he must reassert control over the rebellious and wayward Arden by reincorporating her into the rhetorical system within a safe category, one which will subjugate her to the general order of the system, yet not justify her position nor legitimate her existence. Malthus needs a category to logically control—to name—the dangerously illogical. He achieves this by branding her an "oxymoron," a criminal category at once within the system—a defined and thus controllable construct, albeit nonsensical in its contradictory or incongruous nature—yet by its definition placed outside the viable choices for any "thinking" member of the order. The oxymoron is the rhetorical equivalent of Devil's Island.

The choice of the term "oxymoron" is more than simply descriptive, hiding as it does male-dominance ideology underlying the social logic which Malthus claims to be a universal constant in rational thought. Men traditionally relegate women to the status of "morons" by treating them as grown-up children, that is as feeble minded or mentally defective persons, with a potential mental age of between eight and twelve years old, capable of doing routine work under supervision. They are admired for their innocence (read lack of adult reasoning power) and beauty, while simultaneously considered stupid or boorish. And they must be carefully socialized because they, like children, are sexually curious, even ambiguous, which in adult terms means they are sexual perverts. All of this is directly denoted by "moron," and if women themselves are morons, from Malthus's male perspective lesbians truly would be extreme—*oxi* signifies extreme—examples, or oxymorons. This subtextual meaning of the term, however, ironically makes Arden Benbow the extreme example of classic womanhood itself, revealing the opposition in male dominant rhetoric in which two categories of being, woman and mother, emerge as contradictory. Malthus's position would require women to cease being women to become mothers, sacrificing themselves to the children (male) for the sake of society (male dominated, of course). After years of marriage, Arden came to understand Malthus's concept of the social order on the level of personal relationships: "There was something about Malthus and his needs that I found draining .... Whatever he wanted always took the form of my giving up something. For my own good. Not until years later did I realize that at the center of each of Malthus's desires was a cipher. He wanted the absence of something, not the presence" (75). Ironic undermining of patriarchal logic is a key strategy of feminist writing: it constitutes an intertextual engagement of the masculine sign system through its articulation and simultaneous re- or trans-articulation into another system with a radically different ideological position. It turns the static, symbolic patriarchal text of significance—which rests on the principle of non-shifting sign systems—into a fluidly semiotic, phenomenological space of signifying. As such it fulfills the deconstructive function that Julia Kristeva and other feminists attribute to female letters.

> If women have a role to play. . . it is only in assuming a *negative* function: reject everything finite, definite, structured, loaded with meaning, in the existing state of society. Such an attitude places women on the side of the explosion of social codes: with revolutionary movements. (Kristeva 1980c, 166)

> . . . a feminist practice can only be. . . at odds with what already exists so that we may say "that's not it" and "that's still not it." In "woman" I see something that cannot be represented, something that is not said, something above and beyond nomenclatures and ideologies. (Kristeva 1980b, 137)

The female author's disrespect for patriarchal logic introduces anarchism into the male bastion of writing—a displacement of the readers' eye to a marginal space away from what men deem important.

At all levels of *Faultline* this infusion of dynamism occurs: rules, customs, and values are challenged and subverted. Arden adopts her grandmother's last name to emphasize matrilineal succession; she hires a black homosexual male as a live-in baby sitter to her six children; she leaves her successful husband for a woman, which in turn deprives her husband's boss of his wife; she even refuses to feign social conformity when being inspected by the Child Welfare agency. On the level of discourse, the novel presents the same disrespect for establishing norms. Either as Ortiz Taylor's or as Arden's text, it hardly conforms to the patriarchal monological principal nor to the generic assumptions of the traditional novel—a concept, admittedly passé, but useful as a symbol of equally dated patriarchal concepts of life as a tightly controlled family unit under the sign of strict heterosexuality. As mentioned above, *Faultline* consists of a series of voices dialoguing with an interviewer/investigator and with each other through the meditation of the reader, the only possible constructor of a unified text from the fragments presented. Instead of one authoritative version capable of summarizing all perspectives into one narrative voice—like a forty minute lecture from Malthus—the text offers a multiplicity of versions in search of authority, in search of a sympathetic judge who will be convinced to allow the voices to exist in their individuality while relating them into a unit.

The singularity of authorship, another bourgeois concept associated with patriarchal order, is itself subverted in as much as Arden completes her aunt's novel when the older woman dies, and then later constructs and ends her own life-text according to an alternative model envisioned by her aunt: "a loud-tender party" (75). In this way, two texts are co-authored, each encompassed within the other. The one we read, furthermore, is composed of a series of authors who find themselves involved in Arden's dynamic movement, carried along by the sheer power and attraction of her ever fluid, never static, style of life. But if "authority" lies in a supposed creator of meaning, a constructor of order, then from the start that responsibility is shifted to the reader, who, it is hoped, will abandon her/his exterior stance of solely "thinking person" and join the party to participate in the field of play as one more force in the text's continually shifting dynamics.

The temptation to read *Faultline* in terms of Kristeva's female characteristics of negativity and anarchy is certainly attractive. From the beginning, the text simultaneously sets up a system of logical, bipolar terms (witness/jury, accused/accuser, text/reader) and infuses the system with apparently anarchical, even chaotic content and form. Arden sets the tone by opening the text with a rambling explanation of why she has three hundred rabbits. The strategy is to associate the apparently unrelated existence of the rabbits and Arden Benbow's criminality: "I realize" the text begins, "that my three hundred rabbits are the most serious piece of material evidence against me. People will think only an unstable mind could not only produce but sustain that kind of absurdity" (1). She seems to be preparing us for a plea of insanity, yet Arden does not allow the reader time to focus on the absurdity and apply prejudice—a preconceived sense of what is logical. She quickly shifts directions, displacing the reader's vision or concentration to another consideration that on one hand forces suspension of judgement, while on the other recontextualizes the previous set of elements to be judged. The effect is like following the narrative thread down dim passages and being forced to take an unexpected turn before reaching the end—an end that turns out to be an ambiguous illusion, or perhaps only a partial and fleeting glimpse of the eventual final revelation.

This tactic, fundamental to the text's strategy of stringing the reader along until having them drawn deeply into it process, in the opening dialogue takes the form of Arden asking the reader for tolerance and patience, for appearances can be deceiving: "Yet absurdity is really just an event out of context, like a beached whale" (1). (One might state that female writing within the male dominant literary canon is an event out of context.) Note how the metaphor which she employs takes creation's largest animal, which also happens to exist in the fluidity of nature, and immobilizes it on the edge of land, the beach, that frontier strip where the two poles of land and water meet, overlap and intermingle, water being sucked into solidity and land being rendered fluid. This simple metaphor is typical of Arden/Ortiz Taylor's strategy. On the one hand it is surprising, effectively distracting the eye from the subject in question by introducing another image designed to make the reader question the new element's relation on the topic. This suspends judgment, extends the argument, and engages the reader in the narrator's game. On the other hand, as an image it significantly transects what could be read as a dividing line—the edge separating land and water, a metaphor for all dividing lines in bipolar logic—and creates a space of interaction, the beach, a constantly shifting space, redefined by the movement of the apparently opposed elements. This space is opened beneath and around the whale, a mammal—by all rights a land animal—who nevertheless inhabits and rules the world of fish.

Thus, Arden has arrived at a sort of oxymoronic symbol of what she depicts as the central proof of her condition. But her reasoning and purpose are quite different from her ex-husband's. Where as Malthus moves from the oxymoron to the need to maintain the established polarity of logic by respecting the separating line between elements, Arden insists on the possibility of varying and even contradictory interpretations of any event, of the joy of interpenetrating fields, of intersecting lines and dialoguing spaces. To the essentialistic tradition of a priori categories of meaning posited by Malthus, Arden counters with a phenomenological existentialism. Apparently Arden, and with her Ortiz Taylor, offers here feminist fluidity, multiplicity, and anarchy as a alternative to male stasis, duality, and order. And by introducing this alternative, not as a response to her ex-husband's position, but as a contextualizing preface, Arden relativizes her text, undercutting it before it can assume the place of first principle in the argument. She, in effect, pro-logues the societal logo-centric prejudice which Malthus has formulated into an accusation.

The opening strategy, therefore, is aimed at preempting the right to set the terms of the debate and the rules of the court by drawing the line, or possible lines, of "fault" in order to refocus attention in such a fashion that the judge will not limit his or her vision only to the obsessive point of apparently common-sense logic of mainstream, patriarchal society. The line Arden draws is far from straight—no pun intended—drifting as it does from one point to another in a seemingly chaotic manner. Thus, just as she does with the whale image, Arden suspends judgment by extending the panorama to be considered into an interesting game of intertwined lines of thought and imagery; that is, she forces cross-stitched slashes of interaction over the straight-edged line dividing the polarized zones of a yes/no verdict. Like the jagged trace of a faultline in the earth, Arden's discourse insists on the multiplicity of points and their interconnectedness, even more, their interdependence. After her presentation, it should be impossible, or at least difficult, to reduce the question of fault to the simplistic terms of strictly binary and mutually exclusive oppositions.[2]

The ex-husband would have the reader act as a subject viewing facts as objects within a confined field of action within which elements can be isolated out of context and artificially set in clean opposition. That is, subjectivity is assumed to be a given within a symbolic order, yet outside, and thus free, of the action itself. That Arden differs in orientation is obvious. Actually, from reading the first two chapters the reader could draw the conclusion that the "crime" to be judged—the object being investigated—is itself in question: is it the matter of three hundred rabbits, or Arden's lesbianism? If we delve just beyond, taking another turn in the web of allusions, the two are linked: Arden addresses her lesbianism obliquely, having first attired it—recontextualized it—in the mythical garb of Diana, the goddess of nature, the huntress and ruler of the forest. It is this web of allusions that link all terms into a interlocking relationship that undermines the attempt to separate them into oppositional systems: poetic allusions subvert prosaic logic, and Arden repeats many times that she is a poet.

Taking yet another step into Ortiz Taylor's verbal space we discover that she proposes that action happens within the subject, because the real action is semiotic, in this case reading and judging.

That significance of action—which in a text is the signifying process as realized by the reader—is clearly dependent on how the subject relates and responds to the action. Furthermore, as Arden learns from her novelist aunt, readers are like Michael Raven, the detective sent to track Arden and her Aunt Vi when they travel to Mexico. Readers pursue with only a partial knowledge of what they seek, informed or ill informed by the instigators of the search, here the accuser and plaintiff. However, readers will become actors if they can be strung along long enough and allowed to participate in the story. When Aunt Vi is asked if she is planning to elude Raven, she responds in the negative and then explains: "The question is, What is he after me for? I doubt Michael knows that as well as I do. . . . My dear, losing Mr. Raven in the desert would be child's play. . . . That is not my plan. I regard Mr. Raven as a member of my party. That's why we've been waiting for him. Naturally" (63). Readers can be seduced into becoming the subject-object-of-action if judgment can be postponed, suspended long enough to divert attention away from the abstract logic of prejudgment and on to the complex phenomenology of real, material existence and playful interaction.

Subjectivity itself breaks down, identity becoming a fluid matter open to redefinition. Mr. Raven, among many others, illustrates the point by finally joining Aunt Vi's group, going from detective to fellow traveler, a change in identity followed by the more profound change into the lover of the young man who helped Aunt Vi escape from the rest home into which her husband had had her committed. Aunt Vi had already practiced the same transformation on the young man, changing him from a rest home orderly into the magician he wanted to be. Arden, of course, is the ultimate proof, becoming a writer under the influence of Aunt Vi's repeated presentations of her as a poet, and finally by leaving her niece an unfinished manuscript which Arden then completes and has published.

In the diachronic order of reading, however, the first identity in question is the crime, closely linked, naturally, to the identity of the accused and culprit, identities disputed by Arden and her husband. While self-identity may seem to be a personal choice Arden and Malthus can make freely as the ultimate authority of her and his individual sphere of existence, this is an illusion. As the epigram to Adrienne Rich's *Diving into the Wreck* states, "there is no private life which is not determined by a wider public life" (2). That between the two of them the interpretations of their respective identity is a matter of debate supports Rich's position. In the context of the novel, their social identity is synonymous with textual identity, which is a matter of convincing representation in a field of signification in which the reader/judge is vested with final authority. How the reader will judge is of vital significance to the characters.

If Malthus has his way, readers will judge from the perspective of establishing codes of conduct and meaning—that is, they will prejudge on the basis of prejudice. Arden, realizing this, must preempt that process, delaying and eventually derailing it. If she has her way, the system of identification itself will undergo a redefinition, which undermines the originally inscribed role of the reader, allowing her or him to abandoned the position of external "thinking person" and transform into one more fun seeker at the party which is the text. Aunt Vi teaches Arden that the traditional endings for novels—death or marriage—are unsatisfactory. For the novel she would prefer a party, not "one of those stiff affairs where debts are being paid, but a party of people who belong together, celebrating. A loud, tender party" (75). In Aunt Vi's aesthetic, which here takes the form of feminine wisdom being passed down across generations from the dying Sophia to the young apprentice high priestess, the ultimate goal of the reading is the pleasurable participation in a joyful gathering of many fellow travelers, a gathering of a true society bound by common interest. Obviously, this smacks of chaos to the guardians of the static order as represented in Malthus and the implied canon of the traditional novel. Aunt Vi and Kristeva seem to agree: the female novelist must say no, that's not it, and suspend judgment through and in anarchic playfulness.

If Ortiz Taylor's argument would remain at this point, however, we could well apply to her the perceptive criticism that Elizabeth L. Berg has made of Kristeva's position.

> It is not sufficient to say that woman, like libidinal drives, has always been disruptive of the symbolic order (as Kristeva does, for example); this disorder is precisely what has always been necessary to the constitution of order itself. In claiming value for the devalued term of an opposition, one still allows the opposition to remain in place and to perpetuate the same order of relations. (Berg 1982, 19)

Fortunately Ortiz Taylor moves beyond this simple opposition of terms to something closer to Sarah Kofman's third woman position.

> Kofman's third woman effects the displacement of the opposition and breaks the bondage that holds woman in an inferior position. The third woman, as both masculine and feminine, is no longer the incarnation of truth, but neither is she the representative of falsehood or deception. In. . . refusing castration—she has moved beyond the economy of truth to affirm, simultaneously or in turn, both her masculinity and her femininity. This third instance beyond the alternative of masculine or feminine is not a synthesis of masculinity and femininity. It is not that there is no sexual difference for the affirmative woman; rather sexual difference is seen as undecidable, producing an unresolvable oscillation between masculine and feminine. . . . What she. . . refuses is perhaps, in the end, the resolution of the paradox of bisexuality. (Berg 1982, 19)

Kofman and Ortiz Taylor share this third-womanist position, or, we could say, an oxymoronic view of sexuality, understanding the term through an ironic displacement of it to an affirmative dynamic similar to Derrida's supplementary reading. As Barbara Johnson explains in her introduction to *Dissemination*, "The logic of the supplement wrenches apart the neatness of metaphysical binary oppositions. Instead of 'A is opposed to B' we have 'B is both added to A and replaces A.' A and B are no longer opposed, nor are they equivalent. Indeed, they are no longer even equivalent to themselves. . . . Rather, the very notion of their 'identities' is put in question" (xiii).

Ortiz Taylor continually dialogues with the societal intertext—present in language and readers—to force this supplemental juxtapositioning of the feminine and masculine. Many instances are subtle, as in making of the strongest male in *Faultline* not only a homosexual but the live-in baby sitter. The male detective in *Faultline*, incarnating all the stereotypical machismo that the U.S. detective novel traditionally has infused into the figure, becomes an active member in Aunt Vi's game of self-creation by coming out of the closet and declaring his love for the male orderly who helped the aunt escape from the hospital. Arden herself is at once so beautiful that men fall in love with her, and so good with tools that she can play the role of the proverbial handyman mechanic.

In a sort of parody of Robert Pirsig's popular cult classic *Zen and the Art of Motorcycle Maintenance* (despite the promising allusion to a philosophy of yin/yang gender harmony, yet another male on the road, rite of passage narrative), Arden executes a feminization of that arch male symbol, the motorcycle.

> Those of you who tend to be quiet and thoughtful I would like to leave right here for the time being, following my aunt's gaze into the patch of grass springing through strewn motorcycle parts.
>
> The rest can come with me. You are upset about the motorcycle. Or maybe motorcycles in general upset you, and the thought of a woman on a motorcycle, especially when she is not a mannequin passenger, drives you wild. Step to the rear of the bike, please.
>
> Well, part of your problem is that you are thinking about men on motorcycles. You are thinking of arrogant noise and sideways leers through tinted face shields. You are thinking of sprawling legs and phallic innuendo. [To this point we have the articulation of the societal sign system. What follows is feminist rearticulation.]
>
> Motorcycles do not need to be noisy. They can hum. The hum means they are well cared for and do not require your attention. And the rider does not require your attention. The rider's attention is elsewhere.
>
> The rider is watching for wild flowers. She is feeling the ripple of asphalt, feeling for the bank of a curve, listening for the bird call or the thunk of a manhole cover. She is with things, as things. She is reaching, at odd moments, for what they stand for. Between her and the wind there is nothing but her own calm mind. (66)

It should be lost on no one that the fragmented motorcycle is a metaphor of the fragmented narrative. What is to be reconstructed is to some extent limited and determined by the parts available, but how it will be used—read—is a matter of interpretation, so the narrator is also working yet another metaphor of lesbianism and motherhood. If it is to be the offensive male chauvinistic image or the harmonious third-womanist combination of male/female can only be resolved in the reading by how well readers learn the text's lessons.

The ultimate image of "male/female" flux is achieved, as we might expect, in the lesbian couple as described by Alice, Arden's lover:

> Arden and I had been living together a year but I never stopped feel-

> ing warmed by the easy way we moved from being the supported to the supporter and back again. That was the joy of it. Nobody got locked into limited, tedious, unchanging expressions of self. I held her now as if she floated in still water, my hand under her back. (111)

Just like the image of the whale, or the example of the rambling narrative of chapter one discussed above, this image of the lovers belies the possibility of a straight line of definition, preferring to allow the two zones to intermingle in a self-creative dialogue, to float and reshape themselves according to needs and desires, yet linked by a love that is apparently as out of place in society as a whale on a beach.

The lesbian bed and the novel are synonymous spaces of flux and transformation, although decidedly linked to the female pole in traditional terms. Texts themselves are questioned in the novel. *Faultline* is a series of texts, some of which are written and signed as official documents or diary entries. One letter (chap. 17), by a professor of geology, recommends the combination of myth and science as a truer version of natural phenomenon. The latter is also utilized to explain faultlines as natural reminders of the continual process of creation, which denies static definitions of a world order. This geologist's text directly dialogues with and refutes Malthus's pseudoscientific argument. That all of these texts are transformed into a narrative is the virtue of the novelistic space in its dialogical dimension. The monological, monogeneric text and traditional patriarchy are synonymous; to subvert one is to attack the other. So when the novel/bed is transformed into the space in which definitions—especially generic ones, both literary and sexual—can remain fluid, the monologic patriarchy is subverted.

To some who might protest that Ortiz Taylor is not conscious of this third-womanist position, I offer the proof of the title. In *Faultline* Ortiz Taylor, through Arden, says "we choose our own metaphors, not the other way around" (1). As the primary generative image, the title *Faultline* sets the action in a geological in-between zone of dynamic tension and inevitable movement. Two apparently opposing systems touch at the line which marks their separation and union, similar to the example of the oxymoron. And we come to understand that life should be lived in that ever shifting zone, the most fertile and natural of all spaces, never static nor stable because it is always in the process of transformation, rearticulating its intra and inter relationships. Moreover, what is posited is a new recognition that identity is not either/or, but the process itself which binds elements in constant flux. Life is that signifying process.

Sheila Ortiz Taylor offers for our consideration a utopian proposition. Her novel, on all levels, joyfully spurns social norms, and at once invites us to look at facts in a different way. If one allows this alternative a chance to function, by giving it credence, at least as a viable fiction, then the space for its existence is established, simultaneously outside and inside the space of literature. This is the condition of utopias: they exist as fictions, yet they consistently set themselves off from the other genres, just as the societies and worlds they describe are set off from the normal society and world which readers inhabit. Utopias are fragile creations. Brought into existence by an act of the will that insists on naming reality as something other than it is—the lesson learned by Arden from her aunt, who demonstrates her skill at poetic transformation several times—Arden's utopia exists in constant danger of being exploded by outsiders who refuse to participate in the game. Ortiz Taylor knows that average readers are just such outsiders, so she strategically engages them in an obtuse fashion, dangling fascinating but ambiguous tidbits of information in front of them which she then moves out of reach before they can decipher their meaning and make them their own, seducing them, slowly drawing them into her web, into a labyrinth, into a world apart, where rules can change, because identities themselves are variable. The actual discomfort experienced by some readers upon entering a "lesbian book"—some of my students, for example, have voiced their opposition—can be related to the fear of entering, not just the unknown, but something akin to a web or a labyrinth, a space with its own intricate system of passages, one that has been traditionally burdened with negative connotations. Yet if one trusts in the mythological thread if Ariadne (for which Arden is ciphered anagram), safe voyage is assured and eventual pleasure guaranteed. And when seen from afar, with all their carefully contrived lines of intercommunication, labyrinths and webs reveal themselves to be fascinating works of art—quite similar to illustrations for treatises on utopia. It should be unnecessary, but perhaps useful for some, to mention that labyrinths and webs are traditionally female symbols. *Faultline* is that utopian space, one marked with the sign of the third woman.

Space does not permit me to elaborate fully on the relationship between Ortiz Taylor's work and Chicano cultural production.[3] To me what Ortiz Taylor does and says in her literature is what Chicano literature has done in some of its best moments, and the desire to create a utopian space apart from the prejudiced society that surrounds us is nothing new to Chicanos—it is called Aztlán. However, we must admit that perhaps more often than not, Chicano authors have maintained the traditional binary system of dichotomous polarity in their imaginary societies and the texts in which they are postulated. Certainly within Chicano cultural production there exists still the same chauvinism that Ortiz Taylor attributes to traditional patriarchal society, and thus the bipolar system of oppositions prevails. As I have pointed out elsewhere (1985), two leading Chicana poets, Bernice Zamora and Lorna Dee Cervantes, open their respective books by displaying patriarchal rituals in which women are excluded and victimized. Their texts then assume the form of response and alternative proposition to the patriarchal order; thus they are the negative response similar to Kristeva's position. Both strive for self-determined equilibrium, Zamora apparently opting for androgyny, while Cervantes moves closer to traditional heterosexuality within marriage. Yet the structure of their texts privileges the male origin of traditional signification. Ortiz Taylor, recognizing the unavoidable circumstances of traditional patriarchal dominance, chooses, however, to shift into the third woman strategy, avoiding the bipolarity of response and re-action.

The struggle to achieve an alternative self-image in the face of a dominant sign system which attributes negative polarity to the writer's group is another point shared by Ortiz Taylor and much of Chicano writing, as are the deconstructive strategies. Yet the alternative of a fluidly dynamic, in-between state, neither this nor that, but the on-going process of relating possibilities without having to accept predefinitions nor any definitive identity is not shared by all Chicanos. A brief example can serve us well here. As I have explained in numerous essays, Chicano literature displays a penchant for creating traditionally ordered spaces of centralized orientation, quite similar to the process of sacred cosmicization studies by Mircea Eliade. The desire is to recuperate the cultural or ethnic *axis mundi* from which the circle of the group's space can be accurately compassed. This manner of viewing social structure is so ingrained that it seems a given. So when in chapter one Ortiz Taylor addresses it by making it the context of her first meeting with Malthus, the representative of traditional order and her eventual accuser, the deconstructive process may be missed.

Arden recalls visiting Griffith Park Planetarium in Los Angeles and sitting "watching the giant pendulum below swinging back and forth, knocking down wooden pins for upwards of an hour without troubling myself or anybody for else for an explanation" (3). Having accepted the faultline as her essential metaphor, Arden seems untroubled by the display of instability and potential destructiveness that underlies the apparent stability of "normal" perception. She needs no explanation. However, she adds that she had just graduated from the University, thus having been thrown into a state of disorientation. This can be taken as a classic threat of chaos which so often sets up the Chicano response (Bruce-Novoa 1975). Malthus steps in to offer order and assurance. His "forty-minute" lecture places the phenomenon of the pendulum in a rhetorical perspective, a manageable cosmos of static principles based on his work as a graduate student in city planning. The passage is revealing.

> He was fascinated, he said, that nature should be so orderly while society was so sloppy. He thought society might be tidied up a bit, and that if you had ample parking, convenience markets, community centers, and nightly bingo, crime and suicide might will disappear. If the earth had an axis then so might society. And if it didn't, then you could always build it one out of high-impact plastic. (5)

The irony is that Malthus so misreads the phenomenon of the pendulum which generated the meeting and his lecture. Arden was observing the proof of the ever shifting world axis that in effect topples the human illusion of centeredness and corresponding definitive periphery. Malthus counters by making a fixed point outside the field of play, himself, the apparent stable center of definition. This he would also practice on society, thus forcing a fixedness unnatural and eventually untenable. To hold the earth's natural movement would produce pressure and eventually slippage along the lines of resistance—and we discover the underlying web of allusions and associations that the apparent anarchism of playful narration, Malthus's stand, makes it inevitable that somewhere down the line the fault line will burst, shifting relationships and redistributing the elements in the field into a new order. When Arden finally breaks with Malthus's order, it is just such an event that throws her and her lover together, but more significantly it throws her back into her original state of recognizing that the underlying process of nature is its fluid state of change.

This deconstruction of the myth of *axis mundi* stability, the revelation that all claims of fixed centeredness are actually rhetorical discourses of territorialization, undermines a whole series of centralizing projects, from nationalism to tribalism to ethnicity, and in passing much of what Chicano literature has postulated as an alternative to U.S. social order. Yet it is a healthy sign that from within the ranks of Chicano authors this challenge can arise, because it bespeaks the possibility of realizing what some of us have called for all along: the non-defined state of process which allows for continuing exploration of identity as something to be created not inherited (Bruce-Novoa 1975).

We have much to learn from Ortiz Taylor, but we also have much to be thankful for, because from one of our own we will learn that through her, as well as others of our sisters, Chicanos already participate in the nurturing of a reconstructed image of ourselves, more liberated and liberating than that which existed just a decade ago. Ortiz Taylor's version of Utopia seems much more appealing than the limiting nationalistic ones created by many Chicanos in their literature.

## Notes

1. Ortiz Taylor made her ethnic background clear in the novel's introduction: "The family I knew in Los Angeles was my mother's family, thirteen children presided over by my Mexican-American grandmother, who made flour tortillas so thin you could read a book through them" (ix).

2. This image of cross stitching over binary opposites recalls Hayden White's (1978, 4) description of discourse itself. "A discourse moves 'to and from' between received encodations of experience and the clutter of phenomena which refuses incorporation into conventionalized notions of 'reality,' 'truth,' or 'possibility.' It moves 'back and forth' (like a shuttle?) between alternative ways of encoding this reality, some of which may be provided by the traditions of discourse prevailing in a given domain of in-

quiry and others of which may be idiolects of the author, the authority of which he is seeking to establish." Stitching and weaving, of course, are often conceived of as women's activities.

3. I will address the question of *Faultline*'s Chicano specificity in another article.

# Beyond the Anti-Aesthetic: Reading Gloria Anzaldúa's *Borderlands* and Maxine Hong Kingston's *The Woman Warrior*

*Alvina E. Quintana*

> The Asian American woman's voice dissolves binary opposition of ethnicity and gender, American and Asian American, male and female, "I" and "not-I," eluding the fraudulent objectivity and totalizing grids misreaders male and female, Asian and non-Asian, attempt to place over it. Located at the intersection of race and gender, Asian American women's writings insist on identity and difference in multiple layers of selfhood and community.

In the above passage Elaine Kim describes an unfinalizable characteristic that is also apparent in Chicana literary production. This quality is not formed in a vacuum but rather emerges as a direct response to the position women "writers of color" occupy at the "intersection of race and gender." I am fascinated by the strategic possibilities this converging terrain provides Chicana and Asian American women writers and would like to focus this essay on exploring the ways in which these writers, motivated by their marginal subject position, use their literary endeavors to resist dominant and minority systems of representation. More specifically I want to reflect on the autobiographic works of Maxine Hong Kingston and Gloria Anzaldúa considering the challenges their texts advance to a politics of domination that seeks to render them nameless and voiceless.

Blending creative writing with autobiography, both of these authors take their readers on historic and mythic journeys which ultimately provide a firsthand look at Chicana and Asian American female realties. Kingston's is a voice that struggles to name the unspeakable as she compares life in China to life in America; likewise Anzaldúa writes about life on the borders of American and Mexican cultures. Astutely both writers speak of their need to overcome a tradition of silence. When we consider the narrative strategies they employ, blurring fact with fantasy, as they attempt to sort out "what is real" from what is illusory, it becomes apparent that Kingston and Anzaldúa are involved in complex intellectual projects that not only problematize conventional literary form but also challenge a politics of female domination that is perpetuated by so called "traditional" interpretations of culture and history. Although speaking specifically about Chicano history Rosaura Sánchez has outlined the difficulty women of color face in the United States, maintaining that Chicanas find themselves "interpellated by a series of different, competing and overlapping ideologies, including class and non-class ideologies" (Sánchez 1990b, 5). This subject position, marked by its overlapping systems of control has motivated many women of color to write. Anzaldúa and Kingston have produced texts that problematize dominant modes of representation, as they confront Asian American male and Chicano (male) writers, who have up until quite recently dominated "minority" discursive practices. Both writers respond to "tradition" by developing heteroglossic responses that are reminiscent of Fredric Jameson's notion of pastiche (114).

Drawing upon the practices of anthropology, history, and women's studies, the Anzaldúa, Kingston dialogues articulate an alternative perspective. As these cultural descriptions unfold we are made aware of our preconceived notions and quickly realize that much of what is commonly referred to as tradition, in reality can be attributed *not* to Chinese or Chicano heritage, but simply to externally imposed stereotypes. The implications are vast when we consider how so-called "traditions" are often based on categorization(s) that are created to facilitate understanding for someone who is unfamiliar with the culture in question. The Anzaldúa, Kingston projects seek to deconstruct stereotypic representations and as a consequence make us aware of the contradiction that comes into play whenever an "insider" attempts to define herself or her culture by applying an "outsider's" notions of convention.

*Woman Warrior* and *Borderlands* challenge essentialist notions of identity. Through their subject position as insider within a "minority" culture both writers are able to point to difference as they give voice to the silent, and as a result help dissipate the belief that

Chicanos and Asian Americans constitute a homogeneous or strangely predictable community. With their emphasis on difference Anzaldúa and Kingston help emphasize what in poststructuralist terms has been called "the death of the subject." Elaine Kim suggests that one of the most critical contradictions facing the Chinese American woman in *The Woman Warrior* (and I would add the Chicana in *Borderlands*) is the relationship between her perceptions of her heritage and American realities. "This contradiction is explored primarily through the question of the women's status and role in both only obliquely understood societies" (Kim, 201). Because Anzaldúa and Kingston seek to create a new space of inquiry for coming to terms with "old" and "new world" traditions, they seem quite naturally drawn into literary experimentation. In "No Name Woman" Kingston subtly raises questions regarding the reliability of traditional history as she challenges common perceptions of objectivity.

> Chinese-Americans, when you try to understand what things in you are Chinese, how do you separate what is peculiar to childhood, to poverty, insanities, one family, your mother who marked your growing with stories, from what is Chinese? What is Chinese tradition and what is the movies? (5)

Similarly Anzaldúa, when confronted with the same new/old tradition dichotomy, focuses her attention on the social construction of culture:

> Culture forms our beliefs. We perceive the version of reality that it communicates. Dominant paradigms, predefined concepts that exist as unquestionable, unchallengeable, are transmitted to us through the culture. Culture is made by those in power—men. Males make the rules and laws: women transmit them. (16)

Both texts can be characterized by their self-reflexive tendencies. These writers effectively undermine our expectations of form. When they juxtapose myth with reality, we are forced to reconsider what constitutes an autobiography, to ask ourselves whether or not "talk stories" or "cuentos" are acceptable in this regard. One response to such questions could ostensibly come from cultural critics, who motivated by an interest in aesthetic form might be tempted to explain the Anzaldúa and Kingston projects by simply cataloging them as postmodern texts. I find this tendency to focus primarily on general classifications a bit dangerous because, more often than not, the categorization accentuates a superficial reading that diverts attention, depoliticizes or disregards any internal critique(s).

Hal Foster's meditations on postmodernism, for example, have led him to develop his concept of the anti-aesthetic. For him the "anti-aesthetic signals that the very notion of the aesthetic, its network of ideas, is in question." He argues that postmodernism (like the 'anti-aesthetic') marks a cultural position on the present, which questions whether or not categories afforded by the aesthetic are still valid. The anti-aesthetic also signals a practice, "cross-disciplinary in nature, that is sensitive to cultural forms engaged in a politic or rooted in a vernacular—that is to forms that deny the idea of a privileged aesthetic realm" (xv). What Foster describes in simple terms is a form which allows for diversity and difference by creating the space for articulating minority viewpoints. Because of the nature of their writings we understand that Anzaldúa and Kingston wish to deconstruct the idea of a privileged aesthetic and that their autobiographic texts thus fall well within Foster's rubric of the "anti-aesthetic."

The semi-autobiographical mode of writing Anzaldúa and Kingston employ makes it evident that they are challenging conventional perceptions of genre. It does not take long for students, who are confronted with either text, to state that "this is not autobiography—this is fiction" or to dismiss these works as radical misrepresentations of autobiography because they blur oral history with history, myth with reality, poetry with prose, and in Anzaldúa's case Spanish with English. (One of my students even told me that she felt "personally" betrayed by Anzaldúa and Kingston.) By experimenting with content and form, both authors inscribe a new culture (Anzaldúa's *una cultura mestiza*) as they confront dominant modes of perception. Consider for example how both authors use their narratives as an opportunity to play with language. Kingston's innovative use of the term "ghost" and Anzaldúa's use of the word "border" are important in this regard.

In the opening pages of *Borderlands*, we are moved from the familiar and the literal (the U.S.-Mexican border) onto the figurative:

> The U.S.-Mexican border *es una herida abierta* where the Third World grates against the first and bleeds. And before a scab forms it hemorrhages again, the lifeblood of two worlds merging to form a third country—a border culture. Borders are set up to define the places that are safe and unsafe, to distinguish us from them. (3)

Anzaldúa begins by focusing her attention on the line that divides the United States from Mexico, yet on another, more symbolic level she alludes to the politics of space, mapping out the terrain created by power relations. The border is represented as a wound that bleeds and hemorrhages—"the lifeblood of two worlds merging to form a third country." In visual terms Anzaldúa describes the unstable ground between cultures to which Kingston refers. Both authors illustrate how the lifeblood of two distinct cultures merge to form a third culture, a hybrid culture. And thus we comprehend Anzaldúa's meaning when she states:

> The actual physical borderland that I'm dealing with in this book is the Texas-U.S. Southwest/Mexican border. The psychological borderlands and the spiritual borderlands are not particular to the southwest. In fact, the Borderlands are physically present whenever two or more cultures edge each other, where people of different races occupy the same territory, where under, lower, middle and upper classes touch, where the space between two individuals shrinks with intimacy. (preface)

Kingston, like Anzaldúa alludes to the dividing lines created by "old" and "new world" perceptions of reality. It is in this context that her use of ghosts, shadowy figures which appear on the margins of both worlds, becomes so illuminating. Contrary to popular belief the ghosts in *Woman Warrior* do not merely refer to Anglo-Americans. The ghosts in Kingston's subtitle "are not simply white people but 'shadowy figures from the past' or unanswered questions about unexplained actions of Chinese, whites, and Chinese in America." (Kim, 200) By returning to Anzaldúa's concept of border we understand how those who attempt to cross over borders and go through the confines of what is perceived to be "normal"—a word that is also used to signify the "traditional"—could easily be characterized as "ghosts," as haunting souls. What becomes apparent when we consider *Borderlands* and *The Woman Warrior* as experimental, minority texts is that, yes—they are emblematic of a kind of resistance literature which challenges the idea of a privileged aesthetic realm, and that, yes—"the anti-aesthetic" as defined by Foster is useful for initiating a dialogue concerning the limitations that are created by what we view as "classical form." But it would be truly unfortunate if we limited our present analysis to a dialogue which concerned itself exclusively with aesthetic and counter-aesthetic practices. Unfortunate because with this narrow discussion we would undoubtedly run the risk of missing the critique these authors make of their respective "minority cultures." It is important that we remind ourselves here that Anzaldúa and Kingston are not only resisting the politics of traditional literary theory but the politics of cultural nationalism as well, and that these are complex texts that challenge "the margins" as well as "the center."

At this point we realize that Foster's notion of the anti-aesthetic, though useful in structuralist terms, has set us up for a trap that only recognizes minority cultural production in oppositional terms. Paula Gunn Allen has argued that this kind of binary thinking represents not only a patriarchal influence but a Western one as well. Obviously these limitations are especially problematic when considering cultural productions that are influenced by Eastern or matriarchal traditions. In a passage which could effectively be used to describe Kingston's text, Anzaldúa states:

> My "stories" are acts encapsulated in time, "enacted" every time they are spoken aloud or read silently. I like to think of them as performances and not as inert and "dead" objects (as the aesthetics of Western culture think of art works). Instead the work has identity; it is a "who" or a "what" and contains the presences of persons, that is incarnations of gods or ancestors of natural and cosmic powers. The work manifests the same needs as a person, it needs to be "fed," *la tengo que bañar y vestir*. (67)

Anzaldúa suggests that she (and Kingston by my implication) is engaged in a project which attempts to rewrite culture by creating a literary space that will facilitate a discussion concerning matriarchal and oral influences. Because it is evident that both of our writers wish to clear and reinscribe their cultural slates, we must appraise the value of employing patriarchal or Western modes of perception to analyze their literary endeavors. In broader terms, we must question whether it is possible to evaluate oppositional aesthetic practices with "standard" methods of interpretation?

In *Feminist Aesthetics*, Silvia Bovenschen surpasses Foster's analysis. Ironically it is due to her interest in defining women's art that she is able to point to the limitations of Foster's anti-aesthetic. No doubt her experiences as a feminist philosopher make her suspicious of aesthetic practices that serve to universalize a male perspective. Therefore, rather than merely building on a discussion based on Hegelian principles, she questions whether or not it is possible for women to create an aesthetic that can be described as truly female, because in her words:

> Art has been primarily produced by men. Men have neatly separated and dominated the public sector that controls it, and men have defined the normative standards for evaluation. Moreover, in so far as the came into contact with this sector at all, women have for the most part acquiesced to its valued-system. (30)

She suggests that because women's art is always placed in opposition to traditional "male" aesthetic practices it can, in reality, only be seen as a response based on rejection or better yet reaction to that which has been deemed legitimate. Thus we have categories such as Art with a capital "A" and women's art, literature with a capital "L" and women's literature, Autobiography with a capital "A" and women's autobiography.[1] Because of this oppositional placement, women's cultural production is seldom seen as autonomous or original. Bovenschen presents a provocative position that begins to chip away at the core of our understanding of art. Raising questions that challenge Western notions, she inadvertently underscores important issues which are relevant to the Kingston/Anzaldúa autobiographies because of the dual challenge their texts convey. It is however important to note here, that although Bovenschen's critique is useful for outlining the predicament "women of color" face, it is an analysis that is at the same time limited because of its exclusive focus on gender oppression. We must then continue our analysis by keeping in mind where the interests of Bovenschen, Anzaldúa and Kingston intersect as well as the point at which they separate. The key then, with this type of inquiry involves the consideration of similarities as well as differences. Consequently we realize how on one level all three writers are involved in similar discursive projects that subvert the power relations brought forth by a privileged aesthetic domain and a privileged "gender-specific" interpretation of culture. Even though on another level the Anzaldúa and Kingston projects explore forms of exploitation and oppression that go beyond the boundaries of gender, there is no denying that each writer, in very real ways, undermines Foster's "anti-aesthetic" as each writes in order to dismantle the very foundations on which his postmodernist rubric is built.

If we consider *Borderlands* and *The Women Warrior* (or Bovenschen's text for that matter) exclusively in Foster's terms, we run the risk of missing the internal critique that each writer makes of her respective culture. Because the cultural nationalist movements of the sixties were responsible for muting the voices of women of color, Anzaldúa and Kingston have virtually been thrust into the position of challenging the politics of the movement in order to establish a literary space that allows for gender difference. It is ironic that both of these writers are compelled to confront the same issues of silencing that their male counterparts addressed in the 1960s (the same with the exception of one minor difference which can be attributed to gender). Consider for example this excerpt from the introduction by Frank Chin and Jeff Chan to *Aiiieeee*:

> There is racist hate and racist love. That is, if the system works, the stereotypes assigned to the various races are accepted by the races themselves as reality, as fact, and racist love reigns. . . One measure of the success of white racism is the silence of the minority race and the amount of white energy necessary to maintain or increase that silence . . .

Kingston, writing in the 1970s, opens *The Woman Warrior* by illustrating how silencing against women has been used as a strategy of ideological containment.

> "You must not tell anyone," My mother said. "What I am about to tell you. In China your father had a sister who killed herself. She jumped into the family well. We say that your father has all brothers because it is as if she had never been born." (3)

"No Name Woman" initiates a theme that centers around silence and passivity, a theme that reappears throughout *Woman Warrior*. In "White Tigers" Kingston reveals how the ideology of female silence is maintained stating that "When we Chinese girls listened to the adults talk story we learned that we failed if we grew up to be but wives or slaves." Focusing on ethnic secrets and silence in a new way, Kingston, in fact, rewrites the *Aiiieeee* introduction to emphasize issues of gender oppression. She moves the emphasis from a simple discussion of racism to a more complex articulation of race and gender. We are thus able to expand the *Aiiieeee* quote so that we understand how one measure of the success of male sexism is the silence of the minority gender and the amount of male energy necessary to maintain or increase that silence. Interestingly, Kingston establishes what we might refer to as "sexist hate" and "sexist love." The kind of sexist hate and sexist love that becomes apparent when we survey some of the critiques of her work. Some of Kingston's critics allege that her "primary concern is the marketplace," that *Woman Warrior* "represents her attempt to 'cash in' on a 'feminist fad.' " One well known Asian-American critic accuses Kingston of "selling out. . . her own people" by addressing herself to a predominantly white readership and gift-boxing old clichés about China and Chinese Americans, thereby obscuring the fact that Chinese Americans are not exotic foreigners but have deep roots in American life. Her work is classified as "white-pleasing autobiography passing for pop cultural anthropology" (Kim, 198).

This kind of criticism almost seems paradoxical. Clearly Kingston's intention is to illustrate that Asian Americans comprise a group influenced by not one, but at least two cultural systems. And by doing so, she—like her male critics—stresses that Chinese Americans are not exotic foreigners. Kingston is not speaking to predominantly white readership, a point that is illustrated by the cross-cultural nature of this study.[2] The Asian American criticism that I have alluded to crudely evokes the notion of Tradition yet on a more subtle level it points to another matter. It seems to me that what Kingston is reprimanded for being a gossip, for talking back. Gloria Anzaldúa's thoughts can be modified to illustrate how the aforementioned Kingston admonishments manifest from silencing practices that are based on patriarchal traditions:

> *En boca cerrada no entran moscas.* 'Flies don't enter a closed mouth' is a saying I kept hearing when I was a child. *Ser habladora* was to be a gossip and a liar, to talk to much. *Muchachitas bien criadas*, well-bred girls don't answer back. *Es una falta de respeto* to talk back to one's mother or

> father. . . *Hocicona, repelona, chismosa,* having a big mouth, questioning, carrying tales are all signs of being *mal criada.* In my culture they are all words that are derogatory if applied to women—I've never heard them applied to men. (54)

Anzaldúa's quote sets the agenda "overcoming the tradition of silence" and brings us back to our original discussion concerning how minority literature should not be viewed solely as an expression of creative power but rather as a political gesture that challenges a politics of domination that would render these writers nameless and voiceless.

*The Woman Warrior* and *Borderlands* take on a multiplicity of concerns as they challenge dominant and minority systems of representation. By the nature of the issues they confront and the experiences they attempt to represent these are texts that exemplify Bakhtin's notion of heteroglossia.[3] Ultimately both writers advance a critique against binary thinking, challenging Western notions of tradition and minority discourse that fail to take into account difference.

When we consider *The Woman Warrior* and *Borderlands* as creative endeavors that go against the grain, we are in a better position to understand the principles of minority aesthetic practices and thereby become more keenly aware of the ideological context from which mainstream and "minority" American literature emerges. What becomes significant is not so much the fact that in the United States, mainstream and minority literary production share a common point of origin but rather that they express different points of view. Because Anzaldúa and Kingston are very effective in challenging our knowledge of what is at issue when the categories of minority and majority are constituted, I propose that we spend a few moments contemplating the presuppositions that are implicit in our labeling practices. When we speak of minority are we (in reality) merely alluding to race and ethnic distinctions or can we suggest that the classification also includes literature with a focus on categories of difference? Isn't it more accurate to say that "minority" refers to those groups that have through one social mechanism or another been marginalized or omitted?

Women writers of color occupy a "minority" social position that is, in Elaine Kim's terms, located at the intersection of race and gender. Because of their doubly marginalized position they are forced to "insist on identity and difference in multiple layers of selfhood and community." Gloria Anzaldúa's "To live in the Borderlands mean you" supports Kim's assertions because:

> In the Borderlands
> you are the battleground
> where enemies are kin to each other;
> you are at home, a stranger,
> the border disputes have been settled
> the volley of shots have shattered the true
> you are wounded, lost in action
> dead, fighting back;
> To live in the Borderlands mean
> the mill with the razor white teeth wants to shred off
> your olive-red skin, crush out the kernel, your heart
> pound you pinch you roll you out
> smelling like white bread but dead;
> To survive the Borderlands
> you must live sin fronteras
> be a crossroads. (195)

## Notes

1. It is interesting to note that women of color are beginning to further define or break down the concept of women's literature, by specifying difference. For an informative discussion on Black women's autobiography see Braxton.
2. In 1989 *The Village Voice* featured an essay by Michele Cliff which was entitled "Women Warriors: Black Writers Load the Canon."
3. Gary Saul Morson and Caryl Emerson describe heterglossia as Bakhtin's term for linguistic centrifugal forces that "register and respond to the most diverse events of daily life, to the prosaic facts that never quite fit any official or unofficial definition." See Morson and Emerson.

# Film

# Chicana Film Practices: Confronting the "Many-Headed Demon of Oppression"[1]

*Rosa Linda Fregoso*

> Your vision is valid, its expression is valid. Don't let your art be judged on their terms.
> —Frances Salomé España

## Introduction

The epigraph is taken from Frances Salomé España's essay, "Artist Testimony and Raza Survival Guide: A Chicana Obstacle Course For the Exile on Her Own Turf." It is point seven of a ten-point lesson she deems "enabled me and empowered me to make art and contend with the world on my own terms" (1990: 3). Written from the perspective of an artist nurtured in part by the Chicano Movement, España's powerful testimony is emblematic for the rebelde (rebellious) Chicana artist who, for years, has felt "exiled on her own turf." That "own turf" is the canon of Chicano cultural practices, dating to the cultural renaissance of the Chicano Power Movement of the 1960s (Fregoso and Chabram, 1990). Through her essay, España draws attention to the imposition of "politically correct" modes of Chicano art, formulas that constrain artistic creativity. She also speaks to surviving or transcending the inner, culturally specific politics of sexism and marginalization.

Like Chicana writers, the cultural practices of Chicana film and video practitioners serve a "metacritical function." Re-assessing the import of Chicana authors to the "canon" of literature, Ramón Saldívar correctly points out that their work "is counter-hegemonic to the second-power, serving as a critique of critiques of oppression that fail to take into account the full range of domination" (1990: 173). Moreover, Rosaura Sánchez notes that "what distinguishes Chicana writers is their relative invisibility," nonetheless, they have managed to create "aesthetically superior work" to that of their male counterparts (1985: 61-62). In a similar manner, I will argue that Chicana film practices represent the most innovative and resonant development in Chicano cinema, despite attempts to relegate their works to a secondary status.

The exclusion of Chicana filmmakers from events such as the Chicanos 90 ceremony hosted in Mexico by President Salinas de Gortari, their marginalization in film criticism like the Gary Keller anthology on Chicano cinema (1985), and their continual marginalization in festivals such as the film series in Chicano Art: Resistance and Affirmation,[2] is a complex issue related to many factors including, but not limited to, sexism. The CARA film series for example, included only three Chicana filmmakers in the program's initial draft whereas roughly thirty male-produced films were to be shown.

More importantly, the CARA film series exemplifies the way in which women are systematically excluded from participation by the reification of an artificial category, derived from arbitrary definitions about what constitutes "Chicano" cinema. For instance, implicit in the choice of films to be exhibited in the CARA series as "Resistance and Affirmation" is the contention that the historical agents of political struggle are mostly men. This narrow view of Chicano oppositional practices is representative of a particular social formation of critics and practitioners whose cultural politics are, from both a feminist and a theoretical standpoint, highly problematic. Not only do their politics ignore the contributions of women cultural workers, but they also exclude the works of certain men who are outside or peripheral to the "legitimate" Chicano political circuit, but whose films can also be categorized as "political" if measured by a different, less dogmatic, yardstick. Cheech Marin's film, *Born in East L.A.* (1987), which was not included in the CARA series, comes to mind.

An additional reason for the marginalization of women derives from the fact that Chicana production is exclusively concentrated in short films, and Chicanas have therefore not benefited from the recognition which accompanies the production of feature films. In a society where feature-length films signify mastery over cinematic practice and in which 35mm symbolizes power, the accumulation of "cultural capital" (Bourdieu 1984) becomes a self-generating process. In other words, making a Chicano 35mm feature film translates into a certain prestige which virtually guarantees greater critical and scholarly attention as well as film reviews in the mainstream media. In a phallocentric society, power is measured by *big-ness* (as in feature-length films), and *penetration* (as into the Hollywood industry). These are the crucial markers or signs of success, of "making-it," of *coming*. . . into fruition, that is. In this respect, there is little evidence among Chicana filmmakers of big-ness, penetration, or of coming into the mainstream, on dominant culture's terms.

Another factor for the omission of Chicanas from the "canon" of Chicano cinema can be attributed to the limited availability of public funds, but also to their exclusion from the "good-ol'-niño-network" of male filmmakers and critics that function as gatekeepers and power-brokers. However, it must be stated that among many Chicanas, their preference for short films and for the status of "independents" are self-conscious choices.[3] They derive from the concern among Chicana film and video practitioners with the artistic properties of cinema, that is to say, their greater commitment to the craft of cinema as an art-form.[4] Obviously, aesthetic innovations are more manageable in the shorter forms and more possible if one resists the temptation of entering Hollywood, for the latter usually forces filmmakers to adopt more conventional techniques and dominant values.

Due in large part to the rationing of public funds for the Arts, in order to make a living Chicana film practitioners often work for private and public media on commissioned pieces for advertising or educational programs. Yet, some of these same filmmakers also continue to experiment stylistically, producing non-commissioned works that are featured in film festivals or cultural centers. Others like Salomé España have chosen to remain entirely "independent."

An analysis of formal aesthetic innovation requires serious attention to the limitations inherent in film production for the Studios, commercial media, as well as in the works made on a commissioned basis for public television and educational agencies, since all of these institutions tend to impose conventional norms and styles, resulting in films which cater to predetermined "target" audiences. The focus of my article is on those films produced outside the domains of institutional media and thereby without the constraints inherent in commissioned pieces. For it is by examining the non-commissioned works by Chicana filmmakers that we can truly guage the outstanding nature of artistic creativity and innovation realized in Chicano cinema during the past two decades. In light of the unparalleled import of Chicanas to the corpus of Chicano cinema, I will highlight elements in their films that articulate both thematic and expressive differences, that is to say, the discursive innovations made by Chicana film practitioners in both content and form.

As a political gesture, I have chosen to discuss three films made by Chicanas during the height of Chicano movement cinema, the pre-Hollywood era (1969-1980). These films are *Chicana* (1979) by Sylvia Morales, *Despúes del Terremoto* (1979) by Lourdes Portillo and Nina Serrano, and *Agueda Martínez* (1977) by Esperanza Vásquez —films that warrant a long-deserved attention. For aside from token gestures of inclusion in film festivals, or paternalistic mention in anthologies of Chicano cinema, these three films have never received critical scholarly examination. I will end by pointing to recent trends in Chicana filmmaking evident in the work of a new generation of filmmakers. In this retrospective analysis that spans fifteen years I would like to pay tribute to Chicana counter-aesthetics.

I characterize Chicana cinematic discourse as markedly counter-aesthetic because Chicana filmmakers have had to counter two kinds of discourses: the dominant culture's which has distorted the Chicana subject; and the aesthetic discourse of Chicano males, which "render[s] them nameless and voiceless" (Quintana 1990: 262) and, in the case of film, imageless, namely as images, functioning cosmetically as backdrops for male history. Thus, Chicana filmmakers have had to counter, challange, and confront what Moraga and Anzaldúa call "the many-headed demon of oppression" (1983: 195).

The works I have chosen represent "woman" as the central subject of their narratives. We must however distinguish first of all between works that are feminist and those that are woman-centered narratives. Rosaura Sánchez notes that what distinguishes a feminist analysis in scholarly work is that its focus on "the condition and experience of women provide[s] a critical feminist account of gender inequality" (1990: 17). And while we sometimes unfairly burden creative works like a film with such a monumental project, both *Chicana* and *Después del Terremoto* are created in that spirit. Both films are illustrative of a Chicana femininist counter-aesthetics.

## The Feminist Re-vision

The first historical film on Chicanas, Sylvia Morales's *Chicana*, counters both the dominant culture and Chicano exclusion of the role of Chicanas in history. We could perhaps read *Chicana* as the female counterpart to the first Chicano film, *I Am Joaquín*, made in 1969. Both *I Am Joaquín* and *Chicana* are epic accounts of Chicano history: *I Am Joaquín* from a man's perpective, *Chicana* from a woman's. Both reproduce the tendency to tell all of our history in one filmic statement—500 years in roughly twenty minutes of film. Both films reproduce the various themes of Chicano cultural nationalism, namely they challenge racism, provide historical accounts of domination (conquest) and struggle. Both celebrate the indigenous legacy of our people. In terms of form, both *I Am Joaquín* and *Chicana* make extensive use of stills, the murals of Siqueiros, Rivera and Orozco, photographs, and music drawn from an oral tradition.

Despite these similarities there are important differences as well, and not just in terms of theme or related to the fact that *I Am Joaquín* tells the story of our male heroes and *Chicana* of our female heroines. There are major formal/aesthetic and ideological differences as well, for *Chicana* critiques all form of domination.

Whereas male-centered cultural nationalism was critical of "gabacho" society and the "gachupín" colonialists and landowners, it idealized pre-columbian society. *I Am Joaquín*'s epic-account of conquest and domination was based on an idyllic, and androcentric depiction of pre-columbian society. *Chicana*'s epic account refuses the tendency to idealize the Aztecs and offers instead a critical re-vision of our lineage. Unlike the artistic productions of male cultural nationalists, *Chicana* depicts the enslavement of women and men under Aztec domination, while its "re-vision" of Malintzín Tenepal (La Malinche) is represented in the context of feminist critiques of Chicano movement ideology (Alarcón 1983).

Formally, *Chicana* draws from an intertextual tradition which combines and juxtaposes distinct artistic practices into a new form. *Chicana* is a collage of dramatic re-enactment, photographic stills, reportage, and documentary conventions. Given her work as a television producer with KABC-TV in Los Angeles, Sylvia Morales adds her expertise in television documentary and reportage to the slide-show of Ana Nieto-Gómez. She also brings to the film a keen sense of irony and satire, as is evident in the opening sequence which subverts common-sense assumptions about Chicana passivity and subservience.

In this dramatic re-enactment that opens the film, she presents viewers with images of domesticity: one Chicana making tortillas, an elderly woman on a rocking chair, a woman washing clothing, and another potty-training her male son. Yet each of these images is punctuated with a voice-over that subverts the image in a humorous fashion. For example, in the potty-training image, as the mother wipes her son's rear-end, the narrative voice injects, "we free men to work," a commentary that satirically draws viewer attention to the serious issue of the extent of women's unpaid household labor.

Morales's epic account was indeed a counter-discourse to man-centered versions of Chicano history. Through its focus on the role of "important" women like Sor Juana Inez de la Cruz, Lucy González Parsons, and Emma Tenayuca, *Chicana* re-invents a lineage for Chicanas, but the film also contests accounts that render women nameless, voiceless, and imageless in the historical process. In these various ways, aesthetically and ideologically, Sylvia Morales is the first Chicana filmmaker to confront the "many-headed demon of oppression" on such a grand scale.

Lourdes Portillo and Nina Serrano's *Despues del Terremoto* anticipates *Chicana*, yet, in a similar vein, the film exemplifies a Chicana feminist counter-aesthetics. Portillo herself has been one of our most misunderstood and distorted film practitioners. Some critics simply don't know what to make of her. She has been called a Nicaraguan filmmaker by Gary Keller in his introduction to the first Chicano cinema anthology, published in 1985. Assuming that only a man could conceive of a nationalist activist association, Keller also forgot to mention that Portillo was also one of the founders of the media arts organization, Cine Acción.

Perhaps, she herself has added to the confusion, for she has made a film about a Nicaraguan immigrant in San Francisco, another film on the Mothers of the Plaza de Mayo in Argentina (*Las Madres*, 1986), and yet another on the Day of the Dead (*La Ofrenda*, 1989), that dares to give a subject-role to gays in their efforts to revive and transform el día de los muertos celebration in San Francisco. Of course, these diverse ways of re-presenting reality may confuse and perplex those who assume that there is only one way of being a Chicana, that there is only one voice that can speak for all Chicanas, or that there is only one concern that interests Chicanas, in sum, to those who assume that there is an "essential" Chicana identity. Indeed, the ambiguity in Portillo's work, the refusal to be categorized, the multi-dimensionality of her subject matter, her concern for many and varied forms of oppression (for instance, military repression in Argentina; the oppression based on gender and sexuality) are what in fact make Lourdes Portillo very Chicana. Not to mention that she herself claims that identity. As Norma Alarcón reminds us, what characterizes the work of many Chicana writers is their rejection of singular notions of cultural identity, that is to say, their preference for "multiple-voiced subjectivity" (1990b: 336). Portillo's cinematic trajectory similarly draws attention to the fact that Chicanas are "interpellated by a series of ideological discourses" (Sánchez 1990: 5). Her film, *Despues del Terremoto*, assigns these multiple registers to the subject-protagonist's quest for her identity as a woman.

*Despues del Terremoto*'s theme may be about the life of a Nicaraguan immigrant woman in San Francisco, but its concerns are ours as well. And, a great deal of the film's sub-text is also about the experiences (cultural, political, and sexual) which affect Chicanas within a dominant culture. In fact, by depicting these conflicts from the perspective of a non-Chicana, Portillo achieves a distance from the subjectivity of Chicana identity—a distance which provides the film its clarity of vision. In so doing, that is to say, by stepping outside of our culture, the film is transformed into one of the most powerful critiques to date of culture and gender conflict within our own "community." By reading the film allegorically, we can grasp its engagement with Chicana's internal cultural and gender oppression.

*Despues del Terremoto*'s theme concerns a Nicaraguan working as a maid in San Francisco. The plot is propelled by an impending meeting between the film's protagonist, Irene, and her boyfriend, who has just arrived from Nicaragua where he has been a political activist, imprisoned and tortured in Somoza's jails. Yet apart from this specificity which localizes the theme as "Nicaraguan," or the film as a story about Nicaraguans in the U.S., the film's various subtexts can be read allegorically. And it is the manner in which the film is formally structured which opens up its allegorical dimension.

The film's narrative is orchestrated around two major events, Irene's purchase of a television set and the event of the cumpleaños which serves as a pretext for unveiling women's rituals. The film opens with the purchase of the TV and closes with an ensuing conflict between Irene and the boyfriend over the act. The television purchase is important given that the filmmaker utilizes the TV as a sign with multiple layers of meaning. On the one hand, it is a signifier for cultural imperialism, the dissemination of U.S. programming to the Third World. But, the TV is also, in the U.S., a signifier of acculturation, for it is designed not only to homogenize different audiences and organize them as markets, but also to acculturate immigrants into U.S. society. The television also marks success, or it can be read as a symbol of the culture of consumption. What TV does is to inculcate the ethic and logic of consumerism within these communities as a route to becoming "American." The ability to purchase a television, for many lower income people, particularly immigrants, registers their successful incorporation into U.S. culture, as consumers. Given that success is measured through consumption, access to TV discourse marks their participation in a naturalized and commodified world of consumerism offered by television.[5]

Despite these multiple registers embodied in the film, the dominant reading of the television revolves around its function as a signifier for the signified, a woman's independence and autonomy. From the perspective of Irene, the decision to purchase the television symbolizes her autonomy as a wage-earner and her independence as a woman. And it is from the act of her purchase of this commodity that Irene entertains the question of her role as either a future (dependent) wife or an independent (perhaps single) wage-earner, and as a consumer, since the consumer has come to replace the producer in an advanced capitalist economy.

Another significant feature of the film's structure is located in the contrast between two back-to-back sequences: the sequence which depicts Irene and her friend in the bedroom, discussing gender-relations and politics while engaged in the ritual of "dressing-up," and the sequence with the two tías (aunts) involved in a kitchen ritual of making tamales while also talking about gender-relations and politics. The contrast between these two sequences is rich with generational conflict and differences. The filmmakers imbue its imagery with the multiplicity of women's discourse, namely, repression through religion but also bonding through ritual. As Irene walks towards the kitchen space of the tías, she glimpses one of them before a home-altar, praying to Saint Anthony for a husband for Irene. The tía has just placed Saint Anthony in an upside-down position, a religious practice designed to insure the fulfillment of the request. After the aunt leaves, Irene returns the Saint to its upright position and then glances at an image of the Virgen de Guadalupe. Unsure of the significance of religious rituals and icons, Irene returns to the bedroom space where she then asks her friend, "¿Qué piensas de la Virgen?" to which her friend responds, "Nada interesante, la verdad."

Whereas Spanish-language use predominates in both sequences, the film also captures the linguistic structure of code-switching within each generation since in both cases the characters code-switch from English to Spanish, and vice versa. Generational difference in linguistic use is punctuated by an additional sequence, taking place in a third space and visualizing two young girls who do not speak any Spanish at all. The film moreover registers the multiplicity of women's discourse in other ways as well.

In this same segment of the film, the complexity and multiplicity of Chicana identity is captured in the following detail. On the one hand, las tías solteronas (spinsters) voice the most traditional values about their desire for a husband for Irene in proverbs like "no se vaya a quedar a vestir santos" ("let's hope she doesn't end up dressing saints"). Yet in a second breath she remarks, "más vale vestir santos que borrachos" ("better to dress saints than drunks"). Indeed this proverbial wisdom exemplifies the sophisticated deconstructive and reconstructive style rendered throughout the film. The film's spatial rendition of the quotidian, the everyday rituals, succeeds in illuminating the subversiveness of women's private space. Impregnating onto the quotidian those elements of "resistance" inherent in rituals, Portillo offers a Chicana feminist perspective that critiques the values which imprison Chicanas, salvaging those which liberate.

In its depiction of a protagonist whose relation to cultural tradition and religion remains at best ambiguous and distant, *Después del Terremoto* re-constructs multiple-voiced subjectivity. In other words, by assigning "multiple registers of existence" to the main-character, Portillo and Serrano capture cinematically the process which recognizes that "knowledge" of Chicana "subjectivity cannot be arrived at through a single discursive 'theme' " (Alarcón 1990: 355-6).

Finally, while strongly leaning toward cinematic realism, the film's formal refusal to tie-up the threads which make up a fictional text, that is, to achieve narrative closure, opting instead for the ending with the subtitle, "y empezó así. . . " ("and so it began . . ."), leaves an opening, a critical space for the viewer to weave her or his own ending to this on-going struggle of gender politics.

## Woman-Centered Re-vision

A woman-centered counter-aesthetics is exemplified by Esperanza Vásquez's *Agueda Martínez*. Also predating *Chicana*, *Agueda Martínez*'s significance rests in its role as a counter to most male-produced documentaries which focus on grandeur, on the important men and sometimes women in Chicano history. *Agueda Martínez* represents the life of the common everyday woman whose life experience and struggle are just as heroic as those of the "exceptional" individuals. Like *Chicana*, *Agueda Martínez* challenges dominant assumptions about Chicanas as passive and subservient, for the film is an elegant portrait of a self-sufficient woman. She owns her rancho, makes her living by working her land that produces various crops, weaves in the winter, has raised eight children, and proudly claims sixty-seven grandchildren and forty-five great-grandchildren. Agueda lucidly instructs viewers on her various crafts, homecooking, child-rearing, as well as on her views about Chicano culture, history, and tradition. Not only is Agueda resourceful, but her crafts are not at all gendered. Just as she practices traditional New Mexican cooking and weaving (woman's work), so too does she plow the field and till the soil (man's work).

The formal properties of the film mark *Agueda Martínez* as one of the most eloquently crafted films of the period. As opposed to the didactic narrative style of documentary films which use the authoritative convention of the voice-over, *Agueda Martínez* imaginatively uses direct dialogue. Since the protagonist speaks directly, the film avoids an authoritative mediation. Specifically, the film's discourse is constructed in a subjective mode, patterning a subject's stream of consciousness. And its central subject, Agueda, slips in and out of narratives of work, cultural tradition, history, interpretive, critical, and self-reflexive commentary.

Vásquez moreover imbues the central subject's monologue with a dialogic quality patterning the narrative form of oral history, a quality whose style explicitly assumes an interlocutor. The representation of Agueda's mode of address is realized in a nonlinear fashion, thereby reproducing the oral tradition, but also positioning viewers as active co-participants in its narrative. For *Agueda Martínez*'s theme, the form of the film's imagery, articulates the matrilineal heritage of many Chicanas and Chicanos in the U.S.[6]

Structurally, the film reproduces the movement of the day, beginning with sunrise and ending with the setting sun. This visual orchestration overlays onto another marker of time, the cycle of the seasons. Indeed, the cinematic representation is designed in a cyclical fashion, opening with spring-time (Agueda's craft of harvesting) and closing with the winter (Agueda's craft of weaving).

While its beautiful depiction of an exemplary elderly woman may strike us as idealized and sentimental, Esperanza Vásquez's portrayal of struggle in a woman's daily-life existence, represents instead a counter-aesthetics and a counter-discourse to what Quintana terms "predominantly masculine interpretations of history and culture" (1990: 258).

## The "Politics of Representation"

The cinematic production of a new generation of Chicana filmmakers initiates a movement beyond the politics of contestation and towards what Stuart Hall calls "the politics of representation" (Hall 1988). The emphasis among these new filmmakers revolves around experimenting with form, that is, drawing attention to the expressive aspects inherent in the medium. Less concerned with "setting the record straight," in other words, with rendering "positive" images of women, the more recent film practices illustrate a greater concern with the artistic properties of the visual form. While they remain committed to a cultural politics insofar as their works deal with the Chicana/o experience, many are less interested in telling it *all* in one film, or with the grand narrative of Chicano history. Rather, the themes embodied in the newer films represent small pieces of the larger puzzle that characterize the Chicana and Chicano social and cultural milieu.

Here, the question of a Chicana cultural identity is less central, explicit, or obvious. Yet a detailed reading of these new cinematic practices discloses that the problematics of identity persist. However, implicit, identity, in its varied manifestations, permeates each of these films. But unlike the cultural politics of previous generations, these newer ones reveal that Chicana identity can mean different things to different women. Indeed, the new film practices subvert the univocal or bifocal character of previous formulations of cultural identity by infusing these with multiplicity and difference (Fregoso and Chabram 1990; Alarcón 1990b).

A cursory look at recent productions by Chicanas indicates that many continue to work within conventional formats and styles, particularly the didactic documentary. However, an examination of videos also shows that many are experimenting with the newer technologies as well. T. Osa Hidalgo de la Riva, for instance, mixes animation with rap lyrics in her imaginative rendition, *Mujería: The Olmeca Rap*. The musical montage exemplifies an innovative way of drawing attention to cultural identity within the specificity of an urban rap-culture setting. Yet, at the same time, the video also makes reference to an indigenous legacy grounded in female Olmec identity.

Sandra P. Hahn's tribute to the Days of the Dead, *Replies of the Night*, visually illustrates a personal voyage of memory rendered with computer graphics video production. Her work is thus not simply a tribute to el día de los muertos, but more importantly, it represents Hahn's desire to come to terms with the memory of her grandfather. Using computer graphics and digital voice-reproduction, Hahn animates photographic images of her grandfather, thereby paralleling the cognitive process of reviving him in her own mind. Interestingly, Hahn's grandfather died on the Day of the Dead in 1946.

Beverly Sánchez Padilla's work-in-process, *El corrido de Juan Chacón*, imaginatively mixes reportage, film-footage from *Salt of the Earth*, and a performance of the corrido de Juan Chacón. Her short documentary deals with one of the major figures in the New Mexico salt-mine strikes of the early fifties—an event that later inspired the film, *Salt of the Earth* (1954). *El Corrido de Juan Chacón*'s depiction of Chacón, a major protagonist in the strikes and one of the central characters in the film, moves away from the more conventional documentary style. Finally, Frances Salomé España, who prefers to characterize herself as a visual artist, is among the newer filmmakers who take full advantage of the artistic potentiality inherent in the art-form.

The three-minute video, *Anima* (1989), a tribute to el día de los muertos, exemplifies a new experimental style in Chicana filmmaking. España's work draws attention to the representational aspects of cinema, for the video subverts both cinematic time and space. In *Anima*, the filmmaker ritualizes the artistic form through the prolongation of cinematic time, as is evident in her extensive recourse to unusual angles and shots, as well as in the introduction of dissonance into shots and angles. The short film alternates between three sequence spaces: the cementery, images of women with painted calavera faces, characteristic of the day of the dead, and a negative shot of the cemetery in freeze-frame. The alternating movement, back and forth between sequences, is rendered through time-distorted cinematic techniques: jagged or abrupt pans of the cemetery, or images of women with painted faces shot through reflection in chrome mylar. The effect of these distortions cannot be dismissed as simple gimmickry, or film tricks, for España effectively captures, aesthetically, the ritual-based practices which in fact define the Day of the Dead.

Her experimental style is a ritual that is self-reflexive. In *Anima* España ritualizes the depiction of a ritual, thereby inflecting the video with a carnivalesque sensitivity. In a playful artistic style, España re-creates a ritualized representation (form) of a representation of a ritual (content) of women's painted faces for another ritual, el día de los muertos. *Anima* stands out for its infinite representational levels, including the rendering of stylized images of women inserted within another ritual, that of sitting around the kitchen table. The film's complexity rests in the visual artist's skillful ability to create a film language that resonates and reproduces the very content of the ritual—a quality which opens up a new phase in Chicana cinematic practices, a movement beyond the politics of contestation.

The work of this new generation of Chicana film and video makers, which includes Olivia Chumacero (*Mbamba* 1989) and Betty Maldonado (*Night Vigil* 1989), charts a new direction for Chicana/o filmmaking, cinema made in the spirit of a politics of representation.[7] However, like their predecessors, Sylvia Morales, Lourdes Portillo and Esperanza Vásquez, these newer cultural workers must also confront the "many-headed demon of oppression." For the forces that exclude Chicanas from the "Halls of Chicano cinema" (or the Halls of Moctezuma), and those that oppress Chicanas in a racist, sexist, class-based society, are still haunting us today, fifteen years later.

## Notes

1. This essay was first published in *Chicanos and Film* (1992). A more extensive treatment of these issues is published in *The Bronze Screen: Chicana and Chicano Film Culture* (1993). This essay was written during my tenure as a Ford Postdoctoral Fellow at the Chicano Studies Research Center and the Department of Film and Television at the University of California, Los Angeles during 1990-91. I would like to thank the Chicano Studies Research Center at UCLA for its generous support of my research. I also received funds for my research from the Interdisciplinary Humanitities Center at the University of California, Santa Barbara. I would like to acknowledge Herman Gray for graciously providing comments on an earlier version of this essay. I would also like to express my deepest appreciation to Helena María Viramontes for urging me to write about Chicana filmmakers. A word on terminology: practioners of cinema make a distinction between film and video makers. Given that my analysis departs from the subject-position of the spectator as the producer of meaning, I use the more generic term, filmmaker, to refer to both forms of the cinematic practice since technical advances, make it difficult for the viewer to distinguish between each form. Moreover, the rationing of public funds may also make the video format a more viable option for non-industry practioners. Besides, most 35mm films are now released in the video format for home viewing.
2. This month-and-a-half long event was held at the UCLA Wight Art Gallery in Los Angeles on October 2-November 3, 1990. In a telephone conversation, Lourdes Portillo told me that, at the urging of Chon

Noriega, she had called the film series organizer Carlos Avila, and gave him a list of additional Chicana films and videos for inclusion in the event. Frances Salomé España also comments on the event in the following words: "Of course I know my inclusion in the UCLA CARA Film Series was an afterthought. The number of Chicana participants was minimal. The place relegated to the women cineastas and videoastas was a marginal one. I chose not to attend." (Personal interview, December 1990)

3. My reference here is to Chicana filmmakers like Lourdes Portillo who have made a self-conscious choice to remain as independents. There are many others who have entered the mainstream industry, producing both commissioned (commercial) pieces, but also more experimental non-commissioned films.

4. Lourdes Portillo, paper presented at the first conference of Latin American Women Film and Video Makers, "Cruzando Fronteras," Tijuana, Mexico, November 29-December 2, 1990.

5. I am indebted to Herman Gray for his insights on popular culture and television.

6. I am always struck by the response of audiences who view this film, either in public forums or in my classes. There is always someone who comments to the effect, "That's the way my grandmother is," or "Agueda reminds me of my grandmother." Hence, the appropriateness of the film's full title" *Agueda Martínez: Our People, Our Country*.

7. I first made this argument about Chicano cinema in my article "*Born in East L.A.* and the Politics of Representation" (1990). See also Fregoso (1993).

# On Filmmaking: A Personal Odyssey

*Frances Salomé España*

My experience speaks to life sobreviviendo the fracasos of beauty and brutal truth. It speaks to a Chicano aesthetic evolving from the fusion of contrasting dynamics within the Chicano experience. And ultimately, it speaks to one's faith in one's own vision of things, and in one's self, no matter what—con safos.

Surrounded by raza in East L.A., the ambiente was actually quite beautiful, strong enough, even, to bring comfort and solace to my mind and body, given the insulting curriculum and instruction that I had to endure diariamente, within the schools. In my case, the contradictions fed an inquisitive spirit. Otherwise, and in reality, education was sub-standard, unchallenging and poor. I studied art during those formative years—experimenting with collage, sculpture, assemblage, painting, drawing, everything. Everything that my sense of myself directed me towards. Everything, within a school system which implied there was no room for dreams in my life, anyway. Never relating to the institutions which never really related to me, it was just me and my heart, all the way.

I credit myself for surviving public education. I credit the spirit of an entire generation of Chicanos for not only helping me transcend time and place in East L.A., but also, for providing the chispa which bore witness to a movement in consciousness, and finally, a city in flames.

Chicano Moratorium, August 29, 1970: A massive purification ceremony and baptism by Fire. A renaissance within the Chicano community which crossed all levels in thought and culture. The prayers that went up with the smoke on the streets were battle-cries of resistance, affirmation, and self-determination. Only 17 y todavía fuera de la onda; old enough to know my salvation when I saw it. It was the catalyst which allowed me, forced me to take my talent seriously. It was the first omen which prophesied my renaissance as Chicana artist, writer, and image-maker.

I have only a vague notion of the artists' spirit—strong—as is this will within: a well of determination and dreams, y más. I will say that these feelings have always had hold of my heart and are ancient, as the first day.

My parents did not nurture me with books, nor music, nor trips to museums. The schools acknowledged my creativity, but institutions don't count—not in ways that were meaningful to me. I received awards, but no relevant preparation, nothing that met my needs or experience, or sensibility.

I had no models, no mentors, no guías, no nothing—only my faith in myself, and the sensations of an environment which did embrace me. I remember images, color, movement and sounds; my mother's sacred poultry, remnants of rancho in the middle of the city; my father, the Yaqui-Chicano, my mother's medicine man, comfortable, firme; words broken from one language to form another. These are laced perceptions, bred in Aztlán with its trademark peripheral cultural fracasos, institutional racism, and capitalistic neuroses; blow by blow assaults on my identity.

My parents were not able to direct me on my path, at least not in eurocentric terms. But did this path have heart? Did I have heart? Did *I* have good carácter? What was my spirit about? These were their lessons.

Making time with destiny, throwing light upon my own reality still, has not fallen easily upon me. Ultimately, those lessons which have enabled me and empowered me to make art, and contend with the world on my own terms, are as follows:

1. Know yourself. Communicate with your heart.
2. Don't worry about an afterlife. Consider this home. Your conduct can bring you happiness here and now.
3. Look for the Beauty in all things.
4. Be educated. Meet things with your mind.
5. Brace yourself. Transcend the racism.
6. Take risks. You have your own sensibility. Use it.
7. Your vision is valid, its expression is valid. Don't let your art be judged on their terms.

8. Don't let yourself be overcome by evil forces; be aware of your influences. Seek the positive.
9. Don't kill yourself. What does it really mean when one contemplates suicide? Know your spirit.
10. Honor yourself. Defend what you are about. Honor all your relations.

This is my Raza Survival Guide, a Chicana Obstacle Course for the exile on her own turf, determined to walk her own way—on Sacred Ground.

Into the University of California, at San Diego, and sustained by the Chicano community on campus, I studied Visual Art. Not until my second year was Communications integrated as part of the major, through courses in filmmaking, video, scriptwriting, etc. It was my own fascination with the potential of both mediums which compelled me to work with the Visual Art in new ways. Film and electronic media are forms which allow me to address nuance, and the rhythm of my own particular vision more clearly, and without constraint.

I make reference to those dynamics which have shaped me, those which lend texture to my perspective and expression as a Chicana artist. These dynamics are fluctuating. The perspective and sentiment within the Chicano Art community is divergent and reflective of several different currents of thought; we speak in many voices. Still, these are the dynamics which not only embrace a state of mind, but foster an experience and give rise to an aesthetic particular to all Chicano artists, north of México, in the environments which have inspired us. This is the aesthetic movement intrinsically linked to the Chicano experience and vision. It is high-art, raza-specific, and international in scope. It is humanistic. The sensibility is global. It is contemporary and diverse, rich, creative, far-reaching, indigenous, and its time is now.

The translation of this aesthetic within my own particular arena is relatively new, given the chronically limited access of artists of color to electronic media art tools. Consequently, I am experimenting with approach all the time, struggling with form and stylistic qualities all the time. Occasionally the work takes me places where I don't know what I'm doing anymore—discarding movie industry standards because these codes just don't always make the connection with my content.

It's my sensibility that brings the work its integrity. It was several years before I realized that my aesthetics were as much a party to my vision as my ideas. If I wanted to work with the medium as art form, make it more applicable to my own experiences, and use it in ways more relevant to me, then these aesthetics needed to be explored.

Always exploring, and always hopeful because time, discipline, and faith in one's vision ultimately give way to work that is clearer, richer, more dynamic in expression. "Anima"; "El Espejo"; "Mannequin Depressive"; "Hecho en Aztlán"; the work is very different, and relative to two things: experience, and imagination. It is contemporary, urban, real, surreal, spiritual, sensual, East of Babylon, straight-up, feminine in perspective. My themes are themes of life; personal impressions of my own history, time and place—woven with humor and intellect. It is video art.

A woman's truth is good medicine. I am offering my world view, all those things which mark my heart's vision. However playful, however serious, or even irreverent the result, my work is true to my vision; it has meaning.

Special thanks to artists/poets/visionaries/Las Meras-Meras—Gloria Alvarez, Ana Castillo, Yreina Cervantez—all around Chingonas and Original Thinkers for their time and for their insights—which run throughout this piece.

# On Chicanas and Filmmaking: A Commentary

*Lourdes Portillo*

I am honored to have been invited to attend this celebration. It marks the recognition that the border is not a wall; that we continue to grow as Mexicans and Chicanas despite this separation (the border) that we are rendering invisible by our presence here today. This celebration is also the official recognition that women are an important element in the film culture of Mexico and the United States.

In this historical moment when women have been able to question their traditional roles, Chicana women have precariously straddled twin roles, the one that our heritage implies as women, and the role economic necessity imposes on our lives.

Since the community of the Chicana does not have the same class restrictions that society imposes on Mexican women, in the U.S. a working-class woman can aspire to almost any profession, and by exercising great tenacity can obtain it. In the U.S. the child of a farm worker can become a doctor, a teacher a lawyer or an artist. This is the American dream—very much criticized but nevertheless persistent as a myth because sometimes it is true. And what's significant is that this dream is not gendered—girls too have this possibility.

If this is true, as I posit, there is a question that has haunted me for years. Why have so few Chicanas ventured to make films? There are many Chicana writers who are talented and prolific, influential, and in the forefront of our cultural resistance. Helena Viramontes, Norma Alarcón, Sandra Cisneros, Ana Castillo, Cherríe Moraga, Lorna Dee Cervantes, Lucha Corpi and many more too numerous to name.

But in cinema we have only a few women directors who exist on the fringes; one could blame the technical complexity of filmmaking, or the variety of skills needed. Or is it perhaps the exorbitant economic risks that have dissuaded most women from entering filmmaking?

It is curious to note that women who struggle to create in a medium that requires a great amount of money will be marginalized, implying that we are still not to be trusted with money. Perhaps you've noticed that a woman who writes poetry is easily accepted and encouraged. Obviously, she's not spending anyone else's money. Poetry is considered a proper profession for a woman. But a film director is one who must wield power in the process of producing a film, and later wields great ideological power with the final product, the film. I believe that producers are not convinced that a woman, or in this case a Chicana, could actually exert enough power to make a film.

In creating a film one has to internalize authority in order to assert it, and in our culture the assertion of authority by a woman is not looked upon kindly. It represents the denial of all of our upbringing as women: we are taught to acquiesce, to mediate, to console, to serve and never to demand, because to demand is seen as a masculine quality. And it is precisely the assertion of authority that is required when we make a film. We assert authority with the funders, with the crew, with the actors, and with the exhibitors. How can a Chicana mediate these conflicting needs when film work goes against all that is culturally expected of us? Many Chicanas cannot reconcile these needs and consequently we see very few images on the screen that ring true to a Chicana. To this day unfortunately, Chicanas have been mostly the spectators of film and television.

What do we see? We see female images that don't quite fit our experience. As God created Eve in Adam's image, male film directors have created the Chicana/Mexicana image to fit their own projections of who we are. In 1990 the Academy Award for best director went to Oliver Stone for the film *Born on the 4th of July*. As you probably know, the film deals with the experiences of a Viet Nam veteran and his political awakening. In this film the portrayal of Mexican women is no different than those of Sam Peckinpah, or John Ford, or almost any director in Hollywood—the Chicana/Mexicana women are still playing prostitutes to their macho boys. *Born on the 4th of July* will invade the Chicano/Mexicano market and will make millions at the box office for some Hollywood studio. But in this day and age, when we are acutely aware of how images on the screen influence our lives, can we give ourselves the luxury of ignoring such an offense and of paying the price of the ticket to be witness to it?

From the venerated, virginal mother to the voracious, vociferous prostitute, nothing has changed in a century of movie-making for the Chicana/Mexicana. In Chicano films women don't fare any better. Ironically, in the few films where women portray the depth of rich and complex characters, such as *Salt of the Earth* by Herbert Bibberman and *The Ballad of Gregorio Cortez* by Robert Young, the directors were neither female or Chicano.

Film production in the U.S. exists on two levels: the corporate high-finance studio formula of filmmaking that is fed to us everyday and dulls the senses; and the independent filmmaking movement that attempts to deal with themes in depth, experimenting with form and content. Independents make films with limited financial backing and the uncertainty of whether or not it will play to any given audience. It is a conscious choice to produce work that goes beyond the surface, work that touches on subjects taboo to the industry, mostly because they are not lucrative. By being an independent it is possible to dream, while in corporate Hollywood the only concern is about what sells, what is marketable.

I am an independent filmmaker who emerged in the 1970s. It was an optimistic time when funding was more generous, an era when many minority directors embarked on their careers. Later, in the 1980s, the country took a conservative turn to the right and what could have been a time of development became a time of closure for many aspiring filmmakers. Funding was less available, and intolerance of minority themes tacitly accepted. In that atmosphere the possibility of Chicanas emerging as film directors became less likely.

The Chicano directors who managed to stay afloat were forced to survive by attempting to enter mainstream Hollywood and television. Chicanas remained outside of the industry, some in television or as independents, either by choice or for lack of opportunity. Today in the 1990s most women directors work at the independent level. In this marginal existence women have been able to develop their own visual language. The future of film and video has never looked as bright. More Chicanas are entering the universities and studying film and video, and the production has multiplied. As we see here at this conference, they are creating images that encompass the diversity of our experience, turning society's definition of a Chicana on it's head. In video production we see a nascent spark of what Chicana production will be in a few years.

I am an optimist, I believe that video production is not only a viable step toward the future for Chicanas, but that a new aesthetic is being developed in the medium. As a result of video's portability and low cost, the director's struggle to impose authority at all levels of production is minimized. And it is precisely that immediacy that frees the videographer to bring about a work of greater intimacy and truthfulness. It is in video and not in film that imagination is being exercised with greater rigor. And it is in video where the conditions for a new stage of development exist for the Chicana director in the 1990s.

# Bernice Zamora: Interview

*Gloria Elsa Li*

Bernice Zamora, poeta chicana, nació en Aguilar, Colorado, en 1938. La naturaleza, especialmente las montañas de Colorado, ha sido un factor importante en su vida y en su carrera literaria. Zamora proviene de una familia pobre donde no se alentaba la intelectualidad y donde el leer era una actividad prohibida. Desde muy temprana edad se percató de las diferencias raciales y culturales existentes en la sociedad, y ha sufrido discriminación tanto en su vida personal como en su vida profesional. Obtuvo su Bachillerato de Southern Colorado University, su Maestría de Colorado State University y su Doctorado de Stanford University. Actualmente, se encuentra enseñando en la Universidad de Santa Clara.

*Restless Serpents* es la colección de poemas que le ha dado renombre. El éxito de esta obra la tomó por sorpresa y ahora se prepara a publicar *Releasing Serpents* que incluirán *Restless Serpents* y una colección nueva de poemas. Se espera que saldrá en dieciocho meses. Zamora se identifica, principalmente, como poeta, pero también ha escrito prosa. Tiene dos cuentos publicados "Flexion" y "Vergüenza," y hay otro, "Tere," que aparecerá dentro de poco. Al presente está trabajando en varios proyectos: una pieza teatral, una novela y un libro sobre la Malinche. También le gusta pintar y piensa publicar un libro de dibujos.

Zamora es una persona muy amable, expresiva y de buen carácter. Dispuesta a ayudarme, me concedió varias horas de charla donde habló de diversos y variados tópicos, como su familia, su niñez, su juventud, su obra literaria, el proceso creativo, el amor, el movimiento feminista, el Movimiento Chicano y comentó sobre falsas acusaciones e interpretaciones de sus poemas hechas por algunos críticos. En cierto modo, podría decir que tuve el privilegio de obtener una entrevista exclusiva con una escritora conocida por su resistencia a ser entrevistada y también por haber conseguido sus opiniones sobre ciertos temas, como el Movimiento feminista, que según Zamora nunca las había revelado antes. La entrevista fue conducida en inglés porque Zamora se siente más cómoda hablando en este idioma.

*Li:* I understand you were born in Aguilar, Colorado in 1938, but spent most of your life in Pueblo. Tell me about your family and the community where you grew up.
*Zamora:* I was born in Aguilar. From there my parents moved us to Valdez, Colorado which is twenty miles south of Aguilar. In the Valdez area, where the coal mine businesses are, we lived in Segundo. The Colorado Fuel and Iron Corporation sectioned the miners' living quarters, so that one group of coal miners lived in Primero, and another group lived in Segundo; we lived in the Segundo section. I think there were three sections. We lived there until I was about six years old. From Valdez we moved to Denver, where we lived for six years. When I was about twelve years old we moved to Pueblo, where I lived until I got my divorce at age thirty-six.
*Li:* So you married in Pueblo.
*Zamora:* Yes, I married in Pueblo.
*Li:* Was your husband Mexican or American?
*Zamora:* Chicano, Mexican-American. He was *Nuevo Mexicano*. He was born in New Mexico. His father owned a lot of territory at one time, and lost all of it just like everyone else in New Mexico. We had two daughters, and both were born in Pueblo.
*Li:* Did you attend school in Pueblo?
*Zamora:* Yes. I got a B.A. at Southern Colorado University. I earned an M.A. from Colorado State University, an agricultural university in Ft. Collins, Colorado, a small town located seventy miles north of Denver. Finally, I got my Ph.D. at Stanford University.
*Li:* What role has your family and background played in your life and in your creative work?
*Zamora:* Well, we were forbidden to read in the house. My father wouldn't permit us to read at home. I guess it's not too odd in Latino cultures, an educated woman was always a danger, but I had to go to school because the law required it. At age sixteen he wanted me to quit and go to work, because we needed the money.

My mother fought to keep me in school, and so I thought if I got a job at night, then I could stay in school, which I did. I worked eight hours every night. I would go to work at four in the afternoon, after school, and work until midnight every night, including weekends, for the last two years of high school.

As for my background, the state of Colorado, especially southern Colorado, provides the scenery and the background in the literature. The landscape, especially the mountains, instructed us in the way the day would evolve. We looked at the mountains to see if it was going to rain. We related to the mountains on a daily basis. The mountains were always for me a focal point whenever I had a chaotic day; and I write poetry where the Rocky Mountains are a dominant setting.

*Li:* Would you like to go back there?

*Zamora:* I would like to think that I could retire there. It's so beautiful and rugged, but I am allergic to the cold; it's very cold there and my allergy causes me to swell up, or to get hives, and I can't function because so much pain is connected with this allergy. So that's why I can't go back. If I could I'd be there today, but the pain is too much of a distraction to write or to study. I went to the doctor and he said this is a condition that's known but is not common, and they don't have a cure for it. All the time I spent in Colorado I just tolerated it, even sipping wine to numb the pain. After coming in from the cold, warming up was even more painful and now it gets more and more excruciating as I get older. Whatever it is I don't know; it may be arthritic or it could be poor circulation.

*Li:* Did you ever go skiing?

*Zamora:* Never. I've gone on ski trips with friends and just stayed on the ski train or stayed in the ski lodge the one year that I explored the sport, but I never went on the slopes. In our family, it seemed an odd thing to do, to ski. There was nobody in my family who skied. We walked the mountains wearing only boots, we tracked deer, and did other things like that, but it was not recreation, it was a necessity. I was most uncomfortable at the ski lodge. To be at leisure, enjoying the mountains as a sport, was just too odd and awkward. When I was a teaching assistant at Colorado State University, most of the students who came to Colorado in order to be in the skiing areas, wanted to write about skiing. All their "how-to-ski" papers further diminished my interest in skiing.

*Li:* Did your parents encourage you in your creative work?

*Zamora:* Well, when I was at home the creative expression was in the arts. I was a painter as a child, drawing things, and I won an art award when I graduated from high school. But we were so poor, and materials were so expensive that I became frustrated because I couldn't afford them. So I gave it up. I gave up the struggle to find the money for paints, canvas. Even the struggle to find privacy to paint was too much to bear. I gave up most everything, especially when I got married. It was important to be married in my young world and it afforded some privacy.

*Li:* You must have married very young?

*Zamora:* Well, at nineteen. You see, in our culture that's rather old, it's normal.

*Li:* How do you identify yourself? As an Anglo or as a Mexican?

*Zamora:* Chicana. That's my main identity for myself.

*Li:* I understand you attended a Catholic school for your primary education. Tell me about your school experiences.

*Zamora:* Yes, I attended St. Dominic's in Denver and St. Leander's in Pueblo, but my parents couldn't afford to send me to a Catholic high school. I remember crying almost the entire summer because I couldn't afford to go. I wanted to study mathematics, but I had to face reality, I went to a public school instead. It was very different in a public school for me. I became interested in boys at that age, and they were interested in me, and I lost interest in mathematics.

*Li:* Has religion played an important role in your life?

*Zamora:* Very important role.

*Li:* Do you believe in God?

*Zamora:* Oh, yes.

*Li:* Do you still practice religion?

*Zamora:* You know, the part of me that's mestiza, the part that relates to the Indian, that part acknowledges that practicing religion is only an act of faith. A knowledge of God is what I craved. It's very hard to look at the mountains, the animals, trees, or plants and not know that God exists. Listen to the wind singing with you or talk to the animals and there are responses. My father taught us to talk and sing with animals, the wind, the trees. I think that's more the Indian side of religious expressions.

*Li:* You say you are mestiza. In what way?

*Zamora:* On my mother's side, my grandfather was a Taos Pueblo Indian. At one time we thought he was Sioux because he moved the family to South Dakota, but I did some research and found out he was a Taos Pueblo.

*Li:* So on your mother's side you are Spanish and Indian?

*Zamora:* Yes. And on my father's side we're not totally sure, but they spoke Spanish too. He's Indian and part French, we don't know much more.

*Li:* Are you, and were you, a rebel?

*Zamora:* No. As long as I was home or at my parents home attached to the church, because I wanted to go to Heaven, I really wanted to behave. Even within the Catholic Church I didn't realize how much of an outcast I was until I was in the eighth grade. There was a little boy who was an eighth grader. He was on the football team because he was so good at sports, and when the players won games they gave the young boys little gifts, like scarves. This small guy on the team liked me and gave me the scarf he won. I was really impressed, and I said "OK. I guess I'll like him," but I really didn't know if I liked him at all. He just gave me a scarf when nobody else did. So I took the scarf home and my mother said: "You'd better give it back, you can't accept gifts." The next day I didn't know how I was going to tell him that I had to give back the scarf. But he came to me and said: "I have to take the scarf back; my mother doesn't want me to be around Mexicans." So that was the first racial incident that struck me to the core. I was crushed and hurt, and then my mother was enraged when I told her, which made me hurt even more because I didn't want my hurt to go beyond me. But it did.

*Li:* How old were you?

*Zamora:* I think about thirteen. In the first real impact, it was clear to me that there was something very different about us. At least in a Catholic environment usually everybody has religion in common, and we all wore uniforms, and there wasn't much distinction to be made by the young mind. I didn't have the presence of mind to analyze the nature of racial difference until my daughter went to a Catholic school. We noticed years later in a class photograph how all the Mexicans were placed on one side of the room. I don't know if it was racism but it was very clear that people on one side of the room got less attention; and that they were on that side of the room for a particular reason.

*Li:* About the incident with the boy, was that the first time you became aware of cultural and racial differences?
*Zamora:* I had been aware of it earlier because my father would come home with stories, but somehow it didn't seem to register. I knew that it existed. But he was out there in the world, and it certainly didn't have anything to do with the Catholic Church or Catholic people. You know, Catholic schools are made of all kinds of cultures. There were lots of Italians and I didn't see any differences with the Italians. In fact, we had quite a bit in common, even with the Irish. But the racist Catholics, I've since noted, seem to come from other regions.
*Li:* For instance?
*Zamora:* The Scottish or British Catholics.
*Li:* How's Bernice Zamora, the person?
*Zamora:* I don't know. I'd like to think of myself as a really honest poet, a Chicana poet, that's all I do. I teach in order to write poetry. Teaching pays the rent. I strongly need to write poetry, I think because I had a brutal childhood. In spite of the fact that I had such a close relationship with nature, it was brutal and I never expressed anything except in poetry. Once I started to study at the university and received assignments to read poetry I felt I could write in the same way, and I did. Right away things poetic started to move. Poetry was the one thing throughout an unhappy marriage that kept me alive, and does so now. It's the one thing I just do, not quite as automatic as breathing or eating, but I just write often without struggle.
*Li:* It comes naturally.
*Zamora:* Well, it comes like the urge to eat, it's a hunger pain. I don't even ignore it anymore, I just do it, daily. I write about a poem a day, at least that. If I see a Shakespearean play, then I usually write about twelve poems that night, but mostly one poem a day is the normal pace.
*Li:* What are your sources of inspiration? Are they internal or external?
*Zamora:* They're internal now. Before, they used to be external. I used to write in reaction to something I'd read or seen. Now, it's more internal, the internal dialogue.
*Li:* Do you write in order to release your emotions? How do you feel before and after writing a poem?
*Zamora:* I write a poem in order to sleep. I don't sleep if I don't

write, I can barely function if I don't write a poem.
*Li:* It's almost like an addiction.
*Zamora:* Yes, in a way, but one enjoys an addiction, to some extent, with dire consequences. I enjoy writing poetry beyond the addictive high. I can't even explain it; it's beyond orgasm. There's nothing I share with any other human being that compares to writing poetry.
*Li:* You feel independent, in the sense that you don't have to depend on anybody to feel this pleasure?
*Zamora:* It isn't even pleasure though. It's about the closest I can get to a spiritual experience, maybe a mystical experience, and then it's on paper and I can re-read it. When I get ill and I don't know what's wrong, I merely go back to my own poetry and read it and I get well. I don't know what it is. There's something there that's very healing, and I have no words to describe it.
*Li:* How long does it take you to write a poem?
*Zamora:* About three minutes, depending on the length of the poem.
*Li:* Did you think of writing as a profession?
*Zamora:* No, I never thought of writing as a profession. I was interested in art. I studied art and also English. I loved English and I wrote well then. I won ten dollars in a contest, but still I didn't see writing in our family as a viable profession or way to live. We hardly had readers in our family. But art seemed like a nice quiet profession; however, I couldn't afford the materials. Later, when I married, I tried to take up painting again. One night I was up all night long and my husband was furious because I was not in bed. He didn't know what I had done all night and I said: "Well, I painted this." He couldn't believe it. I was surprised because by the time I was through with the painting, the sun was up. I was so shocked. It just seemed as if an hour or so had passed. I was so engrossed in it and I missed the whole night. He was furious and I thought: "Well, he should be pleased. Why is he so angry?" He went to bed, and I had to go to bed too. That's the way it was in marriage, you know, at least in those old days.
*Li:* When did you realize you had a talent for writing?
*Zamora:* I didn't know it. In fact, when I wrote poems I was always surprised that people published them. I also won a short story prize at Colorado State University. I was surprised because I didn't know it was good.

*Li:* There were humorous stories that you used to write. But now, you don't write humorous stories anymore.
*Zamora:* No, nothing is funny anymore. I've done some humorous things, but mostly in letters, I think. There is an acerbic tone to my work now. I need to soften up. I submitted a poem to *Caló*, recently, and I think it's a little humorous. Again, whenever I write I never know the effect the piece is going to have on people, because I just don't know what people respond to. I'm surprised at what the literary critics choose to analyze out of *Restless Serpents*, for example. To me, they choose some of the worst poems to discuss or explicate.
*Li:* Have your daughters inherited your talent for writing?
*Zamora:* They both have published, but they married and they gave up writing. Every year I send them a blank book to try to inspire them to write, but both of my daughters have to work. My eldest daughter writes a lot like me, I think. She's going back to school for her Master's. I think she'll probably pick it up then. My other daughter, I don't know.
*Li:* In your interview with Salvador del Pino, in 1977, you said that Emily Dickinson had been a great influence in your life. Also, I read that other authors have influenced you, like Shakespeare, Guillevic, Herman Hesse, Robinson Jeffers, among others. Is there a particular author or a specific book that has determined your literary career?
*Zamora:* No. No one. Shakespeare comes the closest, for influencing my love of the English language, and I do write mostly in English. I write some poems in Spanish, but not enough to be noted, I think. Although Shakespeare is not my principal inspiration, I guess if my back were against the wall I'd say it was Shakespeare, Pablo Neruda, Emily Dickinson, Borges, Márquez, Angela de Hoyos. . . .
*Li:* Have you read a lot of the Latin American poetry?
*Zamora:* Oh, yes. Rubén Darío, Vallejo. And I also read Russian poetry, German poetry. Goethe is my favorite of the German poets. I read the French. I liked the surrealist movement. That was an influence at one time, surrealist poetry. I like Dylan Thomas, Yeats, but I think I have outgrown them in a way I haven't outgrown Shakespeare, for example. And the poems about Robinson Jeffers, Hesse, and Guillevic I wrote as reactions to their poetry, more than as an influence. I always felt, had the arrogance to

think, that there was more to be said about their work. I had the arrogance to think they hadn't finished with an idea. I just felt I could add something else.

*Li:* Let's talk about *Restless Serpents*, the book that made you famous. How do you explain the success?

*Zamora:* I can't explain it. I had no idea it would be successful. In fact, I was absolutely shocked. Tony Burciaga and I gathered our best poems at that time and put the book together quickly because our students needed textbooks, the Chicano students. We had nothing for Chicanos, very little was published then for Chicanos, so we put *Restless Serpents* together as cheaply as possible; we kept the price at $3.50 so the students could afford it. So, the fact that people liked it, and it has been translated in all those languages, Dutch, German, Italian, Chinese, and Spanish too, that fact has really been a shock; I don't know how to explain it. Since 1966 I've been writing poetry, and this book came out in 1976. It is a collection of what I've written from 1966 to 1976. Compiling the book was done while I was at Stanford. The first person I met there was Cecilia Burciaga. Tony is her husband, and we all became good friends. Cecilia is a good poet, too, although I don't think she's published anything.

*Li:* So *Restless Serpents* was born out of necessity?

*Zamora:* Out of necessity, yes, and on two levels: from the private and personal need to write poetry, and then the collective necessity for the class, and not just the classes, but for cultural presentations at the *festivales*, too.

*Li:* What did you have in mind when you organized the entire collection of *Restless Serpents*?

*Zamora:* Actually, we had our community in mind. I was really nervous. I didn't think our community would accept any of the poetry, because I was at a very elite university and had been cut off from the culture in lots of ways. I was certain they would like Tony's however. I didn't know if my people would be receptive to the poetry. I still don't know. My own family are only now discovering what the poems mean. My sister just rediscovered the book. She, my parents, and other relatives read the book once and said: "Oh, that's nice Bernice." That was, you know, in 1976 when they got the poems, and I just got the phone call this year, 1990. But now my sister is finally reading *Restless Serpents* and reading everything else I've written. She verifies all our experiences that I wrote about. That was the good part, verification; it wasn't fantasy all those experiences, it wasn't, you know, make believe or imagination. It was actual experience. When you have this really different reality from all the people around you, faculty, other people in academia, who were brought up wealthy, you think, "Well maybe I didn't go through all that; maybe it wasn't so bad." But it was bad, my sister verified that, and she is very grateful in that I found a way to express that for her. There is a poem in *Restless Serpents* about abortion. That was a poem about a *tía* of my ex-husband. She never had an education or the opportunity to have one, and so I just took her voice to say things that she says in Spanish, and she says them in murmurings. I remember she was so distraught one day. Her whole life fell apart and her husband always in and out of jails, or in and out of the hospital from getting beaten up. He had a potential future. You wouldn't believe it, but he was one of the *ace* fighter pilots during the Korean War. He couldn't assimilate after he returned home, and he became quite a drinker. That made her life, by extension, very miserable. She loved him and she wouldn't leave him. She had many children, and all she would do was follow the man she loved and was careless about raising the children. In any case, it was her voice I used to write about when her husband was taken to the hospital in an emergency. I had been asked to come over to take care of the kids because she didn't have any resources, not even transportation. When she returned home she was just wringing her hands, and I remember her murmuring a lot of the stuff that's in that poem, and I think that I took the collectivity of her thought and placed it there.

*Li:* Does your aunt know you wrote that poem for her?

*Zamora:* No, she does not. Most of my family doesn't know what I write, or realize the consequences of a published book. My Dad only studied through sixth grade. My parents didn't even realize that the book was dedicated to them; you know, it's that kind of distance.

*Li:* Did you have a vision or theme when you put together the collection of poems?

*Zamora:* No, not a thing. I wish I could say I had one, especially for an academician, but the truth is I had no idea that there was structure to the poems. It was another person who noticed the structure in them, and who helped me to select my own poems.

At that point, it occurred to me that the human mind is always trying to make order out of this chaos. I think Bruce-Novoa says that this is what Chicano poets are doing. I began to see a structure, but usually after the fact, never beforehand. I've put together another book in the same way. I have enough poems for at least seven or eight more books, but I don't have the time to sit down and type them out. I haven't had the time yet.

*Li:* Another collection of poems?

*Zamora:* Yes. Well, it's going to be a collection of *Restless Serpents* and another manuscript that I titled "And Everything Will Perish," but it will be under another title. The two collections of poems will come out under the title *Releasing Serpents*.

*Li:* The first poem in *Restless Serpents* is "Penitents." Why did you decide to start the collection with that poem?

*Zamora:* Well it localizes, not only the poetry, but me. I've mentioned that the center of my world when I started writing poetry, and even now in my mind, the center of my world is the Rocky Mountains. If you live in the mountains you can hear the *alabados*, their chants echo throughout the mountains. I spent a lot of time, especially on summer nights, outside. In those days we didn't have electricity, so all we had were the noises and the sounds. More than crickets, we could hear the horses, the cows, and the singing in the mountains that always caught our attention.

*Li:* Which is your favorite poem and why?

*Zamora:* My favorite poem is "Restless Serpents," because for me it describes the entire activity of the writing of poetry, the whole process. The poem came to me in a dream. Prior to the dream, I had a long period where I didn't write poetry. I fell ill. If I don't write poetry I fall either ill or, in those days, into periods of dissipation. I'd drink a lot. I get really *ansiosa* without knowing what to do about it, and it took me a long time to discover that all I had to do to get rid of that was to write a poem. I had this dream and wrote the poem, and the lyrics alone to "Restless Serpents" refer to that process, the poetic process for me. If I don't write a poem, I get really restless; if I continue to ignore it, I get dissipated. I no longer dissipate. Now if I dream, I just write it down, and that's how I get a poem.

*Li:* So you identify yourself with the restless serpents?

*Zamora:* Oh, yes.

*Li:* According to one critic (Sánchez 1985, 218), "the primary de-

terminant of Zamora's poems in *Restless Serpents* is sex, in the double English sense of gender and the erotic." Do you agree with that statement?
*Zamora:* Critics are using the serpent as an image of sex, and that's a very Western-world interpretation. I'm using the serpent, though I placed it in the Western world context—in the castles, for example—I'm using the serpent to mean what it means for the Nahua Indians: serpents are a symbol of wisdom, and no one picked that up. I think when the poetry is interpreted sexually that says more about the critic or the interpreter than it does about my poetry. I've always preferred mixing the images and mixing the definitions, using the images in very Western technological ways but using the symbolic meanings of Indian culture. If you don't know both cultures, just as in *Caló*, if you don't know both street-language Spanish and English you don't get the meaning. I think that's what happens with the critics who describe it as very erotic, they just see themselves.

I was born under the year of the serpent and the day of the serpent in the Aztec calendar. I didn't know that when I wrote the poems. The first time I ever saw a serpent, a snake, I was up in the mountains with my family. We were having an outing; we used to go cherry picking. While we were picking the cherries, a snake came out from the side of an arroyo bank. The men killed it; they were very vicious at killing it. I was just four or five years old. I saw, for the first time, fear and violence and it terrified me. I was so sick I threw up. Everybody thought I was afraid of the snake, but I was afraid for the snake.
*Li:* The same critic I mentioned earlier has also said: "Her strong feminine consciousness leads her to distrust the traditional Chicano male and inspires her to conduct a sexual battle against him." She also says, "What distinguishes Zamora's poetic universe from that of the other poets, then, is her vigorous desire to master the male" (1985, 217). Would you like to set the record straight?
*Zamora:* Well, that statement gives me more credit for having powers I don't think I even want. But in terms of trying to master the macho, what I did was—and I don't think it is feminist—was taking my role on as a female, as a woman does when she sees the male going astray or is in danger. Most Chicano males, in fact, are quite alert to dangers. But when you see a man in danger, it is

the proper role of women to speak up. Of the Mexicans or Chicanas I know, very few are silent, especially in their domain. I was just voicing what I would've done in a household in that situation. I was taking my stand as a woman.

*Li:* But this critic seems to think that you go out of your way to be the dominant one, not only with the male but also with the "dominant culture."

*Zamora:* Well, I'm not talking about the Chicano steeped in his culture, but to the Chicano who is assimilated, moving dangerously into cultural apartheid. He is a danger to himself, and he is a danger to his culture. We have Chicanos who, for example, are saying that Chicanos are not unique, that there's nothing new about them, that Chicanos are doing just what other immigrants did. Our situation is very different. We didn't come here to assimilate, to be white. We were here, and if we are not unique, we are very close to it. There's something very special about the Chicanos, and I don't think anybody will change my mind about that. I think the Chicano male has a great deal of courage to walk the streets. He may be arrested, just to be standing.

Now I'm talking about the male who is culturally committed; he is committed to his family, his friends. Let's just get out of my poetry for a minute. There's a poem written by José Antonio Burciaga—now there is a Chicano—a poem written about another wonderful man, Juan de la Cruz Cuellar, a man who was put in prison for having possession of less than one ounce of marijuana. In prison one thing led to another, and he ended up spending most of his life locked up. If you look at the records of the prisoners, and how they become repeat criminals you begin to see that most started with a mistaken arrest or a racist arrest. Cuellar ended up a very, gentle man, and I don't mean he was a gentleman—a gentle man, but you didn't mess with Cuellar either. There's the difference between that kind of Chicano and a macho who destroys women.

*Li:* That's the one you are against, the one who calls himself a macho?

*Zamora:* Yeah. But even more than that. When the macho becomes assimilated he's even uglier than the Mexicano macho because he's trying to kill everything that he came from; I think there's so much self-hatred that he will kill anything that reminds him of his culture and that includes women and children.

*Li:* Our critic also asserts: "Zamora's desire to master the male and gain autonomy in her relationship with men is also implicitly connected to a desire to master the dominant culture" (1985, 218).

*Zamora:* I can't even master my own appetite. Now realistically, how am I going to do that? Which dominant culture? How am I going to start? With the church? The Pope? What is the critic talking about? I never had such visions. I think that's probably the abyss of intentional fallacies to say such things. I can't even imagine having that kind of power. Given the way I think now and the way I thought then, I feel that anything done should be done collectively.

*Li:* Seeing that you were successful with your short stories, why don't you write more prose?

*Zamora:* Well, because it takes more time. Poetry, I'm inspired to write it all the time. But I might soon move into prose because the poetry seems to me like it is starting to sound like there's nothing more I can say. Maybe there is, but I haven't found it. I was working on a short story just yesterday, and it's going to be included in an anthology of Chicano literature, titled *New Chicano/ Chicana Writing*, edited by Charles Tatum, from the University of Arizona.

*Li:* What's the title of the short story, and what's it about?

*Zamora:* The title is "Tere." It's in the form of a letter that Tere is writing to a colleague. Tere is an entity living in limbo at the moment, between lives, you know, the whole notion of reincarnation. She is writing a letter to an entity called Tynnus. They are scribes living in the realm of souls, spiritually in the psychic world. Their task is to be born into a specific culture and elevate the level of the language of that culture. The entities who are born into female bodies have less success because they get seduced by the human race, which Tere calls the stubborn creature.

*Li:* Who are the scribes?

*Zamora:* The scribes are entities who copy out the sacred texts in pure form so there's no change from generation to generation in the original revelation.

*Li:* In an interview with yet another critic (Bruce-Novoa 1980, 209) you have said: "Those poems I've written in Spanish are an effort to express love. . . something I've not been able to do in English. . . but love is not yet my subject." What do you mean by this? What does love mean to you? Do you believe in it?

*Zamora:* Well, I've come to the conclusion that, with the exception of my children, I've never loved another human being in the sense that everybody else defines love. I can't relate to that definition. It doesn't mean I can't love or that I don't love. I don't know what to say about love. I thought I had a definition like everybody else, and then I met him, the man who fulfilled my definition of the ideal man to love. Our relationship, too, fulfilled my definition of love. What I discovered, though, is that I had the wrong definition. He was handsome, creative, he was a poet, an artist, independent, courageous, his energy was boundless. He adored me, he liked what I did, he liked my poetry and I liked him and his art. We spent lots of time together; we couldn't be apart from each other, and we were killing each other. I lost thirty-five pounds in six months. My parents, my family got worried because I was becoming anorexic. I thought I needed to get away from him because I was becoming anorexic. I thought I needed to get away from him because he was consuming all my time. During that period I couldn't write poetry, he couldn't paint, and he was getting crazier and crazier, so we broke up.

*Li:* How long had you been with him?

*Zamora:* Six months and we broke up, and it took six months more to break away. It was very hard to break up. We cried but we knew it was for the best, something was not quite right; to this day I don't know what it was. I came back to California and the Burciagas took my picture because I stayed with them, and they were horrified at how I looked. I can't explain what happened but I never went with another man after that. If that is love I can't live long under those conditions. I couldn't create, he couldn't create. We were destroying each other, and each other's art. We had to separate. That was ten years ago. What I wanted from him was very selfish and that was just to be with him, and I don't think love is selfishness. If I had another relationship I'd like it to be very different, not so intensely involved. But I can't even fathom that there's a man alive today to relate to and be creative, too. I have a lot of male friends and I enjoy their company. We go out to dinners, lunches, but no intimacies, nothing like that. I'm happy that way.

*Li:* Do you get along better with men or with women?

*Zamora:* I think equally. I have to work harder when I'm with

women. They don't seem to trust me or my friendship at first.
*Li:* One critic insinuated that you are a lesbian?
*Zamora:* Yes, I think she made an innuendo that I was a lesbian.
*Li:* Why would she say that?
*Zamora:* I have no idea. Well, if you follow her thesis that's the only conclusion she could reach, and I think she had the conclusion from the very beginning and had to build a case for it to justify her statement.
*Li:* Let's talk about the *Movimiento feminista*. I've read that you don't consider yourself completely a feminist because feminism doesn't address the racial issue. Can you comment about that?
*Zamora:* That's right. That's one of the things, and there are many other things about the feminist movement I find fault with. It's hard to totally relate to the issues that feminists address; and they can't understand why so many Third World women don't join the movement. But in the context of their lives, we still have to take the back seat. There is still the master/plantation mentality in feminist situations. Empowering women to do masculine things—killing, for example, is nothing I want. Women have power and it's not necessarily sexual. If you look at the Indian woman, look at the power she has, and look at the power in the culture of my own family. My mother has had the power, always, although my father was very demanding she still, in her gentle manner, had her own role. To my mind, the feminists want equality to be in power positions where they can emulate masculinity. I don't have any trouble with equality in pay or anything like that, but to get in a position of power and then turn around and do the same thing to other women or to children that has been done by men, is a greater atrocity. Where are the feminists in the healing situations, for example? Women know how to heal each other, only women can do that. You know, even in conjunction with other cultures, I think, that the Indians have a great deal to show us. Chicanas have a great deal to share, Mexicanas have a great deal too—home remedies, herbal remedies. You don't see feminists in the medical profession giving up all the masculine kinds of brutalizing surgeries. I don't say that's not necessary in some cases, but it has been proven already that so many of those surgeries were unnecessary. Where are the active feminists and the feminine healing arts in the traditional medical profession? I know they're scant. Very few women can get into the profession. Where are the femi-

nists getting behind those women for healing naturally, healing by a female definition? Women are ranting about rape and about the laws against rape. If all that energy could be taken to healing a woman who has been raped then we have feminine activism. Generally it's thought by church women and feminist alike that nothing can be done, that life is over because a woman has been raped. She becomes a mental case or something. We all know that men have been raping women for centuries. And who is there to cure these women? Where are the healers? And as those of us who are from Third World countries who have also been mentally raped, how are we building up our minds? Who is healing that?

*Li:* Do you consider yourself a liberated woman?

*Zamora:* Oh, no. I think no women in the world today is a liberated woman. A woman may think she's free but she hasn't got her eyes open. We don't have the freedom to do anything, except in a male context, anywhere in the world, except maybe on top of a mountain, all by oneself.

*Li:* But do you think there will come the time when women are going to consider themselves completely liberated?

*Zamora:* Once I thought so, but I don't see it happening. I don't even know what "liberated" means anymore. Freedom means so many different things. I don't think any woman alive today is free. The female CEO is still operating under male structures, and there are particular confines, a bondage, a patriarchal bondage that keeps her in prison and she is not even aware of it. I mean, she can go around and throw her weight around too and fire and buy people like anyone else, but those are masculine images she is emulating, and she is not functioning by feminine principles. You see the mental entrapment? What brought that to mind was many things. I just spoke with a woman from Soweto. She's at a university in Soweto. I was telling her I had to go to a meeting of women of color, and she said: "You are a woman of color? But you can pass for white." I could see her perspective. I said, "I know." "Why do you consider yourself a woman of color? You could pass for white," she kept insisting, and I said: "Who would want to?" From my experiences and for other reasons, I do not join the white-woman feminist movement because she's the weakest woman in the world; she's too easily manipulated. You know, women in our culture who are twelve years old, or the *quinceañeras*, are already considered women and are accepting their adult responsibilities. I'm not saying our women know the complete expression of femininity, but I do think they come closer.

*Li:* How do you see yourself in relation to a man?

*Zamora:* In our Chicano culture there are machos and there are hombres, and they know the difference and I know the difference, and we call on that. I can relate much better to Chicanos, more than any other man on earth. In a university setting Chicanos and Chicanas generally had two things in common: we had been raised by the Catholic Church; and secondly, we assumed we were accepted at Stanford because of our Catholic education. Also, there were Chicanos at Stanford whose mothers were *cantineras*. There was a real understanding among us about what mothers and sisters had to do in order to keep the family together, in order to go to school. Chicanos always appreciated what the Chicanas did. But the more assimilated Chicanos became the uglier of our group. Still, the kindness and gentleness of Chicanos, I don't think, is matched anywhere! We can be at a meeting, we can look across the room and just from the pain in their eyes we know what they've been through; and even if you don't agree with what they're saying you know why they are saying it. We still have connections, we still can communicate on telepathic levels. It's very hard to dislike that kind of person. We have nothing but empathy, rarely sympathy, but empathy with what they're trying to do. Just to get up in the morning takes a great deal of courage in the Chicano community.

*Li:* Tell me about your involvement with the Chicano Movement.

*Zamora:* I've been involved since the early 1970s, and I'm involved to the extent that poets are involved. In the early years, we marched. I took my children to boycott marches. At the very last stages of the political movement we marched for the Farm Workers Union with César Chávez, here in San Jose, against the growers. I took my two daughters so they could learn things. They saw a woman spit on my face; it was a nice lesson in Americanism for my daughters. The woman was a grower and came out of the store. She was furious that we were walking with placards. She said to me: "Do you know you are working for the Czar?"

*Li:* What did she mean by the Czar? Which Czar?

*Zamora:* That's right, she was out of the century, she just meant

Russia. There were no Czars; either she was not aware of that or she thought her statement would have a greater impact.

*Li:* And your daughters saw the woman spitting on your face?

*Zamora:* Yes. Maybe I didn't have the sense to be humiliated, but what I was pleased about was that my daughters could see what American economics could lead to in its extreme.

*Li:* What else have you done to participate in the Chicano Movement?

*Zamora:* Well, I have participated in all the Floricanto festivales, all of the ones I knew about, from 1976 and on. Last year I attended the Floricanto at Stanford and I read poetry there. I read mostly on campuses. As for political involvement, I only support, mostly financially, women who run for office.

*Li:* How has the Chicano Movement influenced you?

*Zamora:* Well, it gave me an audience for one thing, it gave me an identity. I could never be fully Mexican, and I was well aware of that. But I could be a Chicana; I was a Chicana. The Chicano Movement identified all of us who lived in a kind of limbo, with no place to be, no audiences. I knew there were lots of people out there, lost between two cultures. Not one, not another, and creating a whole culture, and by the way, not hating either one, addressing both cultures. Out of that came a new language, the *Caló* we were talking about. I used *Caló* as a child, and when I'm with Chicanos or Chicanas. I don't use it in the universities except on rare occasion.

*Li:* But don't you use it for writing poetry?

*Zamora:* Some, but I write in English mostly. I've been reading English since I was three.

*Li:* Do you feel more comfortable writing In English than in Spanish?

*Zamora:* Oh, yes. I like English. I love all languages, but English is the only one I'm really confident enough to manipulate. I like squeezing emotions out of this very unemotional language. It takes a lot more work. It's much easier to write poems in Spanish, I would think, but if I write in Spanish and translate it into English it just seems romantic sentimentalism; my Spanish poems fail. I'm not that skilled at writing in Spanish, neither do I know the subtleties of the poetic techniques since I was not educated by Spanish teachers. But I understand the subtleties of *Caló*. Alurista will tell you that *Caló* reflects our people's fractured human experiences. Alurista writes very well in *Caló*. So does Juan Felipe Herrera. There are women who are brilliant writers using *Caló*. I wish Olivia Castellanos would do more. She has a certain beauty in her narrative expression. Angela de Hoyos also can write in *Caló*; she's a fine writer.

*Li:* Are there other experiences about the Chicano Movement that you would like to recount?

*Zamora:* The most moving I ever participated in was the very first Chicano writers conference at Berkeley, put together by Guillermo Hernández, who was at UC Berkeley at the time. There were three women writers and all the writers who had been published up to that point were invited. We met each other for the first time. Another experience I like to recount is how I had read Alurista's work. I found his poem, "Nuestro barrio." I stepped on the poem at the university I was attending. It had been part of a sociology class assignment and somebody lost it; I picked it up and read it. I knew then that somebody else was writing the same way I'm writing. I never knew who he was, and at this conference I met him for the first time. It was so moving for me to meet all the other writers too. I knew they were writing just as I was, as though we were living in this, people call it marginal life, but it was a state of limbo. To meet Mario Suárez, Lucha Corpi, and Olivia Castellanos was just the most moving experience I've ever had.

*Li:* What are the goals of the Chicano Movement?

*Zamora:* I think it's very different for different Chicanos now. We got scattered during the Reagan years, and only now we're regrouping. The goal of the Chicano Movement is to have the freedom to express, culturally, and not to have the culture aborted. It's a beautiful culture, most of us would like to keep it intact, and not to be dehumanized, not to be exploited in the process. In terms of the Movement, I'm involved mostly with the artistic aspect to preserve the culture. The historians are trying to re-establish, restructure our history. There is a need to re-write the textbooks because we were excluded from the textbooks even though we played major roles in the development of the country. We need to clarify all the mistakes in history books. But also we have Chicanos who want to assimilate and are now trying to destroy what work was done by the Movement. They're mouthing that the Movement is dead, but I don't think so; Chicano poets, dramatists, musicians, artists prove otherwise.

*Li:* Why do you think Chicano literature has received and still does receive, relatively, so little recognition within the U.S. society?

*Zamora:* Because that's a reflection of how Chicanos are viewed. Why bother with the literature of a people you are not going to bother with anyway. Whatever it is we do is going to be perceived as inferior, whether we do it better or not, fault is going to be found. I should think that we don't need to worry about the criticism or the fact that the U.S. ignores it. Our literature is recognized in European literary circles, in Russia, in China, in Latin America.

*Li:* How do you see the future of Chicano literature? Are there going to be more writers or are they going to be stagnated?

*Zamora:* There's more already. There are not even enough publishing houses to cover them all.

*Li:* What are your goals for the future?

*Zamora:* I have to work. I don't have any specific goals. I have lots of projects; they're already started, some are half finished. I have a play in process, a novel, and also a book on La Malinche. I used to be an artist so I bought some brushes and some paints, and I have some other artist's materials. I'd like to try to dabble in art again. I'd like to take a class just to get started. What I'm going to do is publish the drawings I do have. I have a whole book of drawings. When I used to live in Escondido (at Stanford University), I used to hold monthly poetry readings. All the poets would read their poetry together, and artists would come, so while everybody was reading we would be passing a sketch pad so everybody would write either a poem or draw a picture, and I have a lot of those.

*Li:* Is there anything else you would like to reveal?

*Zamora:* I think I've said enough already. I've never told anyone before my views about feminism.

## Works Cited


Alarcón, Norma. 1983. "Chicana's Feminist Literature: A Re-vision Through Malintzin/or Malintzin: Putting Flesh Back on the Object." In *This Bridge Called My Back: Writings by Radical Women of Color*, eds. Cherríe Moraga and Gloria Anzaldúa, 182-190. New York: Kitchen Table/Women of Color Press.

____. 1987. "Making Familia From Scratch: Split Subjectivities in the Work of Helena María Viramontes and Cherríe Moraga." In *Chicana Creativity and Criticism: Charting New Frontiers in American Literature*, eds. María Herrera-Sobek and Helena María Viramontes. *The Americas Review* 15 (3 & 4): 147-159.

____. 1989a. "Traddutora, Traditora: A Paradigmatic Figure of Chicana Feminism." *Cultural Critique* 13 (Fall): 57-87.

____. 1989b. "The Sardonic Powers of the Erotic in the Work of Ana Castillo." In *Breaking Boundaries: Latina Writings and Critical Readings*, eds. Asunción Horno-Delgado, et al., 94-107. Amherst: University of Massachusetts Press.

____. 1990a. "Chicana Feminism: In the Tracks of 'the' Native Woman." *Cultural Studies* 4 (3): 248-256.

____. 1990b. "The Theoretical Subject(s) of *This Bridge Called My Back* and Anglo-American Feminism." In *Making Face, Making Soul/Haciendo Caras*, ed. Gloria Anzaldúa, 356-369. San Francisco: Aunt Lute Foundation.

____. 1991. "Without a Word to My Name." Manuscript.

Allen, Paula Gunn. 1986. *The Sacred Hoop*. Boston: Beacon Press.

Anzaldúa, Gloria. 1987. *Borderlands/La Frontera: The New Mestiza*. San Francisco: Spinsters/Aunt Lute.

____. 1990. "Haciendo Caras: Una Entrada." In *Making Face, Making Soul/Haciendo Caras*, ed. Gloria Anzaldúa, xv-xxviii. San Francisco: Aunt Lute Foundation.

Aristotle. 1974. *Aristotle's Politics and Poetics*. Trans. Benjamin Jowett and Thomas Twining. New York: Viking Press.

Bachelard, Gaston. 1971. *The Poetics of Reverie: Childhood, Language, and the Cosmos*. Boston: Beacon Press.

____. 1969. *The Poetics of Space*. Boston: Beacon Press.

Barthes, Roland. 1979. "From Work to Text." In *Textual Strategies: Perspectives in Post-Structuralist Criticism*, ed. Josue V. Harari, 73-81. Ithaca, NY: Cornell University Press.

Bataille, Georges. 1982. *Story of the Eye*. Trans. Joachim Neugroschal. New York: Penguin Books.

Bateson, Gregory. 1972. *Steps to an Ecology of the Mind*. New York: Ballantine Books.

Berg, Elizabeth. 1982. "The Third Woman." *Diacritics* 12 (summer): 11-20.

*The Bible*. 1974. Reprint. New York: New American Library.

Binder, Wolfgang. 1986. "Mothers and Grandmothers: Acts of Mythification and Remembrance in Chicano Poetry." In *Missions in Conflict: Essays on U.S.-Mexican Relations and Chicano Culture*, ed. Renate von Bardeleben, Dietrich Briesmeister, and Juan Bruce-Novoa, 133-143. Tubingen, Germany: Günter Narr Verlag.

Bourdieu, Pierre. 1984. *Distinction*. Cambridge: Harvard University Press.

Bovenschen, Silvia. 1985. "Is There a Feminine Aesthetic?" In *Feminist Aesthetics*, ed. Gisela Ecker. Boston: Beacon Press.

Braxton, Joanne. 1989. *Black Women Writing Autobiography: A Tradition Within a Tradition*. Philadelphia: Temple University Press.

Bruce-Novoa, Juan. 1975. "The Space of Chicano Literature." *De Colores* 1 (4): 22-42.

____. 1980. *Chicano Authors: Inquiry by Interview*. Austin: University of Texas Press.

____. 1982. *Chicano Poetry: A Response to Chaos*. Austin: University of Texas Press.

____. 1985. "Bernice Zamora y Lorna Dee Cervantes: una estética feminista." *Revista Iberoamericana* 51 (132-133): 565-573.

____. 1986. "Canonical and Non-Canonical Texts: Chicano Novel. *The Americas Review* 14 (3-4): 119-135.

Calderón, Héctor, and José David Saldívar, eds. 1991. *Criticism in the Borderlands: Studies in Chicano Literature, Culture, and Ideology*. Durham: Duke University Press.

Candelaria, Cordelia. 1980. "La Malinche, Feminist Prototype." *Frontiers* 5, 2: 1-6.

Castillo, Ana. 1986. *The Mixquiahuala Letters*. Binghamton, NY: Bilingual Press.

____. 1988. *My Father Was a Toltec*. Novato, CA: West End Press.

Castoriadis, Cornelius. 1987. *The Imaginary Institution of Society*. Trans. Kathleen Blamey. Cambridge: The MIT Press.

Cervantes, Lorna Dee. 1981. *Emplumada*. Pittsburgh: University of Pittsburgh Press.

Chin, Frank, Jeffery Chan, Lawson Fusa Inada, and Shawn Hsu Wong, eds. 1974. *Aiiieeeee! An Anthology of Asian American Writers*. Washington, D.C.: Howard University Press.

Cirlot, J.E. 1962. *A Dictionary of Symbols*. New York: Philosophical Society.

Cisneros, Sandra. 1987a. *My Wicked Wicked Ways*. Berkeley: Third Woman Press.

———. 1987b. "Notes to a Young(er) Writer." *The Americas Review* 15 (Spring): 74-76.

———. 1991. *Woman Hollering Creek and Other Stories*. New York: Random House.

Cixous, Hélène. 1983. "The Laugh of the Medusa." In *The Signs Reader*, eds. Elizabeth Abel and Emily K. Abel, 278-297. Chicago: University of Chicago Press.

Cortázar, Julio. 1966. *Rayuela*. Buenos Aires: Editorial Sudamericana.

Cota-Cárdena, Margarita. 1985. *Puppet*. Austin, TX: Relámpago Press.

Coward, Rosalind. 1983. *Patriarchal Precedents: Sexuality and Social Relations*. Boston: Routledge & Kegan Paul.

Curiel, Barbara. 1991. "Heteroglossia in Ana Castillo's *The Mixquiahuala Letters*." *Discurso Literario* 7 (1): 11-23.

Davis, Mike. 1986. *Prisoners of the American Dream*. London: Verso.

Del Castillo Guilbault, Rose. 1991. "Women's Cross to Bear," *San Francisco Examiner*, 2 June: 2.

Differences 1 (Summer) (1989).

Ecker, Gisela, ed. 1985. *Feminist Aesthetics*. Boston: Beacon Press.

Fernández-Kelly, M. Patricia, and Anna M. García. 1988. "Invisible Amidst the Glitter: Hispanic Women in the Southern California Electronics Industry." In *The Worth of Women's Work: A Qualitative Synthesis*, eds. A. Strathram, Eleanor M. Miller, and Hans O. Mauksch, 265-289. New York: State University of New York Press.

Foster, Hal, ed. 1983. *The Anti-Aesthetic: Essays on Postmodern Culture*. Port Townsend: Bay Press.

Foucault, Michel. 1984. "The Subject and Power." In *Art After Modernism: Rethinking Representation*, ed. Brian Wallis, 417-423. New York: The New Museum of Contemporary Art.

Fowler, Roger. 1986. *Linguistic Criticism*. Oxford: Oxford University Press.

Fregoso, Rosa Linda. 1990. "*Born in East L.A.* and the Politics of Representation." *Cultural Studies* 4, 3 (October): 264-280.

———. 1993. *The Bronze Screen: Chicana and Chicano Film Culture*. Minneapolis: University of Minnesota Press.

Fregoso, Rosa Linda, and Angie C. Chabram. 1990. "Introduction: Chicana/o Cultural Representations: Reframing Alternative Critical Discourse." *Cultural Studies* 4,3 (October): 203-212.

Freud, Sigmund. 1965. *The Interpretation of Dreams*. Trans. and ed. by James Strachey. New York: Avon Books.

Gardiner, Judith Kegan. 1982. "On Female Identity and Writing by Women." In *Writing and Sexual Difference*, ed. Elizabeth Abel, 177-191.

Chicago: University of Chicago Press.

Gonzales-Berry, Erlinda. 1995. "The (Subversive) Mixquiahuala Letters." In *Chicana (W)rites*, eds. María Herrera-Sobek and Helena María Viramontes, 115. Berkeley: Third Woman Press.

Gumpel, Liselotte. 1984. *Metaphor Reexamined: A Non-Aristotalian Perspective*. Bloomington: Indiana University Press.

Hall, Stuart. 1988. "New Ethnicities," *ICA Documents* (Institute of Contemporary Arts) 7: 27-31.

Harlow, Barbara. 1987. *Resistance Literature*. New York and London: Methuen.

Herrera-Sobek, María, ed. 1985. *Beyond Stereotypes: The Critical Analysis of Chicana Literature*. Binghamton, N.Y.: Bilingual Press.

Herrera-Sobek, María, and Helena María Viramontes, eds. 1988. *Chicana Creativity and Criticism: Charting New Frontiers in American Literature. The Americas Review* 15 (3 & 4).

Irigaray, Luce. 1985. *Speculum of the Other Woman*. Trans. Gillian C. Gill. Ithaca: Cornell University Press.

____. 1989. "The Gesture in Psychoanalysis." Trans. Elizabeth Guild. In *Between Feminism and Psychoanalysis*, ed. Teresa Brennan, 127-138. London and New York: Routledge.

Jameson, Fredric. 1983. "Postmodernism and Consumer Society." In *The Anti-Aesthetic: Essays on Postmodern Culture*, ed. Hal Foster. Port Townsend: Bay Press.

Johnson, Barbara. 1981. Translator's introduction to *Dissemination* by Jacques Derrida. Chicago: University of Chicago Press.

Kaye/Kantrowitz, Melanie. 1987. "Sign." *We Speak in Code: Poems and Other Writings*. Pittsburgh: Motheroot Publications. Quoted in *Borderlands/La Frontera: The New Mestiza*, Anzaldúa, 85.

Keller, Gary D. 1985. "The Image of the Chicano in Mexican, United States, and Chicano Cinema: An Overview." In *Chicano Cinema*, ed. Gary D. Keller, 13-58. Binghamton: Bilingual Review Press.

Kim, Elaine H. 1982. *Asian American Literature: An Introduction to the Writings and Their Social Context*. Philadelphia: Temple University Press.

Kingston, Maxine Hong. 1975. *The Woman Warrior*. New York: Vintage International

Knights, Lionel Charles and Basil Cottle, eds. 1960. *Metaphor and Symbol*. London: Butterworths Scientific Publications.

Kristeva, Julia. 1980a. *Desire in Language: A Semiotic Approach to Literature and Art*. Ed. Leon S. Roudiez, trans. Thomas Gora, Alice Jardine, and Leon Roudiez. New York: Columbia University Press.

____. 1980b. "Woman Can Never Be Defined." In *New French Feminisms*. Eds. Elaine Marks and Isabelle de Courtivron, trans. Marilyn A. August, 137-141. Amherst: University of Massachusetts Press.

———. 1980c. "Oscillation Between Power and Denial." In *New French Feminisms*. Eds. Elaine Marks and Isabelle de Courtivron, trans. Marilyn A. August, 165-167. Amherst: University of Massachusetts Press.

Lerner, Gerda. 1986. *The Creation of Patriarchy*. New York: Oxford University Press.

Lispector, Clarice. 1989. *Stream of Life*. Trans. Elizabeth Lowe and Earl Fitz. Minneapolis: University of Minnesota Press.

López-González, Aralia, Amelia Malagamba, and Elena Urrutia, eds. 1990. *Mujer y literatura mexicana y chicana: Culturas en contacto, 2*. México: El Colegio de México/Colegio de la Frontera Norte.

Lorde, Audre. 1981. "The Master's Tools Will Never Dismantle the Master's House." In *This Bridge Called My Back: Writings by Radical Women of Color*. Eds. Cherríe Moraga, and Gloria Anzaldúa, 98-106. Boston: Persephone Press.

Lyotard, Jean Francis. 1979. *La condition postmoderne*. Paris: Minuit.

———. 1988. *The Différend: Phrases in Dispute*. Trans. Georges Van den Abbele. Minneapolis: University of Minnesota Press.

Mariani, Paul and George Murphy, eds. 1984. *Poetics: Essays on the Art of Poetry*. Ocean Bluffs, Mass.: Tendril Inc.

Marks, Elaine, and Isabelle de Courtivron, eds. 1980. *New French Feminisms*. Amherst: University of Massachusetts Press.

Miller, Nancy K. 1986. "Arachnologies: The Woman, The Text, and The Critic." In *The Poetics of Gender*, ed. Nancy K. Miller, 270-295. New York: Columbia University Press.

Moi, Toril. 1985. *Sexual/Textual Politics: Feminist Literary Theory*. London: Methuen.

Cherríe Moraga. 1983. *Loving in the War Years: Lo que nunca pasó por sus labios*. Boston: South End Press.

———. 1986. *Giving Up the Ghost*. Los Angeles: West End Press.

———. 1991. "La fuerza feminina: las artistas de Aztlan." Paper presented at "Cara a Cara: A Symposium on Current Debates in Chicano Culture," 20 July, Fort Mason Theatre, San Francisco, California.

Morson, Gary Saul, and Caryl Emerson. 1990. *Mikhail Bakhtin: Creation of a Prosaics*. Stanford: Stanford University Press.

Nin, Anais. 1948. *Under the Glass Jar*. Chicago: Swallow Press.

Olivares, Julian. 1984. "Seeing and Becoming: Evangelina Vigil, Thirty an' Seen a Lot." In *The Chicano Struggle: Analyses of Past and Present Efforts*, eds. John A. García, Teresa Cordova, and Juan R. García, 152-165. Binghamton, N.Y.: Bilingual Press.

Ordóñez, Elizabeth. 1983. "Sexual Politics and the Theme of Sexuality in Chicana Poetry." In *Women in Hispanic Literature: Icons and Fallen Idols*, ed. Beth Miller, 316-339. Berkeley: University of California Press.

Ortiz-Taylor, Shelia. 1982. *Faultline*. Tallahassee: Naiad Press.

____. 1985. *Spring Forward/Fall Back*. Tallahassee: Naiad Press.

Ortony, Andrew, ed. 1982. *Metaphor and Thought*. Cambridge: Cambridge University Press.

Owens, Craig. 1983. "The Discourse of Others: Feminists and Postmodernism." In *Essays on Postmodern Culture*, ed. Hal Foster, 57-82. Port Townsend, Wash.: Bay Press.

Paredes, Américo. 1978. *"With His Pistol in His Hand": A Border Ballad and Its Hero*. Austin: University of Texas Press.

Paredes, Raymond. 1987. "Recent Chicano Writing." *Rocky Mountain Review of Language and Literature* 41 (1): 124-128.

Paz, Octavio. 1961. *The Labyrinth of Solitude: Life and Thought in Mexico*. Trans. Lysander Kemp. New York: Grove Press.

____. 1972. *The Other Mexico: Critique of the Pyramid*. Trans. Lysander Kemp. New York: Grove Press.

Pérez, Emma. 1991. "Sexuality and Discourse: Notes from a Chicana Survivor." In *Chicana Lesbians: The Girls Our Mothers Warned Us About*, ed. Carla Trujillo, 159-184. Berkeley: Third Woman Press.

Pirsig, Robert M. 1974. *Zen and the Art of Motorcycle Maintenance*. New York: Morrow.

Pratt, Mary Louise. 1977. *Toward a Speech Act Theory of Literary Discourse*. Bloomington: Indiana University Press.

Quintana, Alvina E. 1990. "Politics, Representation and the Emergence of a Chicana Aesthetic." *Cultural Studies* 4, 3 (October): 257-263.

____. 1991. "Ana Castillo's *The Mixquiahuala Letters*: The Novelist as Ethnographer." In *Criticism in the Borderlands*, eds. Calderón and Saldívar, 72-83. Durham: Duke University Press.

Rebolledo, Tey Diana. 1983. "Abuelitas: Mythology and Integration in Chicana Literature." *Revista Chicano-Riqueña* 11 (3 & 4): 148-158.

____. 1988. "The Politics of Poetics: Or, What Am I, A Critic, Doing in this Text Anyhow?" In *Chicana Creativity and Criticism: Charting New Frontiers in American Literature*, ed. María Herrera-Sobek and Helena María Viramontes. *The Americas Review* 15 (3 & 4): 129-138.

Rich, Adrienne. 1973. *Diving Into the Wreck*. New York: Norton.

____. 1976. *Of Woman Born: Motherhood as Experience and Institution*. New York: Norton.

Ricoeur, Paul. 1965. *Civilization and National Cultures: History and Truth*. Trans. Charles A. Kelbley. Evanston: Northwestern University Press.

____. 1981. *The Rule of Metaphor: Multidisciplinary Studies of the Creation of Meaning in Language*. Toronto: University of Toronto Press.

____. 1984. *Time and Narrative*. Chicago: University of Chicago Press.

Rodríguez, Richard. 1988. *Hunger of Memory: The Education of Richard*

*Rodríguez*. New York: Bantam Books.

Rodríguez del Pino, Salvador. 1977. *Conversations with leading Chicano poets*. Guest: Bernice Zamora. Santa Barbara: University of California, Center for Chicano Studies. Videotape.

Rosaldo, Michelle Zimbalist, and Louise Lamphere, eds. 1974. *Woman, Culture, and Society*. Stanford: Stanford University Press.

Ruiz, Vicki L., and Susan Tiano, eds. 1987. *Women on the U.S.-Mexico Border: Responses to Change*. Boston: Allen & Unwin.

Saldívar, Ramón. 1984. "Dialectics in the Chicano Novel: Gender and Difference." In *Mexico and the United States: Intercultural Relations in the Humanities*, eds. Juanita Luna Lawhn, et al., 151-160. San Antonio Tex.: San Antonio College.

———. 1990. *Chicano Narrative: The Dialectics of Difference*. Madison: University of Wisconsin Press.

Saldívar-Hull, Sonia. 1991. "Feminism on the Border: From Gender Politics to Geopolitics." In *Criticism in the Borderlands: Studies in Chicano Literature, Culture, and Ideology*, eds. Hector Calderón and Jose David Saldívar, 203-220. Durham: Duke University Press.

Sánchez, Marta Ester. 1985. *Contemporary Chicana Poetry: A Critical Approach to an Emerging Literature*. Berkeley: University of California Press.

———. 1991. Paper presented at the "Bridging Borders" MALCS Chicana/Latina Summer Research Institute, 2 August, Laredo, Texas.

Sánchez, Rosaura. 1985. "Chicana Prose Writers: The Case of Gina Valdés and Sylvia Lizárraga." In *Beyond Stereotypes: The Critical Analysis of Chicana Literature*, ed. María Herrera-Sobek, 61-70. Binghamton: Bilingual Review Press.

——— 1989. "Postmodernism and Chicano Literature." *Aztlán: A Journal of Chicano Studies* 18 (2): 1-14.

———. 1990a. "Ethnicity, Ideology and Academia." *Cultural Studies* 4 (3): 294-302.

———. 1990b. "The History of Chicana: Proposal for a Materialist Perspective." In *Between Borders: Essays of Mexicana/Chicana History*, ed. Adelaida R. del Castillo, 1-29. Encino, Calif.: Floricanto Press.

Shibles, Warren. 1972. *Essays on Metaphor*. Whitewater, Wis.: The Language Press.

Silva, Beverly. 1983. *The Second St. Poems*. Ypsilanti, Mich.: Bilingual Press.

Spillers, Hortense. 1989. "Interstices: A Small Drama of Words." In *Pleasure and Danger: Exploring Female Sexuality*. Ed. Carole E. Vance. London: Pandora.

Spivak, Gayatri C. 1988. "Can the Subaltern Speak?" In *Marxism and the Interpretation of Culture*. Eds. Cary Nelson and Lawrence Grossberg, 271-313. Urbana: University of Illinois Press.

Suleiman, Susan Rubin. 1982. *Commentary on Story of the Eye, by Georges Bataille*. New York: Penguin Books.

Tatum, Charles, ed. 1992. *New Chicano/Chicana Writing*. Tucson: University of Arizona Press.

Trinh T. Minh-ha. 1989. *Woman/Native/Other*. Bloomington: Indiana University Press.

Trujillo, Carla, ed. 1991. *Chicana Lesbians: The Girls Our Mothers Warned Us About*. Berkeley: Third Woman Press.

Turbayne, Colin Murray. 1963. *The Myth of Metaphor*. New Haven: Yale University Press.

Vigil, Evangelina. 1982. *Thirty An' Seen a Lot*. Houston: Arte Público Press.

Villanueva, Alma. 1977; 1982. *Bloodroot*. Austin, TX: Place of Herons Press.

____. 1978. *Mother, May I?*. Pittsburgh: Motheroot Publications.

Wallis, Brian, ed. 1984. *Art After Modernism: Rethinking Representation*. New York: The New Museum of Contemporary Art.

Waugh, Patricia. 1989. *Feminine Fictions: Revisiting the Postmodern*. London: Routledge.

West, Cornell. 1985. "The Dilemma of the Black Intellectual." *Cultural Critique* 1 (Fall): 109-124.

White, Hayden. 1978. *Tropics of Discourse: Essays on Cultural Criticism*. Baltimore: Johns Hopkins University Press.

Yarbro-Bejarano, Yvonne. 1987. "Chicana Literature from a Chicana Feminist Perspective." In *Chicana Creativity and Criticism: Charting New Frontiers in American Literature*, eds. María Herrera-Sobek and Helena María Viramontes. *The Americas Review* 15 (3 & 4): 139-145.

Zamora, Bernice. *Archivo*. Stanford University Library.

____. 1976. *Restless Serpents*. Menlo Park, Calif.: Diseños Literarios.

____. 1992. "Tere." In *New Chicano/Chicana Writing*, ed. Charles Tatum, 51. Tucson: University of Arizona Press.

## Contributors

Norma Alarcón is Associate Professor of Ethnic/Chicano Studies at the University of California, Berkeley. She is the publisher of Third Woman Press. She has written a book on Rosario Castellanos and published numerous articles on Chicana writers and culture.

Juan Bruce-Novoa is Professor of Spanish at the University of California, Irvine. His books include a collection of poems *Inocencia perversa/Perverse Innocence*, a collection of interviews *Chicano Authors: Inquiry by Interview*, and a critical work *Chicano Poetry: A Response to Chaos*. He has recently finished his first novel.

Ana Castillo is a poet, editor, and translator. Castillo is the author of the following poetry collections: *The Invitation* (1979), *Women Are Not Roses* (1984), and *My Father Was a Toltec* (1988). Her first novel, *The Mixquiahuala Letters* (Bilingual Press, 1986), received the Before Columbus American Book Award. She has published two other novels, *Sapogonia* (Bilingual Press, 1990), and *So Far From God* (Norton, 1993), and a collection of essays, *Massacre of the Dreamers* (Univ. of New Mexico Press, 1994).

Sandra Cisneros is a poet, fiction writer, essayist. Cisneros's first novel, *The House on Mango Street* has sold over 30,000 copies, and has recently been reprinted by Random House. She is the author of the short story collection *Woman Hollering Creek* (1991) and two volumes of poetry—*My Wicked Wicked Ways* (1989) and *Loose Woman* (1994).

Frances Salomé España is a film and videomaker and coordinator in both cable and radio programming. Her work includes *Explorations of Chicano/a Aesthetics through Video*. Winner of numerous awards for her video projects, España is recognized as an innovative and creative communications artist.

Rosa Linda Fregoso is Associate Professor of Chicano Studies and Women's Studies at the University of California at Davis. She is the author of a book on Chicano/a film, *The Bronze Screen*, editor of the forthcoming book *Miradas de Mujer* and numerous articles on Chicano film.

Erlinda Gonzales-Berry is Professor of Spanish at the University of New Mexico, Albuquerque. She edited *Pasó por Aquí* (1989), and coedited *Las Mujeres Hablan: An Anthology of Nuevo Mexicana Writers* (1988). She has written several critical articles and has established herself as a novelist with the publication of the novel *Paletitas de guayaba* (1991).

María Herrera-Sobek is Professor of Spanish at the University of California, Irvine. Her publications include: *The Bracero Experience: Elitelore Versus Folklore* (1979), *The Mexican Corrido: A Feminist Analysis* (1990), and *Northward Bound: The Mexican Immigrant Experience in Corridos and Canciones* (1993). She has edited three critical anthologies, *Beyond Stereotypes: The Critical Analysis of Chicana Literature* (1985), *Gender and Print Culture: New Perspectives on International Ballad Research* (1991), and *Reconstructing a Chicano/a Literary Heritage: Hispanic Literature of the Southwest* (1993). She has coedited with Helena María Viramontes *Chicana Creativity and Criticism: Charting New Frontiers in American Literature* (1988), and with Seymour Menton *Saga de México* (1992). She is one of three women featured in the poetry collection *Three Times a Woman* (1989). She is currently working on a book on the Mexican/Chicano *pastorelas* (shepherds' play).

Gloria Elsa Li teaches at Santa Clara University and is a Ph.D. candidate at Stanford university.

Demetria Martínez is a journalist and a poet. Martínez's collaborative collection of poetry *Three Times A Woman* (1989), has been critically acclaimed. Her poem about two Salvadorean women, "Rite of Life," for which she won the 14th Chicano Literary Contest, was used in a Federal indictment against her. This was the first time the Federal Government brought to trial a reporter who claimed to be covering a story about the Sanctuary Movement. She is currently working for the *Albuquerque Journal* and the *National Catholic Reporter*.

Elizabeth Ordóñez is a professor in the Department of Foreign Languages, at the University of Texas, at Arlington. She has published several articles on Chicano and Peninsular literature.

Mary Helen Ponce is a novelist and a writer. Ponce has published over thirty short stories, and one collection of short stories titled *Taking Control*. Her first novel *The Wedding*, is currently being adapted for theater. Her autobiography, *Hoyt Street*, was published by the University of New Mexico Press. She is a doctoral fellow at the University of New Mexico, Albuquerque.

Lourdes Portillo is a producer, director, writer. Her documentary, *Las Madres: The Mothers of Plaza de Mayo*, which concerns the Argentine mothers of the disappeared, won an Academy Award nomination for Best Documentary Film. Her new film *La Ofrenda* is a documentary which depicts views about el Dia de Los Muertos and its celebration on both sides of the border.

Alvina Quintana is Associate Professor of English at the University of Delaware. She is author of numerous articles on Chicana writers and cultures.

Kathryn Ríos is Assistant Professor of English at the University of Colorado, Boulder.

Elba Rosario Sánchez is a poet, editor, and instructor at the University of California, Santa Cruz. She is editor of the literary journal *Las Mujeres*. She is a former winner of the Chicano Literary Prize, U.C. Irvine.

Hector Torres is an associate professor at the University of New Mexico in Albuquerque in two departments: English and Linguistics. He has written a book on *Issues of Narrative Authority and Chicano Literary Discourse*.

Helena María Viramontes is a poet, fiction writer, and scriptwriter, currently teaching at Cornell University. Her collection entitled *The Moths and Other Stories* has received critical acclaim and is in its fifth printing. She coedited the anthology *Chicana Creativity* and Criticism: Charting New Frontiers in American Literature (1988). She has published in the *Los Angeles Times Magazine* and other literary journals. She is currently working on a collection of short stories *Paris Rats in East L.A.* She has adapted for the screen another short story, "Candystripers," produced by the American Film Institute and due to be released soon. She is currently working on her first novela titled "Their Dogs Came With Them."

Bernice Zamora teaches at Santa Clara University. Her book of poems *Restless Serpents* (1976) received critical acclaim. Her work appears in the *The Heath Anthology of American Literature* (1990), and other literary journals. *Restless Serpents* was reprinted by Bilingual Review Press under the title *Releasing Serpents*.

**Books available from Third Woman Press**

CHICANA CRITICAL ISSUES edited by Mujeres Activas en Letras y Cambio Social. Chicanas of every imaginable intellectual terrain combine their talents in this provocative collection of essays exploring identity and difference. ISBN 0-943219-09-4, $14.95

DICTÉE by Theresa Hak Kyung Cha. A remarkable mixed media text that combines autobiographical and biographical fragments, photographs, historical narrative, calligraphy, and lyric prose poetry in a complex, discontinuous weave. ISBN 0-943219-12-4, $12.95

WRITING SELF/WRITING NATION edited by Elaine Kim and Norma Alarcón. Five Asian American women celebrate *Dictée* while offering reconstructions of ethnicity, feminism and nationalism. ISBN 0-943219-11-6, $12.95

CHICANA LESBIANS: THE GIRLS OUR MOTHERS WARNED US ABOUT edited by Carla Trujillo. Winner of numerous awards, including the Lambda Literary Award for Best Lesbian Anthology. ISBN 0-943219-06-X, $10.95

THE SEXUALITY OF LATINAS edited by Norma Alarcón, Ana Castillo and Cherríe Moraga. An anthology of short stories, poetry, essays, art, drama and more by thirty-seven Latina contributors. ISBN 0-943219-00-0, $10.95

NEIGHBORS by Joan Woodruff. A magical and compelling novel set in New Mexico, by the author of *Traditional Stories and Foods: An American Indian Remembers*. ISBN 0-943219-08-6, $11.95

CHILIAGONY by Iris Zavala, translated by Susan Pensak. This Puertorriqueña's famous short novel is a work of "fabulous inventions and mental witchcraft." ISBN 0-943219-02-3, $5.95

**Books available from Third Woman Press**

My Wicked Wicked Ways by Sandra Cisneros. Now in its third printing, this book by the author of *The House on Mango Street and Woman Hollering Creek* is the most famous, and infamous, collection of Chicana poetry. ISBN 0-943219-01-9, $8.95

Variaciones sobre una Tempestad by Lucha Corpi, translated by Catherine Rodríguez-Nieto. Poetry from the acclaimed and prize-winning poet (*Palabras de mediodía*) and novelist (*Eulogy For a Brown Angel*). Bilingual, Spanish and English. ISBN 0-943219-05-1, $8.95

The Margarita Poems by Luz María Umpierre-Herrera. Intensely personal and moving poetry from the author of *Y Otras Desgracias/And Other Misfortunes*. Puerto Rico's most outstanding poet and essayist. ISBN 0-943219-02-7, $5.95

Speak to Me from Dreams by Barbara Brinson Curiel. Rich, evocative poetry from the author of *Nocturno* and *Vocabulary of the Dead* that captures the essence of growing up Chicana. ISBN 0-943219-03-5, $8.95

Back issues of THIRD WOMAN journal still available at $8.95 each: TW3 *Texas and More*; TW2:2 *International Perspectives*; TW2:1 *Southwest/Midwest*

Also available through Third Woman Press:
Esta Puente, Mi Espalda: Voces de Mujeres Tercermundistas en los Estados Unidos edited by Cherríe Moraga and Ana Castillo. The Spanish adaptation and translation of the best-selling *This Bridge Called My Back: Writings by Radical Women of Color*. ISBN 0-910383-19-7. $10.00

Send for a free catalog. For all orders please add $1.50 for the first book and $.50 for each additional book. California residents add state and local sales tax. Make checks payable to Third Woman Press. Send to: Third Woman Press, Ethnic Studies, 508A Barrows Hall, University of California, Berkeley, CA 94720